MOSTLY MISSISSIPPI

THE FESLER-LAMPERT
MINNESOTA HERITAGE BOOK SERIES

This series is published with the generous assistance of the John K. and Elsie Lampert Fesler Fund and David R. and Elizabeth P. Fesler. Its mission is to republish significant out-of-print books that contribute to our understanding and appreciation of Minnesota and the Upper Midwest.

The series features works by the following authors:

Clifford and Isabel Ahlgren

J. Arnold Bolz

Walter Havighurst

Helen Hoover

Florence Page Jaques

Evan Jones

Meridel Le Sueur

George Byron Merrick

Grace Lee Nute

Sigurd F. Olson

Charles Edward Russell

Calvin Rutstrum

Timothy Severin

Harold Speakman

Robert Treuer

MOSTLY MISSISSIPPI

A Very Damp Adventure

HAROLD SPEAKMAN

*W*ith a *Number of* DRAWINGS *by*
RUSSELL LINDSAY SPEAKMAN
and the AUTHOR

University of Minnesota Press
Minneapolis • London

First University of Minnesota Press edition, 2004

First published by Dodd, Mead and Company, Inc., in 1927

Published by the University of Minnesota Press
111 Third Avenue South, Suite 290
Minneapolis, MN 55401-2520
http://www.upress.umn.edu

A Cataloging-in-Publication record for this book is available from
the Library of Congress.

ISBN 0-8166-4438-1

Printed in the United States of America on acid-free paper

The University of Minnesota is an equal-opportunity educator
and employer.

12 11 10 09 08 07 06 05 04   10 9 8 7 6 5 4 3 2 1

TO MY WIFE

AND FRIEND

RUSSELL LINDSAY SPEAKMAN

PUBLISHER'S NOTE

The Fesler-Lampert Minnesota Heritage Book Series is designed to renew interest in the state's past by bringing significant literary works to the attention of a new audience. Our knowledge and appreciation of the culture and history of the region have advanced considerably since these books were first published, and the attitudes and opinions expressed in them may strike the contemporary reader as inappropriate. These classics have been reprinted in their original form as contributions to the state's literary heritage.

PREFACE

Three characters persist throughout the following pages—a man, a woman, and the Mississippi River.

Of these three, only one is solid, consecutive, enduring. That one is the river. As long as the clouds are, and the forests are, its tawny-maned flood will go foaming down to the dark bowl of the sea. The story of its strength will be told again and again in books, and records, and charts, and relentless dates.

The man and woman are impermanent, perishable. Their journeys will be short and few. They will be seen only for a moment on the face of the river. In that fact alone there may be a certain value—provided we look at them squarely, not as at a pair of wooden mannikins on which to hang a few gay ribbons of scenery.

So, throwing off any embarrassment I may feel, as something quite aside and stupid, I shall look into the man's mind and to the other's responsive presence for the volatile essence of this adventure, always shielding my somewhat delicately exposed position behind the consoling thought that the river, by its sheer magnificent strength, is both the villain and the hero of this book.

Girl, houseboat, river

CONTENTS

ILLUSTRATIONS

MOSTLY MISSISSIPPI

DUCKS & PERSONAE

I

WE drove the canoe forward.

With a noise like the hiss of a breaking comber, the dark line on the water before us tore raggedly upward into flight. A hundred yards ahead, its component parts settled down again—mallard, teal, pintail—thousand after thousand in another broad, sinuous line, as speckled and dusky as though some one had scattered gunpowder far out on the glittering blue surface of the lake. Again and again, with that strange hiss of wings, it broke into flight, cutting the August sunlight into a weird geometry of patterns and shrill cries.

The wilderness was about us. The forest was dark and unspoiled. It had no fear of the girl at the front paddle, nor of the man at the back. A clamorous host of waterfowl came wheeling and pirouetting about the canoe. Clouds of gulls sailed by, their white groups outlined against the dark of spruce and pine. A pair of blue cranes flapped lazily through the sunlight, while whole families of snipe stalked in solemn conclave along the low shore beyond.

There was a fresh, unfinished look to the scene, like Paradise, perhaps, on the evening of the fifth day. What was the reason for that mile-wide strip of bare, flat sand at the lake's edge before the forest began? Perhaps God had not put enough water into the lake.

We waded ashore over the shallows and came to the village of Bena lying dry and disconsolate a mile to the south. God, they told us there, had put plenty of water in the lake, but the river commission had taken it out. To-morrow we would find a large dam at the place where the young river left the lake, whose name was Winnibigoshish.* A few years earlier, nine feet of water had been drawn off through the dam, they said, giving the lake a considerable space to rise in if the rains were heavy. Thus the flow of water into the river below could be controlled.

But it was bad for them at Bena. That evil-looking line of the whitened ribs and antlers of dead trees along the forest's edge marked the height of the old water level.

Returning to the canoe with a few purchases we had made—some vegetables, a collapsible air mattress, honey in a mason jar, and particularly an additional

* Locally pronounced, Winnibigōsh'.

blanket, for the nights were cold—we set off for a promontory to the west.

I watched the paddle blade in front of me sink noiselessly into the water, run along the side with a swift, even sweep, and, rising from its aqueous fold, send a silvery, funnelled eddy racing by. A good canoeist ahead! As for me, I knew nothing about canoes. I was at the back paddle, the important paddle, only by courtesy. Well, perhaps I'd learn.

The vermilion canoe we rode in was of painted canvas with a double border of staring black-and-white checks along the gunwales. Its hilarious gayety had embarrassed us a little, when, three days before, we had left the town of Bemidji under considerable observation. Here on Winnibigoshish its color shrieked and giggled louder than ever under the solemnity of the wilderness. We would repaint it ourselves a little later on, when once the river had emerged from this adolescent tangle of lakes and connecting streamlets that marks its early course.

Bemidji, on Lake Bemidji, where we had begun our journey, is at the most northerly point on this lake-and-streamlet combination. To travel from Bemidji up stream to the river's source, one does not go decently north as one might expect. Elk Lake, twenty-three miles as the crow flies, *southwest* of Bemidji, is frequently called the source. In a very dry season, there are stretches of the dot-and-dash rivulet between Elk Lake and Bemidji that are not navigable for a canoe. Even down stream from Bemidji, we were forced to run for several rather breathless miles through a series of rushing, boulder-strewn rapids on an extra foot of water generously furnished by a power dam, located where the river leaves the lake!

There have been many ponderous and rather futile arguments as to the true head of the Mississippi. For many years, Lake Itasca was called the source. Then Elk Lake was discovered up stream from Itasca. But the water from Elk Lake must come from somewhere too. In a wet season, there may even be a puddle that drains into the puddle that drains into Elk Lake. The whole subject is made a little less plethoric by a perfectly glorious old faker named Glazier who came that way in 1881, and "gathering his little band about him," rechristened Elk Lake after himself and took possession of it in the name of the United States— just six years after it had been surveyed, named, and recorded at Washington by members of the United States Land Survey!

2

We paddled on. White clouds were marching in broken ranks up the afternoon sky, their farthest stragglers lost beneath the tops of the forest. There had been a storm to the south and these were the victorious legions swinging northward toward the Canadian border.

Then from the front of the canoe:

"How far did that man at Bena tell you it was to New Orleans?"

"Nearly two thousand five hundred miles."

She laughed with a little thrill of anticipation in which I could detect the presence of bears on a dark stair behind.

Sunset was approaching, and here was the promontory ahead. We went ashore on the wide, sandy flat. Then, gathering my little band about me, I too said a few simple words about the other great explorers whose names were linked inseparably with the Mississippi—La Salle, Marquette, Joliet—and, looking boldly around, I took possession of the spot in the name of the United States. But my little band only said, "I think you had better pitch the tent."

The tent was a "miner's tent." It was pyramidal in shape and nine feet square at the base. It was supported by a nine-foot iron pipe that stood upright in the center. When not in use, the pipe unscrewed into two parts which fitted nicely under the thwarts of the canoe. The prize feature of the tent was a canvas floor. This was sewn solidly to the sides, and lay flat under-

foot when the tent was pitched. It not only kept considerable moisture out, but innumerable articles in.

After three nights of tent-pitching, the thing was
easy. But at first, in my zeal, I had tried to put up the
tent pole before driving in the pegs, and so had been
forced into a ten-minute wrestling match with what
seemed to be a large, soiled canvas angel who finally
seized his iron backbone and cracked me over the head.
Then I tried driving in the pegs first, and from that
time on, the gaunt wrestler became our good genie,
guarding us to the best of his somewhat limited ability
against wind and rain.

The tent being up, my companion, who had busied
herself where the wood fire was blazing, now removed
certain savory pans and kettles from the folding grill
and called me to her and gave me bacon and eggs and
carrots and young corn all smoking on a plate. And for
those who don't like carrots, let it be noted that there
was plenty of bread and butter, and coffee, and also
some strawberry jam, to which the manufacturer, with
great solicitude, had added a small portion of benzoate
of soda.

We ate. But when we had finished and sat there, very
content and comfortable, the mosquitoes came raging
against us. And when we stood on a root a few minutes
later washing the dishes, one of them bit my sweet
friend and she sprang off the root into the lake which

fortunately was only two inches deep. Then we smote them hip and thigh, and dragged our bags of dunnage into the tent, and let down the net before the door, with the nasty creatures roaring and yapping at our heels. She inquired a little breathlessly as to what mosquitoes ate in a place like that when they could not find any people. But I was busy blowing up the air mattress and did not answer—which was just as well since I did not know.

The air mattress, what shall I say of it? When we bought it at Bena, it had seemed to be large enough for two. It was nearly as wide as the space between the wall and the tent pole, and correspondingly long. But as soon as I began to blow it up, it began to shrink. And the more I blew, the narrower and shorter it grew until at last it looked like a row of eight little olive-drab sausages lying coyly side by side.

"Heavens! Did you ever see anything so tiny!"

"Well . . . it *is* a little small."

"What shall we do?"

"Why, you take it. I'll sleep over there."

"No; we haven't enough blankets."

"Oh I don't need many blankets."

"Yes you do. We'll try it. We'll put those bags beside us and the raincoats along the other edge."

So we went to bed on the sausages, spending the night like two courteous gentlemen shipwrecked at sea on a raft too small for both, each offering the other his share, or at most suggesting with a thump some slight change for mutual comfort.

"Good kind friend—if you don't mind—you have me squeezed between the tent pole."

"That's ungrammatical. How could you be squeezed between the tent pole?"

"Well, the result remains the same."

"You see, you're heavier than I. You press the air out of that side, and raise it up on this side, and then I roll down hill."

So now I lift myself off the sausages, and the air comes hissing into them again through their hidden ways.

"Now you had better double up your knees . . . because . . . because . . ." (One of us is *very* sleepy.)

"Because why, sweet friend?"

"Because if you don't, I'll gradually settle on you."

I move a little and catch a glimpse through the mosquito netting of the white sand and the hillside beyond, all garrisoned by the silent forest.

"It is a beautiful night. See, the stars are shining. I am very content; *je suis très content.*"

"Sh! Don't talk your French."

I am intrigued by that. "Why not?" I inquire.

"Because . . . the mosquitoes might hear you. . . ."

I lie still, considering. Does she mean that the

mosquitoes on hearing a human voice will plan a night attack? Or does she mean that they are French Canadian mosquitoes and may become enraged at my accent? Or does she mean that at the present moment, all languages, domestic and foreign, are superfluous?

All of these, perhaps. It doesn't make any difference. I note that one particular bright star is glowing above the pine trees. A novel idea comes to me: that is probably the evening star. . . .

So into the sunrise of another day.

3

The day began its new world symphony in a cool minor key—blue water reaching to the far horizon, wind in the pine trees, bird cries from the thickets, the recurring lap of small waves against the prow of the canoe. We paddled through a lake of flashing light, coming at last to a sandy, sedge-covered point which cut us off from the direction we must follow. By standing up, I could see a narrow channel in the rushes, with open water beyond. We pushed our way in.

Thick, aquatic moss lay just beneath the surface on the shallow bottom. Wading and paddling, we worked through it until the canoe floated free of the matted stems. The sedge about us resounded with the clatter of terrific duck activities. Ducks were everywhere.

They rose on all sides, craning their necks, splashing, calling; dragging up small sharp peaks of water with the tips of their wings. The morass was a duck natatorium and family hotel, with ducks at breakfast, ducks singing in their bath, ducks scolding their young, ducks practicing their flight song and at the same time doing an aquatic "breakdown" with their webbed feet; ducks so close that we might almost have hit them with a paddle.

Beyond these ornithological apartments of sedge and wild rice stretched a wide, indeterminate bay. The water was clear and shallow, the lake bottom so vividly defined that we seemed to be passing through an element no more substantial than air, now over tree-like clumps of weeds where fish of all sizes darted in and out among the fronds, now over glittering spots of white sand, and occasionally over dim caverns which dropped away to unexpected depths.

After three or four miles, the lake drew to an apex across which reared the buttress of a broad dam, with buildings to the left, and the U. S. flag flying. We approached with some care and tied to a boom beside one of the runways.

The dam was a complicated structure of concrete, with several waterways, a logway, a channel through which fish might travel from the river below up into the lake, and a chute for the passage of small boats.

But there were protruding boltheads in the chute's bottom which made it impracticable for a boat covered with painted canvas. A formidable gray-haired Scotchman in charge of the dam helped me carry our blushing kayak up over the high concrete steps, he chewing nonchalantly on a straw all the while to show how fit he was.

"There s nothing the matter with your wind," I managed.

"Well—perhaps not bad for an old man."

"Old man!"

"Yes. I was seventy years last month." And he walked away chewing victoriously on his straw. Under the circumstances it would hardly do to say, "Here, come back and help us with these bags"; so my voyageuse and I, each according to his strength, wrestled our dunnage over the dam and packed it into the canoe again, first laying the three large, cylindrical waterproof bags of blankets and clothing crosswise in the center of the canoe between the thwarts with the folded tent above them, then putting the bread box, with its load of bread and jam and condiments under the back seat, then fitting other bags of vegetables and bacon and tableware and pots and pans into the ends of the canoe, and distributing the camera, rain coats, fish pole, grill, hand ax, and a small leather Boston bag (already known as "General Ketchall") where they would be least in the way. The final ceremony consisted in covering the flat-lying tent and bags between the thwarts with a waterproof poncho, and battening it down along the sides with the two sections of tent

pole which fitted under the thwarts, thus keeping the poncho from blowing away, and making the canoe very shipshape.

General Ketchall

I took the water pail up to the house and asked the dam keeper's wife for the courtesy of using their pump. The man himself came out, and I spoke of the myriad ducks on the lake. But he made an abrupt gesture of the hand, such as woodsmen and sailors make, and assured me that the ducks I had seen were nothing at all, and that I ought to be there when the north ducks came down. The whole lake was black with them, he said, and it was a big lake too, nearly one hundred and forty square miles.

"Winnibigoshish is an Indian name, isn't it?"

"It is. Most of the lakes and streams up this way have Indian names. You'd think Itasca was an Indian name too, but it isn't. General Schoolcraft, who discovered it in 1832 had a friend of his with him, a scholar. And the scholar picked out two Latin words, *veritas,* meaning truth, and *caput,* meaning head. And he put the last two syllables of *veritas* together with the first syllable of *caput,* and made Itasca, the true head."

Talking, we returned to the dam together; and there was my friend deeply absorbed in dangling a hook on a little piece of line over the edge, while directly above her was a sign which read, "No fishing within fifty feet of this fish run."

As we approached, she looked up excitedly. "Here are lots of fish," she said. But the old man kindly looked away, and I got her aboard before the catchpolls of the law set upon her. Then we paddled down a small canal into a good-sized pond that goes by the name of Little Winnibigoshish, and thence into the young—and from now on, uninterrupted—Mississippi River.

THE YOUNG RIVER

CHAPTER II

I

IT pursued its narrow way sinuously along between marshy banks, now winding among grass-crested knolls, now gliding over a few feet of sandy beach. There were some scrub oaks and discouraged-looking willows here and there, but the forest itself kept well aloof.

Whether because of her recent escape from the talons of the law, or because the morning sun was pleasantly warm, or because we had no more lakes to cross, the bow paddle was very gay.

"See that snipe running along there, Boppo! And that gigantic fish—supper size! Look at the minnows scoot! There's a bluejay flying down the river ahead of us and telling all the other forest people about us. They're the worst busybodies in the woods!"

It was, indeed, extremely pleasant. Three black crows sat on three small trees watching us solemnly. One of them on a branch several sizes too small, did a slow, ridiculous dance, trying to maintain both his dignity and his balance at the same time, but losing both.

A hawk crossed the river ahead of us. Spreading out its reddish tail, it landed clumsily on the bank and peered out into the stream. No wonder! Here was a squirrel swimming across the Mississippi. Hawk or no hawk he went on, keeping as much of his sharp ears and large gray tail out of the water as possible. We paddled along beside him. Better our company than the hawk's! But he only turned a little and looked at us very much annoyed, like an irascible old gentleman with a stiff neck and a very high collar. Should we bang him with a paddle? Here was meat, of course. Squirrel stew would go very well with macaroni and tomato sauce. . . . No, he was out of his element. A man should be a better sportsman than a hawk.

We accompanied him to the bank, but instead of using our proffered paddle, he dove with a curse into the bushes, while the hawk, very cold and impersonal, flew silently away.

Soon the forest disappeared before a wild, flat marshland covered with tall grass and wild rice that shut out our view completely. The young river, now free of bowlders and pebble-bottomed shallows and steep banks, lost its sense of direction entirely in the high-growing sedge and wandered like something gently distraught across a vast, sorrowful expanse that had once been the bed of an ancient lake; while the canoe, like a rabbit in a runway, nosed along between solid walls of coarse grass higher than a man's head.

The sun blazed down with unexpected fierceness, apparently focusing his attention on one spot of bright color moving in the midst of that breathless swamp. For some reason—probably the heat—I decided to remove my hat.

We stopped for lunch in the scant shadow of the eroded bank, with the green marsh grass rising high above. Masses of tangled root fibers, some of them five feet long, from which the river had washed the matrix of earth, hung brown and heavy beside us, their delicate tendrils striving down toward the water below. Above, among the yeomanly green blades, shone the tattered swamp flowers of the late summer—wild aster, golden rod, milkweed, daisy, gentian—ragamuffins and grisettes of the marshes in royal purple and yellow.

2

Onward all day under the fierce stab of the sun, making camp at night in the mosquito-bitten thicket. There was more to making camp, however, than merely the fact of making it. Paddling along the twisted water-course as sunset approached, we watched two anxious hours, seeking a spot in the rank sedge where our feet would not sink to unknown depths. Here at last, was a narrow carpet of white sand, edged by the ever-present marsh grass. We came close to it, and tried it with a cautious paddle, but the blade sank deep into quicksand.

Half an hour more we probed and poked and re-connoitered, coming finally to a fairly solid-bottomed nook behind a log. Dragging up the canoe, I staked down the tent in the slightly quaking sand. Quake or no quake, it was just as well we stayed as there were no camping places in the sedge for a great distance ahead. If we had gone on, we would have been forced to travel all night, with clouds of mosquitoes for company.

So, on into a second day of grilling heat. I decided to wear my hat.

In the middle of the afternoon, my comrade, now for variety's sake in the back seat, inquired, "Do your ears hurt?"

"They feel a little warm. Why?"

"Well, they look thicker than usual. Turn around."

Obediently, I turned.

"Heavens! You're ruined, *ruined!*"

"What's the matter?"

"Your ears! They're as big as tomatoes! They wobble every time you turn your head. And your face! Oh, poor Boppo—your face. Doesn't it hurt?"

"No it doesn't hurt!"

"Well wrap yourself up well. Put a handkerchief under your hat and let it hang out over your ears."

We continued on our way. Boppo! That was a nice nickname for a dignified writer, long a bachelor! Boppo. But what was there to be done about it? If I were to say that she called me Robin Hood, or Bigge Boy, or Lord Harry, or even Sol for Solomon, I might get other people who did not know me very well to believe it. But what about herself?

No. A woman finds out about a man soon enough without his adding anything like that; it must either be Boppo or nothing. But I had lived years enough in a state of single nothingness. Let it be Boppo then. (Damn, but my face hurt!)

We were nearing the end of the ancient lake site. Here was a clump of trees, and a road, and a wooden bridge with an automobile beside it, also a woman, two small boys and a man, all very neatly dressed in city dwellers' outing costume. The man was fishing from the bank. The others watched very intently as he cast, reeled in his line, and cast again. But as we came abreast of them, one of the little boys shrilled out, "Say, Pop—is that a Yindin?" and the woman mur-

mured admiringly, "We had ought to have our ko-dak!"

Ignoring these trivial matters, the heads of the two parties gave each other a manly good day, then as we went on, the same little boy called out, "Good-by, other man." Whereupon the bow paddle, who was wearing a cap, nodded and smiled but said nothing.

"Why didn't you speak to him?" I inquired as we turned a bend into the last of the sedge.

"Why? Because an ambition of my early life has just been realized. Some one has thought that I was a man."

Whether or not that incident induced an exalted mood I do not know. But shortly, out of the silence from the back of the canoe, came this:

"Even a mosquito, when seen quite impersonally against a blue sky looks like a little flower flying." And that—Heaven knows—anywhere on the Mississippi, is a noble thought indeed.

3

Grass-covered mounds with patches of white sand between them lined the banks with miniature foot-hills. As we came out from behind a group of willows, a massive dredge rose like the bulk of a mastodon above the plain. When we reached it after an hour of devious windings, we found it to be a government affair, with two, large, many-windowed quarter-boats nearby, each carrying the red flag of the Engineers.

There was no one on the dredge, but a man and woman came out of one of the quarter-boats to look at us. And that was no great wonder, for the last craft they had seen except the dredge and the two floating barracks was a rowboat that had passed down the river two months before. No, it was not lonely. There was a town called Deer River a mile or so away.

"Those barracks," observed my companion, "would be wonderful places for a dance."

"Yes—if they'd let you," answered the woman disconsolately.

"Well—you're fairly far from Washington," I remarked.

"Not far enough," replied the man.

"I know what you mean," said I. We pushed upon our maple blades and went on down the stream, I with a long-forgotten but swiftly-returning wave of pleasure at the thought of being able to do anything I wanted to do or say anything I wanted to say without the eternal threat of court martial—a calamity that lowered more threateningly over many a regiment in the late war, and with more havoc to nerves and bodies, than a first class gas attack.

Clouds shut out the sun, and a raw south wind began blowing.

The south wind! If I have called him a rascal on the endpapers of this book, it is not without just cause.

The young Mississippi

For more than flood water or hidden rocks or currents or the menace of river steamers, the south wind was to be our worst hazard on the river.

Again for a short time, the forest capitulated to the

sedge. We stopped for lunch on a desolate strip of beach that bore, beside the blackened hulk of an old-time tugboat, a huge pile of mussel shells, a few shreds of clothing, and some broken bones. This spot had probably been used for centuries as a camp site, its pebbly base keeping it free from the rank marsh grass and wild rice. We continued on against the wind.

After a few miles of toil, on the right bank we spied a homestead of rough, unpainted logs, chinked with moss and white clay. Strips of gray, unpainted wood ran lengthwise down the roof to the eaves. Half a dozen out-buildings, all the same shade of deep, weathered gray, grouped themselves, perhaps better than the builder knew, against a dark background of pines.

Children of assorted sizes came running down the bank, followed by chickens, hounds, and a young calf. Chickens! That was an idea. Could we buy a chicken?

"They're running all around—if we could only catch one," said the oldest girl.

"Is there a place to camp nearby?"

"Yes, right down in the pine grove on the bank. . . . If you go there, I'll catch one and bring it down to you."

When the tent was up, she appeared with an indignant white fowl which she gently slapped now and again to make him behave, announcing that he weighed three and a half pounds, and that they got sixty-five cents for that size. Then with some misgivings, I took the hen's son into the woods alone, and despatched him much more pleasantly than either he or I had expected.

Returning, I came upon a log filled with creosote. Now here was something fine, something that would burn, even if we should have rain—which we very well might. I chopped it up, and built a fire near the tent, and went away for more wood. But when I returned, the wind and the creosote had already done their dismal work. I drowned the fire and started another, but the creosote had descended upon the tent and everything else including ourselves, like a black fog; so that when we sat down to dine, we looked like a pair of fire chiefs at the last days of Pompeii, she with a smudge of black abaft her eyebrow, I with a general change of color from Chinese vermilion to terra cotta, with my large, tender ears a delicate and fashionable tone of rose-beige.

"At last we belong to the Great Unwashed," she said, regarding me with something akin to laughter, only more intense. "Boppo, you are simply unredeemable. It is perfectly impossible to know what steps could be taken to fix you up."

It was true. Creosote soot was practically immune to soap. Yet all was not lost. For when we lifted the lid of the blackened kettle, the chicken shone forth in its garland of golden dumplings pure as the purest lily.

4

For three days we stood siege in our nine by nine tent against an almost continuous drum fire of wind and rain. Some of the rain came through, but not all of it. With rain coats and blankets and the poncho we made ourselves as comfortable as we could, blessing the man who first thought of putting a canvas floor in a tent. (For how can a tent blow away when you are sitting on it?) Our badly sunbaked hands were more annoying than the rain. In the torrid weather, neither of us had thought about sheltering them from the sun, with the result that they swelled up nearly round. For days afterward, the matter of reaching down into one of the canvas bags was something to be considered long and well.

During slight lulls in the rain, I made excursions to the river with a steel rod and reel that had been lent to me for the journey. But in spite of the rain, the fish would not bite on pickled minnows or anything else, and the only catch I made was a clam that attached itself to the sinker. About half-past ten of the third morning, the rain stopped.

"What do you see?" asked one.

"I see that the river has risen a little," said the other. "What else do you see?"

"I see a narrow strip of blue sky through the pines." We bundled our sodden belongings into the canoe, and paddled on into a wilderness of small ragged pine, with underbrush of birch and maple. We passed a little, run-down sawmill on the bank. A woman in a red dress came out and waved at us. The forest closed in and we left the sawmill behind, only to have its black chimney appear ahead of us half an hour later, caught like ourselves in the fantastic coils of the river.

Then the wind began to blow from the north—a most disgustingly bitter wind for early September. We realized that we were not only cold, but miserably wet. Occasional small clearings passed by, and log houses, chinked with plaster; and magnificent camping sites among the pines. But we did not stop, for we wanted to make the town of Cohasset. Logs were floating in the slow current. They moved silently and rather mysteriously beside us down the river.

Along came a small boy with hip boots full of water, carrying a bundle of wild rice which he expected to exhibit in the country fair. How far was the town, we asked him; and was there a hotel?

Cohasset was about five miles by river, he said, but there was no hotel because it had burned up. Still, there was one house where we might find a room. The man who owned it, was named Mr. Skelly. He was married and had a wife. Her name was Mrs. Skelly. . . .

5

We beached the canoe beside a general store near the single-span bridge, and I went up the bank to inquire for the house of Mr. Skelly.

It was a good house, not new but comfortable, with a circular, bowlder-edged grass plot before it, and a flagstaff that seemed to be the axis of Cohasset. The house stood in a semi-official position in the very center of a tiny square. About it were tangled dirt roads, from which the village, growing into a town and then a city, would one day perhaps take form, shaping itself not like a civic gridiron, but into the trace of its own pleasantly-curving byways and irregular streets.

I knocked. A kindly, ruddy face appeared at the door; white hair and a pipe.

"Have you a room?"

"Come in."

"My wife and I are traveling down the river——"

"Come in, come in!"

"—and are pretty wet."

He ushered me into a room that looked like a small hall where a select few might foregather nightly on

the shining linoleum about the stove. There was a lit-
tered table in a corner with some volumes of an en-
cylopedia on it. A black safe stood in another corner.
The stove was a huge cylindrical affair raised horizon-
tally like the boiler of an engine on strong supports—
the leading member, no doubt, of any cold-weather
gathering whatsoever.

"How many of you are there, did you say?"

"Two; my wife and I."

"Well now, I'm afraid we haven't anything. Just
wait a minute." He went out, consulted, and came
back. "You can most likely get a room in the house
next door that says 'Lunch' on the front."

Just then a pleasant-looking woman appeared.
"How many are there of you?"

"Two; my wife and I."

"It's too bad, now. We're expecting a priest from
Ireland here, and that's all the room we have. How
many was it you said?"

"Two of us."

She disappeared. "It's a pity, as she says," added
Mr. Skelly. "If you have come all the way by river
from Bemidji, it's a good hundred and twenty miles,
indeed."

"Are you Irish, Mr. Skelly?" I asked.

"I am," said he.

"A beautiful country, Ireland."

"It is. Do you know Ireland?"

"Well, I've traveled some over there—something over a thousand miles, with a donkey."

To my huge surprise, Mr. Skelly rose up, spreading out his hands like a benediction.

"So you're the man!"

And as he spoke, his wife was at the door saying, "How many—two? Well the priest who is coming to-night isn't coming until to-morrow. And if you can't find room next door, come back. Indeed," she added, "go get your baggage. I'll find room for you anyway!"

So I went back for my baggage, and found her sitting very cold and forlorn in the end of the canoe. But that was quickly remedied, for, there is hardly a rigor in the world that will not give way before the combination of a roaring wood fire and warm-hearted hospitality.

THE THICKET

CHAPTER III

I

To the stove at night came five rugged, powerful old men—for the most part pipe-smoking and silent; men who, in the days of their young manhood had hewed northern Minnesota out of the forest. Men who had tracked and hunted through the wilderness at fifty degrees below zero, who had built the roads and the railroads with hand mattocks and spades, and who had felled the giants of the forest with the ruthlessness of youth in a young country. Now they sat smoking beside the stove, occasionally vouchsafing gentle opinions of times and men.

Why, I asked them, was the old boat landing by the bridge so many feet higher than the present Mississippi? What had happened to the river?

They smoked on for a time, then spoke in turn, each adding to the composite opinion that it was mainly the cutting of the timber which had reduced the young river to its present level.* Forests, they said, beyond all other elements of the earth's surface covering,

* For an opposing point of view—W. L. Moore in *The American Mercury*, July, 1927.

caught and retained moisture. A large tree, in order
to keep its temperature down, would "perspire"
through its leaves as much as five hundred pounds of
water a day. Thus a forest would give off into the air
thousands of tons of moisture which descends again
and again as rain.

With the passing of the timber, the river grew less.
Many of the more shallow lakes dried up. Small steamboats that had traveled this northern section of the
Mississippi could no longer pass. Then too, the river
without the forest's moderating control, became more
subject than before to the immediate action of sun and
rain. It lost its steady flow. In dry weather it was reduced to a rivulet. In wet weather, now that the rains
and thawing snows were no longer held as they had
been by the great trees, the streams turned into tor-
rents.

Dams were built to "regulate the flow of water,"
dams which were also of wonderful assistance to the
powerful milling interests in Minneapolis.

Yes, taking out the heavy timber had turned the
trick. The old steamboat landing was certainly high
and dry. Not that it made any great difference. The
railroads had superseded the river, anyway. The latter had been of greatest value when the country was a
wilderness. And as far as water went, there was still
plenty for everybody.

A few miles to the north rose a great continental divide where streams flowed off toward such varied destinations as the St. Lawrence River, Hudson Bay, and the Gulf of Mexico. A year or two before, a farmer near Bowstring Lake had been cleaning a creek that drained north into the Rainey River, but on removing a certain particular shovelful of dirt, he found that the creek had turned and was flowing south toward the Mississippi!

There were other stories about the country and its people, about the old Indian chief, John Smith, who lived to the age of one hundred and twenty-four years; about Drumbeater, who drank alcohol neat; about a dim host of Indians and lumbermen and trappers of the roaring frontier. One could hear in the quiet talk the crash of great trees falling and the shouts of men across the wilderness.

Well, the old guard was dispersed now, its members dead and gone, or sitting, like themselves, about other people's stoves; or out on little farms through the state, like old John Doob. Old John Doob! There was a funny old cuss for you! In the days when Roosevelt was furthering the conservation of water in those parts by building government dams, the back water from one of the latter had flooded old John's hay field and put it a foot under water.

Then the elections came along. "Are you going

to vote for Roosevelt?" some one asked him. "Roosevelt *hell!* Look at my hay!"

2

Cohasset, as the first town on the Mississippi, was certainly entitled to a sketch. Nailing my canvas to a telegraph pole where Main Street meets the railroad, I got out my paints and set to work. The day was Sunday. A group of village youths, very trim and jaunty in knickerbockers and gay jerseys stopped to look at the sketch. They talked intelligently about the color, the paints, the relative position of the several buildings beyond the railroad track. Then one of them chanted, "Ha ha ha! Main Street, Cohasset!" The others, taking up the words, broke into derisive laughter.

Now a man sketching knows when his work is causing amusement. For example, I have been much enjoyed both in Damascus and Ningpoo by observers whose art traditions did not run parallel with those of the West. But these lads were not laughing at my sketch. Gasoline transportation, the moving pictures, the radio, and recent books have done their work. The young men of Cohasset were laughing in a large, cosmopolitan manner at their own home town!

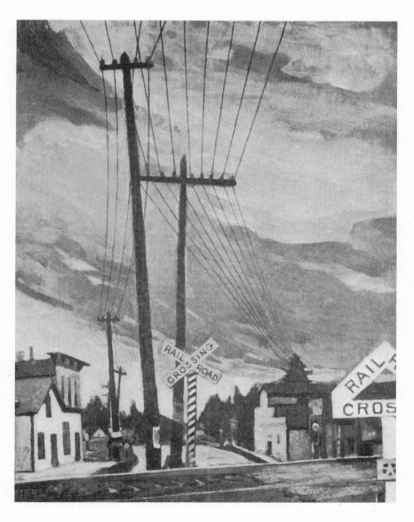

Cohassett is the most northerly town on the Mississippi proper. It has the tang of the frontier about it.

3

Again the south wind, again the threat of rain. Leaving the town, we paddled into high, white-topped waves thrown up by the opposition of wind and current on a river that had widened considerably. Two hours of hard going brought us to a large government dam a mile and a half below Cohasset.

Two young girls sat on the dam fishing with rustic fishpoles. As we approached, one of the damsels squeaked aloud, and, hauling in fishpole and line hand over hand, pulled a thirty-inch pickerel out of the water. Her initial squeak was one of excitement, not incapacity, for she grasped her prey firmly through the gills with one hand and kept the other over its mouth, holding it on her lap like a fretful baby until the fresh air had lulled it to sleep.

"Which is the best side of the dam to portage over?" we called.

"The right side—but there are logs below."

We climbed the bank and looked down. For six hundred yards ahead, the river, closely thicketed by rank underbrush, presented a surface, not of water, but of logs! At the far end, small groups of logs, brought up stream by the wind, were momentarily joining the blockade.

With one of the large waterproof bags on my shoulders, I went along a small path into the underbrush, following the river. The path soon disappeared in a thicket so dense that in order to catch even an occasional glimpse of the river it was necessary to remain within twenty feet of the low bank. The ground became swampy. With every foot, the traveling grew worse. Here were holes filled with stagnant water; charred stumps and black, decaying trunks of fallen trees overrun with brush and creepers barred the way. To avoid the worst of the swamp, I made a detour inland, but on coming back toward the river, I encountered a grove of small birch saplings growing so thick together that the bag could only be dragged through them by the greatest effort.

Here at last was the down-stream end of the massed logs. I cached the bag under a young ash tree that was turning prematurely yellow, fastened a handkerchief to a branch where I hoped it would be visible from the river, and went back to the dam, keeping a lookout as I went, for a better route on the other side. But the bank there was higher and the brush equally heavy.

A slight rift in the logs appeared just below the dam where a canoe might work its way forward a few yards. We piled the rest of our dunnage on the embankment and covered it with the poncho; then portaged the canoe over the bank and paddled carefully down stream, pushing the logs aside until their increasing number made further progress impossible. Working our way toward the shore, we pulled the boat into the underbrush, intending to drag it through the wood to the open water where I had cached the bag.

Now came a few drops of rain, then a soft, increasing spatter on the leaves above us, and finally, such a drenching downpour as one would only expect far to the south. The leaves became small sardonic gargoyles with spouting tongues, the bushes sloshed us with buckets of water, the fallen logs turned black and slimy like the backs of so many giant eels. Slipping and stumbling, we dragged the canoe a few feet into the underbrush. That wouldn't do at all. It was less manageable for two than it would be for one. Yet if I put it over my head, how could we find the way through the bog to the young ash where I had left the sack?

This, at least, was certain: if we stayed where we were, we would shortly be bogged. I turned the canoe over, crawled under it, got my shoulders against the bottom and, with my head in a position of profound thought on my breast, came to my feet. Then, with my well-intentioned companion guiding the inverted bow as well as she could and at the same time fighting her way through the underbrush, we turned inland into a nightmare of swamp and burned trees and brush and lashing twigs and rain.

With an occasional rest, we went on, I from the

dark but by no means cozy interior of the canoe, trying to circle around the swamp's edge and at the same
time attempting to avoid the logs and bogs and bushes
that kept popping up with devilish persistence into my
restricted view. But my feet had lost their accustomed
lightness because of the canoe sitting on my neck, and,
slipping on a log, I went *plop,* the canoe extinguishing
me as a snuffer its candle. Stupidly enough, I lay there
for a moment to get my breath, and on appearing like
Caliban out of his den, I found my sweet friend in
tears, out of fear that I had broken a leg or perhaps a
neck. And I never saw anything so pathetic or so bedraggled in my life, she with her little hat melted onto
her head, and many black smudges from the burned
trees on her face, and the water both from the heavens
and her eyes running off her rain coat and into her
boots, while all the while she wept most sadly, thinking that her man was either sorely hurt or dead.

I made her mind as easy as the situation would permit, and when I had my wind back, tracked off alone
in the direction in which I thought the river lay, keeping well within shouting distance, however; for when
the towns are separated by twenty miles of timber,
even second growth timber, it is not good to travel
alone.

I could not find the river, nor anything except the
rain that was even vaguely suggestive of it. I climbed

a tall pine, but the view was a rim of trees. Sliding down, I worked around the other radii of the circle. No luck at all. We spent perhaps half an hour trying to get some sort of bearings. Then gradually—first with a slight sense of amusement, then without any amusement at all—it drifted in upon us that we were lost. And we wondered if such a trio had ever before been lost in the woods—a man, a woman, and a canoe.

If the man and woman of us could have wandered off together, we might have found some clew as to the direction of the river. But if we left the canoe by so much as twenty feet in that incredible underbrush, it would be as good as gone until winter cleared away its impenetrable screen of leaves.

Then, as we sat in the rain looking wistfully up at the little tent that prisoners call the sky, my companion's face lighted with an idea. "See! The wind up there seems to be blowing from the right. If it hasn't changed, then the river should be somewhere to our left." I got under the canoe again, and we went on through the boscage, banging into certain trees, stumbling over others, now getting the canoe into narrow places from which we would have to back out, until at last she would not let me carry it any farther.

We rested, and then went on, I at the front, breaking the way, she at the back, holding on with both hands, until at last we came to the faint trace of a

disused path, and fifty feet beyond, an abandoned
cabin with its roof grown up with weeds and half the
floor caved in; while there, shimmering faintly beyond an aspen thicket—was the river!

The cabin had a broken stove in it and some dry
boards. I started a fire so that one of us might get dry,
then pushing the canoe into
the river, which at that
point was an inlet full of
logs, I managed, by half-

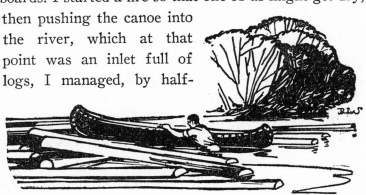

crawling and half-wading, to drag the boat a hundred
yards to open water. Paddling up stream, I came to the
handkerchief which fortunately showed from the river,
and, by pulling the canoe over a few more logs, I got
ashore. Then came three trips back through the underbrush to the dam for the most important of our assembled dunnage—journeys which I haven't any particular desire to remember.

I loaded the sacks into the canoe and returned to
the cabin.

3

She had brought the fire to that mellow state where it consumed even wet wood. The cabin was warm and something like heaven after the sinister, chuckling swamp—but there was certainly a hole in the dirt floor next to the door, ten feet across and five feet deep, and it kept crumbling in at the edges. The passage between the wall and the hole was narrower than when I had left, but the stove was still a good three inches from the rim. Since it must fall in before we did, and thus give notice, we strung a line and dried our clothes, and did ourselves well with some vegetable soup, breakfast by that time being already nine hours away.

But there were still a number of things under the poncho at the dam, and as it was growing late, she insisted on going back with me through the torrent to the branch with the drowned handkerchief on it, and thence through the swamp to the dam, I going ahead and making what path I could, she coming after.

Through the sodden, reeking half mile to the dam, and then all that miserable journey back, she struggled after me with a paint box and the iron grill in one hand, the poncho filled with tableware in the other, and under her arm, the well-wrapped-up sketch of Cohasset—now slipping on the wet logs, now fighting breathlessly through the thicket, the rain upon her, and new stripes of black from the burned saplings across her cheek—but always coming on. And it seems to me that it is not only good for a man to have a memory like that, but to set it down somewhere.

So we returned to the cabin, and whatever discomforts we had known fled away—with the one exception of that ominous caving floor. But the broken stove —bless its soul!—stood like a warm-hearted tutelary god at the edge of the dark pit, and we slept without harm.

LADY INTO CATFISH

CHAPTER IV

I

By morning, the rain and wind had gone. The logs, now released from their place below the dam, were quickly filling the inlet. We loaded our gear into the canoe; then with the good canoeist in the stern, and myself lying out over the prow, we slowly separated the logs ahead, coming at last into open water.

Sunlight on the river. A faint dimpling of the surface by the current. Looking down, we could see the thick foliage reflected as through a slightly uneven mirror. There came a desire to paddle slowly—not through laziness of the paddlers, but through loveliness of the day. The lifted blades tossed out shining rows of pearls which glided along like quicksilver for a few inches and disappeared. The suggested reflection of a hawk passed across the vitreous surface. There, high above, was the hawk itself, sailing down an invisible lane of sky. The floating logs drew close together forming irregular rafts. I lay out over the bow, pressing them apart again in order that we should not join them and become drifters like themselves.

Here was the town of Grand Rapids, with booms of chained logs, a dam, a paper mill, and a portage of nearly half a mile. We passed the boom by pushing one end of a chained log deep in the water while the canoe slid over; and as for the portage, the mill lent us a two-wheeled cart with a friendly horse and driver

St. George and the dragon

thereto. We hoisted the canoe aloft; and the horse, as proud and excited as the steed of St. George carrying home the dragon, pulled carefully to the meadow below the dam, and then, in an emotional moment, nearly spilled it into the river. But his intention had been good, so we thanked him with an apple, and, saying good-by to his master, went on our winding way.

A few miles below Grand Rapids, there came after us a well-built wooden skiff driven by a small out-board motor, with a man, very fine and rugged, standing amidships. This was Lewis Ransome Freeman, a great traveler and adventurer, writing about the river for *The National Geographic Magazine*. He carried a bedding roll in his skiff, great friendliness in his heart, and an expert knowledge of how to cook rice and raisins. For two days we camped together on a high bank where the grass was level as a putting green and shaded by fine elm trees.

He also had first-hand knowledge of lion hunting and fleets and canyons and battle fronts and the jungle —of all terrific adventure, in fact, except marriage. Yet the most astonishing of his tales was a typical story he had heard on the lower Mississippi about two shantyboat fishermen who were tired of their wives and had decided to exchange them. There was a rather fine point involved in the exchange because one of the wives weighed fifty pounds more than the other. Finally they decided that the man receiving the lighter wife was also entitled to a bonus of three times the difference in the weight between the two ladies—that is, one hundred and fifty pounds—of catfish.*

A small well-kept path lead from the camping site up through a ravine to a farm occupied by a numerous family of Finnlanders. The man, a short, power-

* We found later on the lower river that there was every reason to believe this story.

ful peasant with a face marked by toil and kindliness, had come there alone, and, like Isak in *Growth of the Soil,* had hewn his farm out of the forest. It was a strange thing to see his wife, who spoke no English, pattering bare-footed over the well-scrubbed floor to answer the telephone, while beyond the doorsill stood their shining, seven-passenger automobile.

He showed me with pride the first small log house he had built with his own hands and the farmland he had cleared; and when we had drunk his bitter Finnish beer together, he submitted the greatest favor of Finnish hospitality: that since it was Saturday night, we should bathe with his family.

Inquiring for the sake of my lady into the manner and order of the bath, I found that it was a semi-weekly ceremony, that it was accomplished by steam in a bathhouse built especially for that purpose, that it was well-conducted and decorous, and not co-educational.

But when I told her, she would have none of it, claiming that steam always made her sneeze.

Returning to the house in the evening, I found certain members of the tribe glowing pinkly-purple and very merry. With such of the men as still retained their natural hue, I retired down the lane to the bathhouse. The latter was divided into two rooms. A bench ran round the wall of the outer room. We removed our clothes; then the inner door was opened, and one by one we disappeared within into a cloud of hot vapor.

The eyes, accommodating themselves to the light of a dim lantern, saw a rough dais at one end of the room and rough log walls apparently blackened by heat. Near the dais were pails of hot and cold water, and soap, and bundles of laurel for beating oneself on the back. Close by, one of the sons was tending a brick oven that was covered with an iron lid. A round iron container full of good-sized bowlders stood on the oven. The youth in charge threw over them a small quantity of water. There was a sharp, sudden hiss. White vapor enveloped us. We experienced that first delightful pain one feels on getting into a bath tub of too hot water. In order to protect the lungs against the heat, one had to contract the nostrils like a camel and breathe with considerable care.

Gradually we became acclimated. The pores opened sympathetically. There descended upon us the broad expansiveness of opinion so often to be observed in the hot-room of an athletic club. I caught sight of my visage in a small lookingglass. I too, like my neighbors, had turned a rich, crepuscular pink. Rejuvenated, I dressed, thanked the good man of the house, and returned to the tent.

"You missed it!" I exclaimed merrily to the concentric blankets within.

"Yes?" came the response very calm and dulcet—
too calm, indeed, to go unchallanged.

"What's the matter?"

"Nothing." (This, very cool and perfect.)

"Yes there is. What's the matter?"

"Oh—nothing. Only—you aren't so—much."

Thus I found that, while one might bathe by lantern light with water out of a pail, another might prefer starlight and the silent river; and that Saturday
night—venerable institution!—had been Saturday
night for all.

2

Before dawn had so much as peeped, we were up
and about, and breaking camp to be on our way. Then,
appearing over the hill with the sun, came two little
boys and a girl carrying my hat which I had left in
the bathhouse, also two pounds of honey on a plate.
And this was not the pale, insipid honey of the in-
dustrialized town bee, but the rich, mottled spicery of
the buccaneers of the open who have gone roistering
across the buckwheat fields of the north, to come reeling drunkenly back with their redolent plunder.

We thanked the young Finns, and waved good-by,
going southward into a day of glorious sun and sculp-
tured clouds. For the time, the banks of the winding

river had become park-like grass-grown terraces, rising up, one level above another, and covered with groves of young elm and oak and maple. Nature, always capricious, had indulged in a species of forestry almost Teutonic in its efficient neatness. The valley of the Mississippi might well have been the Isarthal. It would have been no great surprise, on rounding a clump of well-regulated willows, to have come on some white swans gliding; and beyond, a white German *Wirthaus* with its green tables, bearing *Augustinerbrau* and *naturschnitzel* and music from the *Fledermaus* rising from among the trees.

In lieu of all this, we went ashore and had some "roasting ears," and eggs, and grilled bacon, none of which were at all difficult in the taking. Then I sat on a rock in the sun, watching my sweet slim friend "plumping out her admirable proportions," as George Moore puts it, with honey and cheese on thin pieces of bread.

"In a previous incarnation, you were certainly a mouse."

"That isn't very nice. Mice aren't so heavenly."

"Well, what do you think you were then?"

"I think I just never saw any cheese before. That's why I'm so fond of it now."

"But what do you think you were?"

"I don't know. I might have been a nun—a bad nun.

Because I have a feeling of fear at being shut up anywhere."

"What! Have you ever been in the hoosegow?"

"Hoosegow?" she inquired.

"Yes—jail."

"No. Anyway, the thing I mean wouldn't be like
that. What would baffle me most would be a domina-
tion I couldn't break because it was too kind."

"Do you ever feel that way about marriage?" I inquired.

"No. Marriage never has had the slightest feeling of
jail at all. I don't see that it has any barriers."

"Just what, for Pete's sake, do you mean by that?"

"I mean that I can do anything I want to. Only
don't be too kind."

"All right; whenever you feel that I'm being too
kind, just bring me that little hatchet and I'll know
what to do."

Instead she came over and sat on my knee, and looking at me very intently said, "Boppo, you have been
sitting in the sun again. Your face is all in chips. What
was that queer-looking man we saw at the circus in
Madison Square Garden a hundred years ago?"

"You can't mean, *'Boy born in the Skin of an Alligator!'*"

"Yes, I do!"

Then in a huge rage I spilled her onto the grass,

and we went on again, quite as pleasantly as before.

Redwinged blackbirds flitted back and forth across the river, disturbed by the distant shooting of pre-seasonal duck-hunters, who, like small boys with fire-crackers before the Fourth of July, simply couldn't hold out any longer.

Half-submerged logs, with their heads pointing down stream, occupied our attention, though only casually, for we were becoming more and more expert at paddling together. "Bobbers," these logs are called; while their completely water-logged brethren, lying, no doubt, in great numbers along the river bottom, are known as "deadheads."

If a hundred million logs have floated down the river, how many deadheads are there? No one knows. They lie there, perhaps a million of them, year after year, unhurt by the running water. A small percentage is hooked, chained, and dragged to the surface by river men who make their living that way. Many logs have been found bearing the marks and symbols of lumber companies that are now forgotten. Men have looked up the symbols in the old forestry records in St. Paul and have found that some of the salvaged logs—still as good as new—are sixty years old.

Bobbers make excellent resting places for turtles. So easy to climb up, so easy to slide down. For some reason or other, the river turtles were very shy. We never came within forty feet of one. Perhaps that was attributable to the red canoe.

For ourselves, we were getting quite accustomed to the canoe's flaming color. People admired it so! We spoke about repainting it less frequently than we had before.

As the afternoon wore on, great numbers of gossamer-winged Mayflies came flitting and dancing out over the river. What were Mayflies doing on the river in September? Committing suicide, it seemed. Sometimes, lured by their own reflections, they dipped to the surface of the water only to find themselves caught and helpless in the strange, cold terror beneath. Others, fluttering above, would brush one of the captives with their wings, and she, or perhaps he, feeling the warm stir of life, would struggle desperately up, freeing herself from the clinging death; or more often, falling back, would flutter a few times and then lie still.

As the shadows lengthened, others too, over-zestful of life, or perhaps very tired, would sink down and embrace the river. Then some hidden eddy, some whim of the current, would sweep them slowly into line and send them down stream in a conclave almost stately— the mourners and the mourned—all dead.

SSS-BANG!

CHAPTER V

I

OBSERVE the town of Palisade, Minnesota, with all twelve buildings on the main street wearing high, wooden, false-fronts, as so many Muenchner burghers their dickeys, and great excitement on the street below. Here was a man with a huge red mustache coming up to me and saying:

"Well, stranger, ye're jest in time ta-buy a ticket fer our fair. There's goin' ta-bee great doin's at the grounds jest across the river. There's goin' ta-bee a hundred and fifty Indians, and a sham battle, and two hundred and fifty dollars' worth of far-works. If ya stay ta see it, I'll tell ya, ye'll be comin' back next year, no matter whar ya-bee!"

"Good! We're in a canoe. Is there a place to camp on the river?"

"A canoe? Surest thing ya know! There's a cornfield jest across from the fairgrounds with some young trees on it. Ya can put yer tent under the trees and rest comfortable, I'm sure."

First, being short of supplies, we went to the gen-

51

eral store and bought butter and raisins and sugar and oatmeal. "Have you any brown rice?" we inquired.

"No, not brown rice—but wild rice, brought in by the Indians," said the storekeeper. And he went on to tell us how the red men, two in a canoe, could gather seven or eight bushels a day, one paddling and the other bending the tall rice stalks over and beating them into the canoe. The price, he said, was twenty-five cents a pound. We bought as much as we could manage, remembering the distant city of New York where wild rice might be had—sometimes—for two dollars a pound. Then returning to the canoe, we went down past a bridge and a few small rapids to the spot across from the fairground designated by the red mustache.

The brush had been recently cut along the bank, and some one had rigged up a wooden framework facing the river, a sort of rickety fort of log slabs. Cut saplings lay under foot. The bank was slippery and muddy. As we were removing our dunnage with some care, suddenly the opposite bank bristled with little boys. They formed an appreciative, nay, enthusiastic audience as I hauled the bags up the slippery bank and carried them to the edge of the cornfield. "There's the settlers," they shrieked excitedly, and sat down on the bank to observe our efforts more closely.

Now their number was augmented by the appearance of thirty or forty adults of both sexes. We heard the word "settlers" being passed back and forth among them in animated tones. A brass band in a grandstand back among the trees struck up a march of the yester-year, and the crowd, drawn by the new attraction, dis-appeared; while the settler's wife, still all aglow from the unexpected house-warming, retired to the cool depths of the tent, expressing in winged words her de-sire for perfect and immediate solitude.

"But, sweet friend, this is really a good place to pitch the tent. How was I to know that——"

No use! I climbed sadly into the canoe and went to the fair alone.

Its grounds, enclosed by the river and an encircling fence, were pleasantly shaded by many large trees and held several new, unpainted buildings, one for garden and household exhibits, others for refreshments, and still others for the horses and cattle. The crowd was gathered about the bandstand where the man with the red mustache had taken command.

"First we'll have a bar'l race. I want four men quick, the quicker the better. There's the bar'ls hangin' side-ways on ropes halfway down the course, one bar'l to a man. You've got ta-climb through twice, once goin' and once comin' back. Here's two Indians ready ta-run. Whar's the white men? Finer'n silk! Now when I say go——"

He kept up a running comment during the race.

"Good boy! Look at John, stuck in the bar'l! He'd make a horse laugh! Look at that bugger go! Hay, John, ya better save ya money becuz ye're goin' ta-stay a long time in that bar'l!" While he was talking, one of the underfed Indians slipped through to the finish, winning almost at a walk.

All out for the tug-of-war! A great event this, between the Indians and the whites. A rope is laid on the ground between the goal posts, and a number of white men take their places. But there are not enough.

"Come on, Homer!"

"Naw, I've got a headache."

"Tug-o'-war's good fer a headache! Come on, Bill."

"Nix. I don't want to get scalped by those men from Sandy Lake."

"Git in there, Roy."

"I hurt my hand crankin' my car."

"You then, Jake!"

"I got the baby."

"Give me the baby. Now one more white man. There you are!"

The Indians, a scrawny crew in smoke-darkened, nondescript clothes, stand ready at their end of the rope—fifteen in all, some large, more small, one negroid, one with traces of Chinese blood. Another—a replica of a dark-skinned Kentucky colonel with gray goatee—holds them steady with raised hand.

"When I say 'three,' " calls the red mustache, "then go. One, two—go!"

The rope snaps rigid. For a tense moment, the handkerchief at its center remains motionless.

"Pull, white men! Pull, Indians! Pull, you scalpin' braves"— Still the handkerchief remains quiet. Then the white men get together. Heave! Heave! *Heave!*

Inch by inch, foot by foot, the dusky ones give way. Instead of facing their decline with savage resolution, the Indians begin to grin. The grins disturb their equilibrium. They pull not as a team but as individuals. As their efforts are overcome, they give a final grunt, and break into giggles like so many schoolgirls. They're done. That's the end of the Noble Red Man. . . .

But suddenly the line stops. The Indians themselves look surprised. They take heart. They seize the rope and pull. Now the white men are tugging and grunting like red Indians, but in vain. They stagger. They give way. More than that, they go down on their backs, their legs passing by like abject signals of distress through the air. Amid great excitement, the Indians walk away with the rope. Good work, Chippewas!

What has happened? Has anyone helped them by pulling on their end of the rope? Certainly not!

Nobody but those four husky white men from Aitken. . . .

2

I paddled back to her whose need for solitude, I hoped, had moderated a little. It had. Together we returned to the fair, arriving just in time to hear the red mustache announce: "Ladies, it has been hinted that we're neglectin' ya. Since that's the case, we want twenty-five women for a rooster race. Make a circle, then we'll let loose a rooster, and the one that ketches it, gits it."

The ladies, however, demurred. Perhaps the memory of the finale of the tug-of-war deterred them.

"How about lettin' 'em chase a man?" some one suggested.

"Good! Mr. Olsen, will ya let the ladies chase ya?"

"Chase me? I've been trying to get the ladies to chase me for twenty-five years. How about yourself?"

"Me? No! They want a good rooster. I'm only a Long Island Red."

"Good fer you!" Great laughter.

"Now, ladies—" But the rooster race did not come off; so he of the roseate tushes announced a squaw dance, which was to be the final event of the afternoon.

A few Indians seated themselves about a meagerly-decorated war drum. As before, they wore dingy caps, mackinaws, and undistinguished trousers. For color, one mangy-looking head bore a green celluloid eye-shield. They sat laughing and joking lazily together and trying out the drum, each with a mallet like a flex-ible, long-handled wooden spoon. The squaws, it seemed, were dressing in the garden exhibit building.

Now, to the accompaniment of a faint falsetto chorus, the drum spoke out in unhurried but insistent rhythm. Three squaws appeared. They wore black sateen dresses trimmed with red bands, and bangles of tin. They were fat and pleasant-looking, and one had her hair in a pair of short braids. Two similarly dressed little girls with bobbed hair and square bangs tripped like colts at their mothers' heels, squaws and daughters all doing a sort of lame-duck step about the men, very stiff and stupid and out of time.*

Two braves in soiled shirts and blue denim pants which were festooned by bright rags joined the squaws, and the lame-duck went on *ad infinitum, sauve qui peut*. There was one feeble consolation. These peo-ple were considerably more Indian than the several full-rigged "princesses" in the distant lodges of Man-hattan, whose calliope altos pour sky-blue water into one's afternoon tea.

---

* Later, one of the little maids posed for the sketch at page 58. Her great-grandfather was Mis-qua-dos, chief of the Sandy Lake Chippewas, who made early treaties with the white men.

It was over. I sought out Long Island Red and asked him a question that had been smoldering in my mind all afternoon.

"When we pitched our tent over there, why did the people come running to the bank and call us settlers?"

"Well, ya see, to-night we're goin' to have an attack by Indians, with far-works, just at the place whar ya landed. And I took the liberty to tell folks at the fair that you were the settlers the Indians were goin' to attack. I hope ya'll excuse the liberty."

Excuse the liberty? With pleasure! *Sweet land of liberty.* . . .

But in the evening a drama took place, which, for want of a better title may be called, "The Settlers' Revenge."

3

Evening, but neither silence nor darkness. The fairground echoed to the raucous howling of motor horns. A huge pile of logs and kindling that had been assembled to light the battle refused to ignite. The spectators, not to be disappointed, brought their cars to the bank and turned a battery of lights upon the river and fort.

We did not cross to the fairground, but stayed on our own bank near a few other stray or defiant souls

This is Ega-bi-a-no-gue (Girl of the West Country). She found it necessary to cry a little after being sketched, but a chocolate bar consoled her.

who hid their identity in darkness. The voices of these came to us through the night.

"What's going on?"

"Nothing, yet."

"This side of the river is better than the other."

"Sure, fifty cents better."

"They've got two boxes of blank cartridges over there for the battle."

"Let's get your gun," said a mischievous lady whose bulk loomed large through the dusk, "and shoot a few good ones in among 'em."

A truck drove along the river road, stopped, and deposited several men and a number of gunny sacks. The men crawled down through the bushes to the fort.

"The real battle's going to begin to-morrow," observed the stout lady. "That bank's covered with poison ivy."

Now an anemic war-whoop sounded from down the river. The red men were about to attack. Here they were, two boatloads of them creeping timidly into the area illuminated by the headlights, their pathetic old clothes blowing about them in the night breeze. They lighted their Roman candles; the attack began.

The defenders of the fort replied with similar ammunition of their own, shooting of course, not into the boats but into the river. But the Indians in their zeal aimed directly at the fort, and their fiery balls came popping in between the slabs, causing the defenders to jump about like grasshoppers in a smudge, and at the same time giving great cheer to the stout lady on the bank.

With another war-whoop, the Indians cautiously came ashore; the white men disappeared above, the fort burst into gasoline flames. One might have believed that the battle was over, but in that case, one would have been very wrong. The real battle had just begun.

Sss-bang! A rocket went up from the bank above the fort. It burst into a cluster of variegated stars, spraying out in delicate tendrils of fire above the Mississippi. The stick, describing a wide, beautiful arc, disappeared with a dull thud among the cars on the opposite bank, leaving in its immediate vicinity a small ripple of excitement. The crowd, however, went on talking merrily.

Sss-bang! Again the burst of illuminated balls; again, the stick, nosing its way downward like a near-sighted watersnake, landed among the cars with a hollow thud. A hush fell over the throng.

Sss-bang! Now there was a gasp of anticipation. *Plop,* said the stick followed by silence. Sss-bang! Another gasp of anticipation. *Plop,* said the stick this time followed by a grunt. Then out of the ensuing

hush, a familiar voice inquired, "How hard did it—
hit ya?"

Sss-bang! Sss-bang! Sss-bang! *Plop! Plop! Plop!*
The cannoneers were warming to their work. Sss-
bang! The air was full of cries.

"Say, you!" some one yelled, but the sound of rock-
ets filled the air. Sss-bang! Sss-bang! Sss-bang!

From the opposite bank came the noise of engines
being started and the wild call of horns. *Plop! Plop!
Plop!* The cars backed away from the river, and like
a stampeding herd of buffaloes on wheels, disappeared
into the grove beyond. Sss-bang! Sss-bang! Sss-
bang!

Plop! Plop! Plop!

The last rocket rose over the Mississippi and
thudded to silence on the now deserted bank. The cannoneers came marching up the road, smirched but
happy.

"I guess we gave them their money's worth," said
one.

The stout lady rose up in the darkness, wiping her
eyes. "Yes, brother," she said, "you certainly did!"

SOME WHO STRAY

CHAPTER VI

I

RAIN and cold, cold and rain—the river lying with
all the gayety of a corpse in a French morgue, under a
steady, congealing drizzle. Above the layers of clouds
that furnished the rain, spread other layers of cloud.
It was very well thought out. The upper strata pre-
vented the sun from drying out the reeking ones below.

We shivered, we froze. We went to bed in everything but our shoes. In a fury of frigidity, I donned
two suits of wearwithalls, three pairs of socks, two
vests, a brace of sweaters, and a suit of pajamas!
What weather for September! There were reports of
snow in Iowa and Illinois a hundred miles to the south.
One morning we woke—after a night so cold that we
wore caps to bed—to find that the frost king had indeed come down the river, touching the banks with
his transforming garments as he passed. Gray sky
above, gray water below, but beside us, a carnival of
green-yellow and golden-yellow, lighting up the fore-

ground as though with splashes of sun against the dark, judicial velvet of the pines.

Here were delicate maples with leaves pink as peach blossoms, dun-colored poplars, oaks and elms still clad in Lincoln green; while sumac, with its vermilion danger signal, flashed the way southward toward the sun. The trees seemed taller now. Early deforestation had not so ruined these river banks as those farther to the north; or if it had, twenty-five years had reclothed them very lavishly again. But it was necessary to rush on past all this beauty; otherwise we might have remained to observe it from a canoe stuck in the ice.

Cold or no cold, we had not yet become entirely gelid. We were still able to enjoy our food. One evening my voyageuse stopped at a solitary, semi-dilapidated little house set high on the river bank among vegetables and flowers. She wished to buy a few of those lowly but robust pearls of the soil that give such kingly relish to a stew. A woman with unmistakable refinement about her and sadness back of her eyes, came out of the house. They talked together about a number of things, as women will, but when it came to paying for the tubers, she refused to take any money at all, adding that there was a good place to camp at the bend of the river, and that she and her husband would like to have us come to see them in the evening.

"We have a nice warm fire," she said.

Later, with the beam of the flashlight leading on, we picked our way through the dew and darkness to the house. Beside the woman, there was a pretty, acquiescent girl in the cheerful room, and a man with an ascetic, birdlike face, a man who looked like a bird that had been swept along on a far flight and that had come to earth lost and buffeted by the elements.

Shortly a preacher came in with his wife and baby. He was a simple, untutored man with a great frame, and a heavy, jovial voice which he could make super-hearty—a sky pilot of the wilderness, with a circuit extending across a hundred miles of timberland. His huge voice wrapping and warming us like a good woolen blanket, he told us about his work of the last eleven years in the lumber camps and settlements, his ruddy, hardship-strengthened face shining large and friendly across the room.

The baby, unimpressed, had immediately fallen asleep. Its mother, a robust young woman, sat listening to her man, content in the knowledge that he was holding his audience.

He told of the logging camps—the long, low interiors of double-decker bunks with the stove at one end and the grindstone at the other—and of how, on a winter's night, when the temperature was thirty degrees below zero, and when all the men were in after a day's work, and smoking their pipes and drying their socks and shirts around the stove with the door and windows sealed, the atmosphere was nearly enough to bowl you over. It had been even worse in the old days, he said, for then the bunks which were called "muzzle-loaders" had been three tiers high, with the heads on the aisle; and six men—two in a tier—had occupied a space only four-and-a-half feet wide. Now conditions were somewhat better. Two men, one in the upper bunk and one in the lower, had a wall space of six-feet-and-a-half.

Most of the time, the men were very decent about listening to him. He had had to strip off his coat to fight a few times, but usually the job was taken out of his hands. A few weeks earlier, for example, he had been talking to the men when a Swede in the back of the barrack had started the grindstone and held a kettle against it. The preacher had remonstrated in a friendly way, and the Swede had stopped. But when he went on with his talk, the "kettle-music" began again.

After the third repetition of this discourtesy, a nearby Irishman arose, and in a voice that shook the camp, announced, "Somebody tell that —— if he does that once more, I'm going to land on him." The kettle sounded off again, the Irishman jumped, and a pair of Scandinavian heels "cracked like a gun" on the floor.

They dragged the now unconcerned Swede to the door, and the sky-pilot went on with his sermon.

One thing about the lumberjacks was, he said, that they had no hypocrisy about them. If a man shook hands with you, it meant that he liked you. If he didn't like you, he wouldn't shake hands. Of course there were a lot of yeggs and criminals among them. "If a murderer gets into a logger's costume and leaves a few days' beard on his chin, the Lord Himself would have difficulty in picking him out from the rest."

"What is the greatest hardship in your work?" I asked him.

"It's the funerals," he said. "Weddings aren't so bad, because they let you know a few days beforehand. But when it comes to dying, folks die most any time, even if you have just left them and are fifty miles away over terrible roads. Then you have to come back; and perhaps you have word that some one at the other end of the circuit is very sick and wants to see you. When a man drives a Ford over these roads for forty or fifty hours without sleep, he begins to see people in the road where there aren't people at all."

So he talked on, stopping at last to ask the man with the birdlike face how things were coming on about the new dam.

A power company, it appeared, held a concession from the government to build a dam a few miles below the little house, and if it were built, all this land would soon be under water. Of course, the power company would pay for the land, and pay the taxes too, and the man would build again on higher ground on the other side of the river. "It makes it bad about the big bridge, though," he said. "The bridge has to be raised seven feet. That is going to cost the county a lot of money—five million dollars, or something like that."

"Five *thousand,* isn't it?" said his wife, looking at him gently.

"Well, maybe it is. Five thousand, then." Conversation died down into a contemplative silence, but the preacher revived it with further stories of the lumber camps, inquiring at last about our journey and listening with visible enjoyment to the narration of certain of our adventures. Finally we talked about cities up and down the river, while the man with the eager, distant look in his eyes listened but never said a word. Well, we must think about going back to the tent. What time was it, anyway?

But now the birdlike man, quietly leaving the room, returned with a cardboard box in his hands. And in the box were dozens of beautifully carved objects of wood—chains made all of one piece; intricate nests of cages; pincers and pliers for every use and trade, each exquisitely carved and finished from one piece of wood, opening and shutting on pins that were also a part of the same piece of wood. Undirected, his artists' spirit had spent itself with infinite, pathetic care on these useless things.

As he showed them to us with a strange, suppressed eagerness, his wife kept looking and looking at him. But I think I was the only one who saw that. For my own companion, who has a first hand knowledge of wood-carving cried, "This is wonderfully fine work."

"He hasn't done any for a long time," said his wife soberly.

"How did you come to make them?" I asked.

"Well—when I was in the fields alone, and there wasn't anything to do, I passed the time working this way. I enjoyed it." He brought out a large card, handsomely mounted with other sets of chains, puzzles, tableware, and pincers. "I sent these to the county fair, but they didn't have a class for them—so they came back."

Then his wife said in a quiet voice, "He has been making ax handles lately. How many is it you have made?" she asked him.

The distant, eager look died out of his eyes.

"Twenty," he answered. "Twenty."

2

Not until the Mississippi has traveled a hundred miles below Palisade does it take on the first semblance of majesty. The vast marshes of sedge and wild rice to the north of Cohasset had not dignified the river, for it had run like a pale thread through their midst. Such broad stretches of water as we had met lasted only a mile or two. Frequently it would have been easy to toss a pebble underhand across the stream.

But now the shores drew back into low hills arabesqued with the jagged magnificence of spruce and hemlock, while the river, spreading out under the wide sky, passed on with fuller curves and contours toward a ripening maturity.

Above the town of Brainerd, we found the way blocked by a double boom of logs under a bridge, and beyond the bridge, a vast mill like the one at Grand Rapids, for turning logs into paper. By virtue of some careful study, we threaded the canoe through the upper boom. But the timbers of the lower barrier were chained solidly together. We could find no place to penetrate it.

A hawk-faced old man was tinkering with a launch beside the bridge, but he walked away as we approached. Two women were fishing from one of the piers. With them was a horrible little infant, sex unknown, who whanged first one, then the other of them with its own fishpole, and in return received a series of cuffs over the head, which it appeared not to mind at all.

"How do we get through the boom?" we asked. They paused long enough in their divertissement to reply that as far as they knew, we didn't. But a youth with a shot-gun strode across the bridge and said, "Just go up to the mill, and ask for Mr. Long. He'll help you across—whether he wants to or not." *

Shortly, we crossed the lower boom, and were assisted around the dam below, and went on between high banks to the town. But Brainerd, which rises nearly a hundred feet above the Mississippi, did not expect guests by river, and so had no suitable spot for pitching a tent except in a tourists' camp high above our heads. We paddled back to the best bank we could find, with the uptown sewage polluting the river, and the town refuse dump functioning not far away, and made camp to the distant accompaniment of trains snorting, dogs barking, children calling, and some one playing a cornet.

So, sitting there near the town but not of it, and listening to a particularly spurious blat of the cornet, I thought—without any ill-intention at all toward Brainerd—of old John Bunyan's town of Vanity "where a lusty fair was kept." But when I mentioned

* Contrary to current opinion of many dwellers along the banks, it is not compulsory for companies having dams or booms across this section of the river to assist voyagers. We found however, that in every case, help was most generously and courteously given.

it to my tentmate, I found that she had a far lovelier picture in her mind.

It reminded her, she said, of France and an early evening in Chartres, when she had walked out into the little park on the hilltop where the cathedral rises above the valley. And from the valley came the sound of music like a light, quivering murmur of birds—a sound which thrilled and gladdened her, for she had never heard anything just like it before in her life. Then she walked to the edge of the balustrade back of the cathedral, and looking down, she found that the gentle, unknown sounds were the voices of human beings in the little valley far below.

3

As the towns on this section of the river lie fifty miles apart, it was necessary for us to buy supplies at Brainerd. The only possible hitch in that plan would lie in the non-arrival of a letter we were expecting in the general delivery. Rising early, we climbed the hill and went toward the town. Brainerd, high on its bluff above the river, contains some nine thousand for-the-most-part friendly people. Even the county jail, which has all the charm of a parsonage, held its modicum of sociability, for as we passed, one of the inmates spying my companion's cheering yellow slicker began to chant, "There ^she^ goes, on ^her^ toes—" changing at that point to "I wish I had some one to love me——"

"Is that a hoosegow?" inquired the subject of the serenade.

"Yes," I answered and hurried her along out of ear-shot before any sentiment should arise which might mar the beginning of an otherwise propitious day.

At the post office we found much mail, but not the particularly desired letter. We looked in our pockets again. No luck. Hardly enough for lunch. Indeed, we had traveled the last seventy-five miles of river on the tag end of a five-dollar bill. At least, we had our other mail. We would try a local bank.

Finding one nearby, we entered, went to a small, precise man who was the manager, and attempted to get a check cashed, with no more means of identification about us than the following:

A letter from the editor of a well-known magazine.

A letter from Dodd, Mead & Company, containing a royalty statement and check.

A bank receipt for money recently deposited.

A letter from Alderny Castle, in Ireland.

Two reviews from English papers of my last book.

Two wedding announcements.

The banker looked over my papers, very courteous and grave, and when he was done, he shook his little mouse-colored mustache, saying that he was very sorry. I could see that he thought I had like as not forged these papers in some kitchen of hell and come all the way to Brainerd and to his bank to get the money; and I could tell by his eye that he thought we were a couple of peculators of the first water. Or it may be that I do him wrong, and that he considered the wedding invitations liabilities that completely over-balanced all the rest. And yet again, it may have happened that his agents up the river had seen my feminine accomplice emerging silently from a cornfield carrying a dozen ears of corn. . . .

At any rate, "So many checks come back," he said. "So many tourists go through. . . ." Then I noticed a neat brass tablet on his desk bearing the legend, "Mr. Peefendinkel," or something like that, and I said to myself, "God help us," and to my companion, "I think we had better go."

Leaving him to his fate, we repaired to a telegraph office, and with our few remaining coins, sent out a telegraphic S.O.S. Then, seeing another bank, we went in to the manager, whose name ended, not in *dinkel,* but in the very proper Minnesota syllable of *quist.*

"Do you ever cash checks for unidentified people?"

"We do almost anything sometimes," he answered merrily. So we left him a few minutes after with our pockets comfortably lined. Then the money came by telegram, and in the afternoon, the expected letter.

"I have an idea! Let's go back and buy Mr. Peefendinkel's bank!"

"No, we could never get it into the canoe."

So we bought our supplies instead, and, sitting in state in the town's most official taxicab, we returned past the now silent gaol to the enfolding silence of the river.

4

On through the forest with its increasing variations in autumnal color. On past lonely farms with sheep and cattle staring strangely at us from the bank; on past deserted log cabins and neglected fields covered with rank overgrowth. Now the river had got well out of its infancy, and, responsive to the quickening rain, it flowed along full and silent between its banks. On through the constantly changing landscape, with only the substantial realities of ourselves and the red canoe fixed firmly in the shifting pattern of days.

Sometimes one sat in the bow, sometimes the other. When she took the front paddle, I steered, and vice versa. There was considerable difference in our technique as steersman, also an accompanying discussion that was as long and as flowing as the river itself.

Longer, in fact. For while the river stops at the sea, our affirmations as to how to travel down the Mississippi will probably go on forever.

On the whole, the current throughout the length of the river flows like this: That is, the momentum usually forces the current away from the shallows and in toward the overhanging banks. One of us, feeling that directness was best, wanted to travel thus:

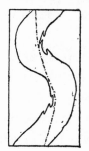 Whereas, the other, believing that the current was an important factor in helping us, liked to travel thus:

The truth is, of course, that either method has its advantages. In following a straight line, there is danger of being caught on a sandbar at a shallow point, or of getting into a backwater where the river actually travels up stream. On the other hand, in following the channel too persistently, there is likelihood of losing a lot of time by going back and forth across the river.

So our various judgments, estimates, opinions and appeals furnished us considerable amusement and a little grief, and occasionally kept us nicely warm even though the weather was cold. For if marriage is "a

state of balanced tension," what, in the name of Count
Herman Keyserling, is marriage in a canoe?

But we adjusted the balance by agreeing that we
take turns steering day by day at the back paddle, and
that he at the back should steer on his day as he chose.

Varied by stretches of less classic timberland, the
park-like banks of the river continued. As we came
around a sharp curve in the valley on the second afternoon beyond Brainerd, the sun burst through the astonished clouds and shone gloriously on a group of
yellow willows against a landscape of deep blue gray.
A painting in that!

We stopped. I unloaded the canoe, set up a canvas
and began to sketch. She watched me for a while; then,
"I'm going to look for a well," she said.

Taking the water bucket, she paddled off across the
river to an opening between the trees which showed
the corner of a badly neglected field. Pulling the canoe
up onto the bank, she disappeared.

Half an hour passed. Then the sun dived behind the
clouds, causing a total eclipse of color, and changing
the mood, the quality, the very composition of the
subject. I worked on; but the sketch, which had not
progressed very far, grew weaker and weaker, dying
at last of acute alteration. I scraped it down, cleaned
up the palette, pitched the tent, and collected some
firewood.

Another half hour passed. I fished a little but the pickled minnows caught nothing. Collecting more firewood, I looked frequently toward the opposite bank. No one in sight. I got out a few of our small, blue-covered volumes from Girard, Kansas. (Whatever their limitations from a bibliophile point of view, they are superlative for light housekeeping in a canoe.) But somehow or other, "The Three Strangers" did not have its expected appeal. I was getting worried. It was now an hour and a half since she had gone to the opposite bank. I could see the canoe lying there, its bow pulled a foot or two up out of the water.

I walked along the bank, whistling a signal whistle that we both knew. I stopped now and then to shout "Hello!" at the top of my voice. There was no response, no echo, even; only the underbrush, the corner of the ragged field, and an exceedingly empty silence.

Taking my Savage .38 to the top of a nearby knoll, I fired several shots at intervals of a minute or so. The shots might help her establish her direction. Yet from the crest of the knoll, I could see that the river did not go a hundred yards before twisting away in a series of perplexing loops. Even if she heard the shots, she might come toward them only to find herself confronted by an entirely strange section of the river.

I imagined a dozen possible situations. She was lying in a ravine with a badly wrenched ankle. There were tall ferns in the ravine, half-hiding the trunks of fallen trees, and over one of these she had plunged headlong. I could even see the water pail she had been carrying. It had rolled among some ferns and there were drops of dew on its new tin surface. . . .

Now she was wandering through such a thicket as we had met at the abandoned cabin up the river. She still carried the water pail, but her face was scratched with briars, and she was crying, but very quietly. . . .

She had gone half a mile down the field and knocked at the door of a squalid house. A long-armed, chinless brute of a man had come to the door.

"May I have some water at your well?"

"Yes—come in. The pump is in the kitchen. Are you alone?"

"No; my husband is with me. He is on the other side of the river. I crossed in our canoe."

"Then he can't get across?"

I do not know that I allowed my mind to visualize beyond that. At any rate, there came a slight feeling of nausea, and it became urgently necessary for me to cross the Mississippi. And I remember thinking to myself, "What I do now must be done right."

More methodically than usual, I made everything snug about the camp, slung the holster of the Savage Automatic high around my neck; took the flashlight and hatchet; put matches inside my hat; caught up the remaining paddle, and returned to the river with the urgent feeling that I must hurry.

A raft of logs lay along the bank buried in the mud. I tried to pry it loose but it was immovable. Heavy chains and railroad spikes held it together. Even to cut one log from it would have taken an hour. A half submerged tree lay beside it. I pushed it off, but it refused to float.

On a sandbar there was another tree, short, heavy, thick, with a huge fist of roots sticking out of the water. I managed to shove it off. Getting astride the trunk, I began to paddle. First came the knob of roots rising like the head of a charger from the Mississippi, then myself, apparently sitting waist-deep on nothing at all and working the paddle, then a small limb of the tree, rising out of the water behind like the charger's tail. I remember looking around and thinking that the situation should be humorous, but somehow the element of humor was entirely lacking.

The water was swift, I had to paddle hard. As the current caught the log, it lunged and jumped about in a surprising way. But I managed to keep the holster around my neck dry, and landed on the opposite bank some distance below the starting place. There was no trace of footsteps leading from the canoe, nor across the ragged ·field. Apparently she had walked on the grass at the edge of the wood. To eyes untrained in woodcraft, no marks of any kind were visible. I cut across the field away from the river. She had been gone more than two hours now and darkness was coming on. *I must hurry.*

And then, as I stumbled over the weed-grown furrows in my water-logged boots, out from behind a cluster of trees far down the field came that dear, familiar figure.

She was walking quite wearily, tugging with both hands at the handle of the water pail. Reaching her, I took the pail from her silently, and, wet clothes or not, put my arm about her, and we walked to the canoe. It was no wonder she was tired. Going and returning, she had carried the pail nearly five miles.

"At the end of the field," she said later, "I saw a sharp-roofed house standing beyond a fringe of trees. I went up to the house, but it was abandoned, and the well was full of rubbish, and there were a lot of old boots and other things around the yard. A sandy road ran into the wood, and I followed it a long way, but I could not tell how much farther I should have to go because the woods were very thick. I went on and on. I thought, it can't be much farther now; and I thought, if I go back now, I'll have to walk all that way without the water; and I thought, we haven't any water anyway; and I thought—oh *Lord*——

"Then I came to a clearing, and before me was a vast, flat plain, level as a floor, with tiny distant groups of farm buildings on it, each with its own barns and its own windmill, and the whole scene looking wide and thunderous like a woodcut by Rockwell Kent—black, newly-plowed fields, a blue strip of hills, and white groups of buildings cut fresh and sharp against the blue. There were motor trucks too—four or five of them—traveling at great distances apart over the wide plain like little mechanical toys.

"I came to a house with hundreds of sheep in the yard, and a woman gave me water from the well. Her nearest neighbor, she said, lived two miles away across the plain, and we could see every detail of the neighbor's house through the clear air. But the woman who never got away from her work, had never called on her, and did not know her name. . . ."

Thus my companion found that we had come out of the wild timberland of the north into the Minnesota plains, and that a pail of water is heavy.

And her companion found that there may be a strange and rather grim adventure of the spirit where there is really no adventure at all. And that he would rather, oh, considerably rather, do without water at all, than travel on alone.

GOOD-BY CANOE

CHAPTER VII

I

So, despite the heavily-wooded valley of the Mississippi, with its trees and undergrowth as thick as ever, we had left the actual forest country behind. And now all the clouds that had gone north in wet, impenetrable blankets, came south again in flint-like shards driven by an even colder wind. We pitched our tent in hollow banks, in gravel pits, in dense brush, even in ruined cabins—anywhere for protection.

Just in the nick of time came the well-lighted town of Little Falls perched at the edge of its high power-dam. We stayed at a hotel there two days, and warmed our warping bones. But ice was in the gutters. We must go on.

A second huge dam, holding back a forty-five foot head of water blocked the way seven miles below Little Falls. Between the two dams, the river became an elongated lake. As we started, a chill north wind was blowing across the wide water. Shortly it changed to the northwest. We made our way down the lake with great care, but a violent squall of wind struck us, tearing the poncho off the canoe and causing us to ship water over the side. The strain of the wind was very great. Only the fact that the heavily-laden canoe exposed not more than three inches of its sides to the wind kept it from taking that position made famous by the turtle, but which no self-respecting turtle will voluntarily take.

At any rate, we shipped water badly, and had to stop at once on a promontory covered with young oak trees. There was a pyramidal mound on its top built of rounded field stones—a government surveyor's mark, we thought, set here to mark some territorial division in the wilderness.

A bronze tablet showed among the stones. We read it and received a thrill; for what we had stumbled upon by sheer accident, was this:

THESE ASSEMBLED STONES FORMED THE CHIM-
NEY OF THE FIRST BLOCK HOUSE BUILT IN
WHAT IS NOW MINNESOTA IN OCTOBER
EIGHTEEN HUNDRED BY LIEUT. ZEBU-
LON MONTGOMERY PIKE EXPLORER
AND SURVEYOR OF THE LOUISIANA
PURCHASE.

Thus we had happened upon one of the earliest historical relics of the United States in the Chippewa country.

The wind moderated. We crawled into our frail boat and went on. What a river! Always panoramic, always changing its character. Always shifting the painted canvas of its scenery. Now, among the pine and spruce and tamarack, were powdery clusters of gray-green sage. The contour of the shoreline reflected a new swiftness of current. Instead of being clothed in foliage or sedge as before, one of the banks, sixty feet high, dropped sharply down to the water like a railroad fill, baring itself, in a half-mile bend to the devouring teeth of the current. While on the other side —long since conquered and forgotten by the shifting river—a low, indeterminate shore rose from the water; a swampy, willow-clad thicket where roots and branches and dead leaves assisted by earthworms, would form new soil and again give contour to the river as it ate slowly into the opposite bank.

Here were some small rapids, the swiftest we had so far met on our journey, with the canoe starting forward like a horse under the touch of a whip as submerged steps of rock, well below the surface, dropped us forward to slightly lower levels. On the shores were clean, tall groves of standing pine, with the unfit trees thinned out and lying in neat piles on the banks,—this being a sign of a scarcity of timber and government supervision; for men in the Northwest were seldom economical of their timber until they were ordered to be.

The river too, bore traces of further economy, for we passed a number of two-man rafts, each raft built like a horseshoe, with a derrick and capstan above the opening for raising deadheads from the bottom of the river. The men poled the rafts slowly up stream with long pike poles, feeling at the same time, for deadheads along the river bottom. On finding one, they raised it a little with their poles, slung a chain under it, lifted it to the surface with the capstan, and moored it to a raft where it would not sink again. Simple enough to tell about, but to accomplish—not quite so easy.

We passed the piles of timber, coming at last to a place where the river seemed to have a wooded island in its midst.

"Which side, left or right?"

"We shall have to go to the right," she said. "That isn't an island, because the channel on the other side isn't cut through at all."

"I think it is," said I.

"I don't," said she.

"All right, cigarettes against nut bars?"

"Correct!" We reached the lower end of the so-called island, but it was a long one, and it was impossible even from that point of vantage, to see whether the left-hand channel was cut all the way through.

"I'll pay you your cigarettes," she said magnanimously, "—but it's not an island."

"Come back up the left-hand channel, then," said I.

"No," said she.

"That's not good sportsmanship," said I.

"Why not?"

"Because you say it isn't an island, but you won't give me a chance to prove that it is."

"All right, we'll go back then."

So, like a couple of idiots and in spite of more than two thousand miles to go, we turned the canoe around and fought half a mile up the left-hand channel against the wind and current. As we progressed, the channel widened out, and I saw that the island was an island after all and that I was going to win. As I looked at her struggling at her paddle ahead, compassion came over me, and I came very near saying, "I'm wrong, it is not an island. You win." But that unfailing urge which husbands have for making their wives always finer and nobler kept me silent. Then she said in a rather subdued voice, "I guess it is an island, all right." I answered, "Yes, it seems to be." And we turned around again and went down stream, I not feeling half so magnificent as a winner ought, nor very much like anything else except a spanked pup, full of shame.

2

The logs gave place to rocky shores. The current became swifter, with rocks above and just below the surface. These made ominous, V-shaped ripples which appeared to travel up stream with astonishing speed and were upon us before we knew it, giving us many a desperate pull at the paddles and many a corresponding moment of relief.

Here was a landscape from an earlier, more romantic century than ours, with unctuous groups of autumnal trees, and the broad, golden vistas of a Sixteenth Century tapestry, turning, toward dusk, into something still simpler and more tender, like a wall painting by Puvis de Chavannes.

We stopped at a farm lying halfway back into the landscape to buy some vegetables; however, the farmer insisted on giving us not only cucumbers and corn and carrots but a pail of butternuts as well. He was a young man, apparently Anglo-Saxon, with wife and children, and was farming one hundred and ten acres alone. His name was Wolhart.

"You don't look like a German."

"No, I'm not," he answered. "My grandfather's name was Willard, but there were so many Germans on this part of the river, that he changed it to Wolhart." That was the first time I had ever heard of a man in this country changing his patronym from an English to a Germanic name.

"There are rapids below the Watab paper mill," he said as we made off.

"Are they bad?"

"Well, I came up stream once from St. Cloud in a canoe with my brother-in-law, and we were green at it, so we carried the canoe around. But it will probably be easy for *you*." (Did you hear that, mate? There's a man of perception!) We waved him a hearty good-by.

From a distance, the mighty Watab paper mill, rearing its decorative bulk against the sky, seemed to block the way. But just in time, the river veered to the right, bringing up, as usual, at a dam. As we sat before it considering ways and means, the chief engineer sent four good men to our assistance. We lowered the canoe over the rotting wooden barrier of a dry spillway, carried the cargo down by the same route, and took off into the swift water below.

The purling and mantling of the river did not stop. The current became stronger and more constant than we had ever seen it before. Now came a series of rapids, with ourselves all at the alert as the brown, half-hidden rocks flashed by; then safety, and with it a pleasant sense of elation. A bit of a village huddled on the left bank, and there was a bridge over the river with a few people on it who seemed to be watching us even more intently than the gay canoe would warrant.

We had gone on perhaps for a mile more when the steady sound of rushing water came to our ears. Before us, under another bridge, was a glint and sparkle that meant more rapids. The bridge put us a little off our guard. One didn't expect much in the way of rapids near a bridge. For the moment we had forgotten that there is also a bridge at Niagara Falls.

Looking at the line of foam, we decided to keep to the left, and we headed in that direction. It might be well to stop and consider, a little. Then—before we knew it—the current seized the canoe and shot it forward into a seething chute of water. Here and there, flat, boiling surfaces flashed by, but they gave us no comfort for we knew that rocks were under them. Being well caught, and since there was nothing else we could do anyway, I shouted, "Right through the middle!"

"Go to the right bank," came a faint voice just audible through the rushing waters from the head of the canoe.

"We can't!" I shouted. We couldn't. Then came a noise like an express train in our ears, a glimpse of twisting, boiling waves, and we were in it, bearing directly down on one of the black circles edged with foam. No time to try for the side! Right through the middle, nerves set for a crash and a sudden deluge of cold water.

Somehow, we slipped across the submerged rock without hitting. Now came the stone abutments of the bridge, and a bowlder to the right as big as a ten-ton truck, and now . . .

Directly before us, the surging current curved, in two successive billows, down a four-foot drop into a wall of foam. The canoe did not hesitate, after the manner of the best fiction, for an undecided moment at the top. It turned its nose downward in a thoroughly businesslike manner, and plunged. *Splash!* We twisted a little sideways and shipped several buckets of water. I gave a desperate wrench at the paddle. *Splash!* Hardly touching the bottom of the second step, we dove into the barrier of foam, rose over its boiling surface, righted ourselves and went on—into quiet water.

For the sake of the complete verities, I must add that in St. Paul a few days later, we again met Lewis Freeman, who, among his other achievements in the open, has probably shot more rapids than any other man in America. And I learned from him that from a professional standpoint, these particular rapids, though the worst on the Mississippi, are not a great affair, being what is generally known as a "riffle." On the other hand, when one is a novice in such matters, I submit that shooting the Sauk Rapids, catch-as-catch-can, without any preliminary study, is a rather breath-taking episode that carries with it an indescribable feeling of exhilaration.

A hilltop near St. Cloud

Fortunately, there are neutralizing elements in nature which prevent man from remembering his successes too long or too well. On the very next day after the great rapids, we came into a series of insignificant riffles below St. Cloud; and as we were looking at the dozens of small, beautiful islands that divide the river at that point, the canoe stuck crosswise on a rock, and it was instantly necessary for one of us to tumble into the water to keep the canoe from capsizing. So one of us did.

3

Monticello, Elk River, Anoka. . . . Quiet villages, these, on a quiet, lovely stretch of river. Dayton too, the quietest village of all, hiding like a memory of New England among avenues of ancient trees; a village still holding gently and a little sadly to the knowledge that once, in the long ago, it had come within two votes of having the state capital just across the river bank. But the two votes had been lacking, and so St. Paul had won.

"We never growed," said the old ferryman there; "in fact, we're only half as big as we were twenty years ago." And very likely he knew whereof he spoke, for he had been at that spot for twenty-five years— and nineteen years logging on the river before that.

"How high have you seen the water here?" I asked.

"Right up to my doorstep," he answered indicating a spot some ten feet above the present level. "It's goin' to come again, but next time, *big*. One of the old dams up the river is goin' to give away, and then another and another, and carry everything before. It may not be in our time—but it's comin'." As I remembered back over the twenty portages we had made in that four hundred and forty odd miles of river, it seemed to me that the old man's idea might bear some serious pondering. So I add my statement thereto, that several of the dams seemed to be old and rotting. It would do no harm at all if some good Minnesota legislator were to find out whether or not the dams are being properly inspected.

Below Anoka, the valley took on that squalid, half-settled, factory-ridden look which frequently means the approach of a great city. On a scrubby, marshy-looking bank all lined off with stakes and bits of string, was a new, vulgar tin street sign with "River Terrace" on it—placed there, perhaps, by George F. Babbitt himself; for undoubtedly by this time, that gentleman has a Minneapolis office.

Here was a workhouse on one bank, and a handsome new filtering plant like a palace on the other. A dam was being built for the filtering plant, but there were still spaces under the low, temporary bridgeway where the current was running swiftly and where a canoe could pass. However, as we approached, a foreman came running along the scaffolding and told us in no uncertain terms not to go under it.

Following his directions, we made for the side of the river, nosed around a dredge, lay flat on our backs, and shot under the bridgeway into a pile of clay which the dozen or more workmen who had come up, had failed to tell us about. Extracting the canoe, we asked why we had not been allowed to go through the middle section as we had planned. They answered that the day before, two boys had tried it, and that their canoe had been smashed and one of them drowned. In the weeds near the bank half a mile farther down the river, we saw one of the halves of the canoe, broken off across the middle with surprising sharpness.

Beyond, making a last stand against the city, were several small, wild islands covered with young cotton-wood trees and underbrush. Then came a bridge with a by no means attractive tourist camp at one end of it, and a little creek into which the up stream current had blown the floating gray filth of the city. We beached the canoe and poked around amongst the tents and automobiles. But the place had a greasy, bread-and-buttered look; and I, for one, when I sit down to contemplate the wildwood, don't enjoy rising up off a half-eaten chocolate cream.

Then too, some tourist had cut himself a nice, slick little pile of firewood, and had piled it just so, with a sort of ant-like efficiency, beside his tent. But we had had five weeks of sky-freedom and had been freed from the hokus-pokus of how things should be done, by the wind and the rain. We went back to one of the wild islands with its cottonwood trees, and pitched our tent for the last time.

4

A day or two later, we paddled under the city's dozen or more bridges to the Pillsbury flour mill at the head of the series of concrete coffers that have replaced the once beautiful Falls of St. Anthony in the middle of the city. Half a dozen husky millers in white aprons and caps helped lift the canoe out of the water and up to a truck on the street. A few squares beyond, we turned down into a winding path below the last cluster of dams, launched the canoe again, and, passing another short rapid, we found ourselves in a beautiful, heavily-wooded gorge flanked by fine residences, university buildings, and parks. On the left bank at the river's edge hummed the expansive, embattled factory of Henry Ford, with the arc of a splendid concrete bridge cutting the sky overhead.

Ford cars will soon be shipped down the river for five hundred miles by barge, supplying a territory sixty thousand square miles in area. The great plant beside the new bridge marks the northern end of actual navigation on the Mississippi. From that point, river packets and tow boats can run all the way to New Orleans.

New Orleans. . . . We continued our way down the river. Loiterers on the bank might have wondered at the slowly-drawn paddles of the two voyageurs in the red canoe. The fact was, that the change from portage navigation to the uninterrupted possibilities of the two thousand miles ahead marked an approaching change for us too. In St. Paul, eight or ten miles below, we would be leaving the canoe for a stronger, roomier craft—and we had certain regrets.

It had been a staunch friend. When unloaded, it was sensitive and skittish. But with ourselves and two hundred and fifty pounds of luggage aboard, it had been admirably suited for river work, lying not too deep in the water to endanger itself from rocks and waves, and not too high to cause trouble from the opposing force of the south wind.

We had reciprocated by a constant watch against rocks and logs, and by keeping it free from mud. Inside, there were a few pleasantly uncertain inch-long places where the wooden veneer had chipped away, showing the canvas. We had had a can of marine glue aboard for possible accidents, but we had not needed it, for the canoe did not leak a drop.

And that statement about a boat leaking or not leaking brings me almost automatically to the *Isador P. Finkelstein.*

SHANTYBOAT

CHAPTER VIII

I

As we came riding down the current to the commanding bluffs where St. Paul stands, I kept my weather eye out for the *Isador P.* What a change in the water front! When I had left the city five weeks earlier, there had been a wide strip of something that might by courtesy be called beach below the Robert Street bridge, with several houseboats high and dry on it, and several others swinging lazily in the slow eddy at its edge, their gang planks firmly ashore.

Now, where the beach had been, there was water, with strange houseboats and familiar houseboats and masses of nondescript lumber all jumbled together and floating around in a disorganized mess. At the lower side of this hodge-podge, near some piling, three large houseboats were moored to each other in a row out from the shore. The boat farthest out I recognized as belonging to one John Lierrick; and beside it I espied the object of my search.

"There it is," I said.

"Where?"

"There. Do you like it?"

"It's *beautiful!*" she said.

The *Isador P. Finkelstein* was indeed something pleasant to contemplate. Small enough for one man to handle, it was big enough to hold two men, or even a man and a woman. The external length of the hull from one end of the deck to the other was twenty feet. The width of the hull was seven, but there was also a little runway along each side on which, with luck, one could travel from the back to the front deck without going inside or overboard. The cabin, sitting solidly upon the barge, was seven feet by fourteen. It had two windows on each side and doors at the ends. Standing on the deck in front of one of the doors, you could just see along the top of the gently-rounding tarred roof. In order to enter the cabin, it was necessary to bend the head a little and go down two steps.

We knocked at John's door. No one answered, but a slight, wiry man with gray hair and a rather ascetic face who was puttying windows on the boat nearest the shore told us that John was away at work. Then a rather pretty, black-haired girl came out, followed by a little boy and a yellow old woman who had a goitre and who was playing with a puppy on a string. A few other people strolled out on their decks.

I inquired of the gray man if he had come from down the river.

The St. Paul Cathedral from the river.

"Oh, I belong here," he answered. "I was down the river, but I've been here off and on longer than any of them. Is that your boat?"

"Yes, the small one."

"It will make a good little boat for you, with a bit of fixing. John left the key with me."

We moored the canoe, went on board the houseboat, and looked it over. Old John had promised to clean it up when I had bought it from him for a hundred and twenty-five dollars, five weeks before. Perhaps the time had been too short.

"Let's get some paint," said my friend.

"Right," said I, "but we'll have to hurry because it is late and to-morrow will be Sunday." We went ashore on the long mutual gangplank before the row of house-boats, crossed under the railroad tracks and raced up a steep hill past some warehouses and water front cafés to the town. But when we returned with the paint, we found that we need not have hurried so, for it was only Friday—a slight miscalculation on our part which seemed to put the boat people considerably at their ease.

We unloaded the contents of the canoe onto news-papers in the houseboat, filled "General Ketchall" with the things we needed most, and took ourselves off to a modest, friendly hotel on Robert Street.

"So you like the boat," I said.

"Like it? I love it! There's only one thing . . ."

"Yes?"

"Why, for Heaven's sake, do you call it the *Isador P. Finkelstein?*"

"I call it the *Isador P. Finkelstein*—so we won't forget New York City." She looked at me solemnly for a moment, and then turned away, gently shaking her head.

"Or if you prefer," I added, rather wilted, "we'll just call it the *Isador.*"

2

With a galvanized tin pail and brushes, overalls and washing powder, I went down alone to the boat. Old John had left the place in a vile mess—ragged hats, shoes, clothes, rags everywhere, and an unnameable collection of grimy chattels under foot. I cleaned it out and down, and scrubbed it; then, prying up several square sections of floor boards, I shoveled out the mud and water that had accumulated on the bottom. Shortly the mate appeared. While I was busy on the outside of the boat, the painting began within. She painted the ceiling, the walls, the cupboard that stood in one corner, the table that folded against the boat's side. The walls were two shades of gray, the ceiling white. In the city she bought a gray, two-burner Perfection oil stove for cooking and to keep us warm; and a bed, half of which pulled out from underneath itself. She bought some cloth, not green nor blue but both, and from it she made curtains for the windows, and a table runner, and a cover for the bed. Since the battered aluminum dishes from the canoe would now be very *infra* in our new *dignitas,* she bought a magnifi-

The last of the red canoe

RLS

cent set of china from the five-and-ten-cent store. She bought a lamp and a book-rack for the blue-covered library, and towels and a mirror, and pots and pans and tableware.

While she busied herself arranging these things within, I was at work without. The tar-paper roof needed re-pitching; all the exterior paint must be scraped and re-painted—sides white, deck gray, windows and trimmings green-blue, and the chimney, English red. I traded the canoe for a rowboat to be fastened as a tender to the back of the *Isador.* I bought a four horsepower, two cylinder out-board motor, new and shining. With Pete Groshan, the gray, kindly fellow who had greeted us first, I rigged a step-like extension on the back deck just above the waterline. We cut a hole in the step and set the fifty-five pound motor temporarily into place. The horizontal flywheel lay parallel with the deck. Directly beneath was the flat gasoline tank and the cylinders, then the long shaft running down into the water, with the propeller and a small aluminum rudder at the end. Would a four horsepower motor run a four ton houseboat? Would the *Isador* respond to the tiny rudder? These matters were in the laps of the gods—with the possible exception of the god Mercury. For whatever the result, it certainly would not be a matter of speed.

A large window was built into one side of the house; a pair of seats were installed on the back deck to hold the five-gallon cans of gasoline; a hundred feet of good rope was bought. It smelled splendid.

We bored a four-inch hole in the overhanging roof and another directly underneath in the back deck, threading a long, heavy pole through the two holes and allowing it to rest on the shallow river bottom for an anchor.

All these things came under the head of pleasure. But there was also a secret sorrow. The *Isador* leaked. The day after I had shoveled it out, there were again

2 inches of water in the bottom. I pulled up some more sections of flooring and investigated. Several of the front planks were dubious. One was plainly bad. A slow succession of minute bubbles rose from the black, wet wood, and with them escaped a trickle of water.

The thing to do, of course, was to remove the plank and put in a new one. But how take out a plank when the *Isador* was sitting on it?

"That's easy," said Pete. He found a block and tackle on his work scow and came wading back in his hip boots, pushing a rowboat full of tools. We turned the houseboat endwise to the bank, laid a runway of wet timbers under it, and with the tackle and jacks, heaved its four tons quite easily up out of the water. Then Pete hit the condemned plank a tap with his maul and it broke into three pieces.

"By gad," he said, "we just got that plank out in time! The tail of a yellow-bellied catfish would have finished you. A little boat like that sinks quick, too."

"How long would it take?"

"About five minutes."

"Old John said it was seven years old. Should a plank go rotten in as short a time as that?"

Pete picked up a piece of the plank and scraped off some of the old pitch. "Look here." A small, rust-colored nail hole was visible.

"That boat's made of second-hand lumber." He ex-

tracted a good plank from his floating lumber pile,
ripped it up, planed it down and set it into the hull.
Then, digging a hole in the river bottom so he could
swing the maul below water, he pounded five great
spikes upward into the boat's timbers. We caulked it
with oakum—not too tight, for the new plank would
swell—and then Pete covered the bottom with soft
pitch. There was the *Isador*, black-bellied and motionless, standing on its four jacks like a contemplative tor-
toise; and all the time the mate was painting and painting on the inside, with the doors and windows wide
open.

I talked to Pete about the roof leaking. He said he
had some tar we could have cheap; but the mate, in a
sudden frenzy of economy, called out, "Why can't we
use the gallon of ebonol that we got at the paint store?"
Pete, interpreting her remark as something a bit de-
rogatory, and being a sensitive soul with no commercial intentions against us, closed up like a clam—which
was very unfortunate, for his conversation about the
river was more valuable than the price of much tar.
But she went on painting unawares, and presently
called out, "Why don't you let him fix the hinges on the
cupboard?" Then I had to go inside, and shut both
doors, and make a gesture of trampling her underfoot,
explaining *sotto voce* that if she wished for the best,

she would treat Pete a little less like an employee and more like a friend.

So later when he was putting on the hinges, she laid down her paint brushes and devoted herself so much to him, now helping him with the door, now holding the hammer for him, that the poor man was quite breathless from her attentions.

"Your missus is making a pretty good job painting," he said to me later. Which in the bashful, inhibited code of the river, was a compliment *de luxe*.

Now there was nothing to do but let the paint dry. Good! We would look at St. Paul.

OFF

CHAPTER IX

I

OF two cities lying near each other, I have often thought that the smaller city gains infinitely more than it knows by its proximity to the larger one. I am sure that the jovial city of Milwaukee understands its place in the cosmic universe much better than it would without Chicago. Rock Island and Moline see the light with considerably clearer eyes, thanks to Davenport across the Mississippi. Berkeley is not less the priestess of learning on her hillside because of the earthy presence of San Francisco beyond the bay. St. Paul too, holds an eminently human attitude of civic mind. Like those others, it is able to think of itself without swelling up and going off in a loud series of pops.

Quite aside from the informing influence of Minneapolis, St. Paul is highly intelligent in its own right. It has a home rule commission that works. It has eliminated its ward boundary lines. It publishes annually a number of excellent books; and one of the local papers runs a daily column on the finer arts by a man named

James Gray that is as erudite and distinguished a column as any in the country.

Here is a quaint, mellow city of distinct charm, rising on irregular bluffs above the river and culminating in the high cross of its cathedral which towers three hundred feet above the portal. Several massive bridges link the city with South St. Paul across the river. Like Minneapolis, it splays out into a charming countryside of parks and small lakes and agricultural units of the University of Minnesota.

Its early days rest firmly on the establishment of a military post at Fort Snelling, in 1820. It was not until January, 1841, that the village was christened St. Paul by Father Boltier. It has grown considerably since then to reach its present population of three hundred thousand—not however, as fast as its younger confrère, Minneapolis. The two cities, originally ten miles apart are now joined by several quite solidly built up thoroughfares.

2

One day, through another voyageur on the river, the daily press found us and took photographs of the *Isador* and its crew, and set us on the first page with a column containing names of books and distant places. We wondered what effect this would have on Pete and our other shantyboat friends. But I think that by that time they liked and trusted us, so it made no difference at all. Indeed, the fact that we had not pestered them with our grandeur worked to our credit. As I sat one night on the back of Pete's work scow with half a dozen other river rats, one of them said with a sort of vicarious approval in his voice, "I've got a cousin who has traveled all over the world. Jeez—there's nowhere he ain't bin! Borneo, Alaska, the Philippines. . . . He's a good skate, though. You could be working by him and talking to him all day, and he'd never say a word about it *unless you asked him.*"

The fact that I was taking notes on the river, seemed to draw Pete out rather than the reverse. Sitting together in the evenings, we had long talks in which he told me of his life and the life of the shanty people. Sometimes, we would sit silently for a while looking out at the reflected lights from the bridge, swaying and balancing on the dark river.

"I was thinking about my kid," he said one night. "If he'd lived he'd be fourteen now."

"Then you lost him when he was very small?"

"Yes. There was a sort of strange thing. . . . Two weeks before, I was going along through a thicket of spruce—or it might have been pine—a little way up the river thinking about a boat I was building, when I heard some one call, 'Pete!' I stopped and looked around, but there wasn't any one near, and there was no house within a mile. I went on, and then, just as plain as day, I heard the voice again. I stopped and went to the thicket and looked all over—thought it was some fellow I knew playing a trick on me,—but it was empty, so I went on. Again some one called 'Pete!'"

" 'What is it?' I asked. And it said, 'You're not going to raise your kid.' Two weeks later, the kid was taken with cholera infantum. The next day at noon, he was dead. He was a fine little kid. . . . Whenever any other children were fighting, he'd cry until they quit. He was a great little feller. . . ."

The shanty man stopped talking and drew long and deep on his mellow pipe. "That was the only time I ever heard voices, but I've had lots of hunches all my life. When any of the family are away, I can tell when they are coming home almost to the minute. I didn't use to pay much attention to my hunches, but I do now. A man's got to keep himself free from being all tied up by this or that if he wants them to work."

We went on talking about hunches, both agreeing that too much domestication spoiled a man's instinct; and I told him how Mary Austin, had written about hunches in a book called "Everyman's Genuis," telling about a gambler who forgave himself for leaving his family because his child's crying spoiled his gambling hunches.

Pete said with conviction, "By golly, that's right! There's gamblers on the Mississippi River who won't let you put your foot on the rung of their chair. There's Indians in the North too, where the women won't let the men do any work around the house because it might spoil the men's hunches."

That was entirely correct, we agreed. Men ought to be free. . . . But we weren't able to talk about it any longer because the mate was waiting for me to fill the lamp from the five gallon can; and when I looked out again, Pete's wife was standing there watching him as he went up to the freight house after a pail of water.

3

Now the *Isador* was ready. But it listed badly to the left rear.

"That's all right," said Pete. "Get you some ballast." So we went under the railroad viaduct and up the street, my friend and I, and, no policeman being in sight, we borrowed six large cobblestones from the affable city; and these were a great help to us all the way down the Mississippi, first in one corner, then in another, depending on the condition of the cupboard on the left side and the water keg on the right.

We got into our river clothes, ate in our last cafe-

Pete of the Mississippi. He believes in hunches.

teria, went to a final picture show, and then, for the
last time, came down the hill past the dark factories
and warehouses and the dimly lighted cafés filled with
toughs and drifters of the river front.

She was dressed in a sort of tan sweater and skirt
and a small tan and orange hat,—with no collar and
cuffs showing because she wore none. I too, had on an
ancient sweater, and breeches, and lumberman's boots
and a cap. As we passed the river cafés, she laughed
and said that I looked a lot tougher than any of
those within; and that was exactly my intention—considering the two thousand unknown miles ahead of us.
So I seized her like a particularly villainous apache
would and dragged her roughly under the viaduct and
down the gangplank past the silent house boats, and
we disappeared into the *Isador,* stifling our laughter.

4

Friday, the thirteenth of October. Great activity
on the deck of the *Isador.* How were we to get past the
rows of piling of the old bridge below the shantyboats? Should we have to row up stream far enough to
swing the boat into the main channel where the water
was open, or should we try to ease it down between the
piles in the narrow space at the side? We decided on
the latter. I tied the rowboat, nose up stream, to the

front of the *Isador*. Pete made his dingey fast to the stern, then while the mate stood ready on the deck with a pike pole several sizes too large for her, we warped and woofed the *Isador* down through the piling and into open water.

Now came a more serious question. Would the rudder on the little out-board motor steer the ship? I started the motor, and we turned down stream past the buoys that marked the channel. Now for the test! I pulled hard on one of the guide ropes. Groaning, the *Isador* turned and with deliberation,—oh extreme deliberation,—headed back up stream. I pulled the other rope. Cumberously but perfectly the boat performed the figure eight! Good!

With a farewell grip of the hand to Pete, we turned down stream. *Sans doubte,* we were on our way. Now, beside the customary black buoys and the red buoys, we saw the first of the white wooden shore marks set up by the Lighthouse Service as guides to navigation. The government engineers in St. Paul had given us a small book called a Light List which told the name and number of each shore mark or buoy, its distance in miles from St. Paul and its position to the left or right of the channel. We were to pass to the left of the white buoys and to the right of those that were red.

Also we had with us a set of one-inch-to-the-mile maps from St. Paul to the mouth of the Missouri

River, six hundred and fifty miles below. While the original drawings of these maps had reached the venerable age of forty-eight years, they had been partly redrawn and posted up to 1915,—and that was infinitely better than no maps at all.

Coming into the woodland beyond the scattered factories of several great Chicago packing companies, we saw that while we had lingered in St. Paul the autumn had been advancing to the south. Even the hardy oak groves on the far hillsides had turned russet against

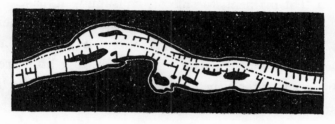

Seventy-five wing dams in five miles of river!

the gold and scarlet of the more delicate trees along the river. Long lines of willows ran out into the water at right angles from the shore and extending nearly halfway across the river. These marked the first of the hundreds of wing dams that had been constructed by the engineers for the purpose of guiding the current and helping the river to dig out a permanent channel.

These wing dams are solidly built of crushed rock, and their saw-tooth tops, which are frequently submerged a few inches below the surface, give foothold to thick rows of willow saplings. As we continued across the morning and down the afternoon, it seemed as though the wind, observing us, had said, "What first lesson shall I teach these two who go so recklessly down the river?" Then it came on us from behind and blew against the cabin; and instantly the fact became plain that in a good breeze the flat-bottomed *Isador,* with eight feet above the surface and ten inches below, would do whatever the wind advised.

At that moment, the motor, consuming its last drop of gasoline, coughed, swallowed, and stopped; whereupon the wind laughing at our efforts with dingey and pike pole, bundled us into the mouth of a little creek hardly wider than the boat itself and held us there like some fussy old nurse maid, saying, "Now take good heed of what I am doing so you don't get caught again!"

We did, observing that there is no craft so difficult to handle in a breeze as a houseboat, and particularly a houseboat named the *Isador.* And that was the lesson of the first day.

5

The sun is getting low. Time to tie up for the night —but how do you do it? Certainly not by running into the shore when you are going down stream at six miles an hour? Here are some trees on a pleasant bank, with no wing dams in sight. The current is rather swift but the trees are something to hold to. I swing the boat around with the bow up stream and we nose in toward the shore, the mate gauging the depth of the river with the pike pole.

Six feet, four feet, three feet. . . . Now we are within a few good jumps of the bank. I shut off the motor and drop the "spud" or anchor pole. The latter catches on the river bottom and the boat, swinging around, places its nose against the bank. I carry a rope ashore and fasten it to the trees before the *Isador* can start out again. The spud pole, resting on the sand bar, keeps the back of the boat steady in the stream; the ropes hold it to the trees on the bank. All's well on the Mississippi.

6

That is, all is not entirely well. For a slight coolness had arisen between us over the manner in which we had left our mooring in St. Paul, she holding that it would have been necessary only to drift easily down stream between the rows of piling, whereas I still stuck to the safer way of tying the small boats to the front and back.

So we went to bed very aloof, and considerably troubled within; I, determined in spite of all, to navigate in the *Isador* with the greatest care. Because when it comes to the final analysis and obituary after an accident, it is the man who is the responsible party. So, in a matter of this kind, he may as well avoid the frying pan and jump with both feet right into the fire at once, hoping that in time his sweet friend may come to understand that the very one he is being sizzled by, is the one whose life he is protecting,—noble fellow!

I dreamed that night that there was a great storm on the ocean and that I was saving a strange lady on a snowy pier; and that, as I carried her up the pier, I asked her where she lived and she gave me a certain address. But when I got her to a taxicab, she told me she did not live there after all, and I said to her very indignantly in my dream, "What do you change your story for?"

In the meantime, my companion dreamed that she was gathering crab meat; and as she walked along the beach she came upon several sizeable crabs, one of whom seized her by the foot. But she very neatly cut off his claws with a little ax she had brought for the purpose and put them on a dinner plate, and chopped all the claws off all the other crabs she could find, and marched triumphantly back to the place she had started from.

At breakfast we told each other our dreams and made certain comments thereon, each secretly taking stock of the other's state meanwhile, and observing, with rising spirits, that a calm was brewing. Soon we were great friends again, and in the exuberance of the moment I untied the *Isador,* pulled up the spud pole, and we drifted down the river. But a little breeze came sneaking along, and in spite of great activity in the skiff, we bore down with speed on a submerged wing dam covered with bushes and small trees. The *Isador* caught it broadside, and stuck there like a dead fish on an intake grating.

I tried to pole out around the dam, but without success. We would have to stay there, it seemed, and let the sand drift up around us, and found a new city, with the boat for the city hall.* But finally, with the help of the very wind and current that had traduced us, we managed to squeeze our four tons out between the young trees and into the open water beyond.

Voyaging on, we came to the Pretzel Islands, deciding that if that was not their name, it ought to be, for they look like this:

The Pretzel Islands

* Many of the islands and bars in the Mississippi are actually formed over the wrecks of old packet boats and barges.

Beside them perched the town of Red Wing, with a small sudden sky line of grain elevators and semi skyscrapers, and a trim grass-covered water front spread out before it like a clean green bib. A great rock called LaGrange (the barn) stood over against the town; it was named by the French who settled there so long ago that no man alive remembers their coming.

There is an editor in Red Wing who can tell you more about the countryside in the course of half an hour than another man could tell you in a month. He will relate, perhaps, that the island directly across from Red Wing was the worst hole in Wisconsin, but that he drove the desperadoes out, and that it has been turned into a park for the city. And when he is through, he will doubtless take you to the intersection of the two main streets of Red Wing and say to you, with a twinkling eye, but also with an emphasis born of conviction, "Here, my friend, is the center of the universe!" Who knows? He may be right.

A WRECK OR TWO

CHAPTER X

I

THE *Isador* had traveled only a mile beyond Red Wing when the wind came up and the night came down, both with great suddenness, and we took shelter, in a deep, narrow, outflowing channel to the left of the river between two islands with heavily wooded banks.

While dinner was preparing, there came a sound of a heavy body passing stealthily through the underbrush across the creek. "Probably a cow," said the mate, pulling down the shade. That seemed plausible, but at the same time, I remembered that we were some distance beyond the place where the editor had cleaned up the islands for the town.

An hour passed. We finished our meal and sat down with nothing more on our minds than the pleasantly reasonable thought that this had been another day. Then, out of the calmness, came the slow, put-put-put of a powerful one-cylinder engine. It turned from the river into our slough. I had not thought it necessary to light the lantern on the cabin. But if the slough were being used by other boats, it might be well to take that precaution, for the government will criticize you severely if another boat runs you down when you are showing no light. I went out on the deck.

A long low-lying power boat was approaching from the river. Then the engine stopped, and the boat, under its own momentum, came on through the darkness.

"Hello," I called. "Who's there?"

Silence. The boat came on.

"Hello there! What do you want?"

Silence.

"Who are you, and what do you want?"

"I'm nobody," came a low voice.

The boat was only six feet away now. At that moment, some one came gently up behind me put my Savage .38 and a flash light into my hand.

The man on the skiff rose up, a great bear of a man —and put his hands on the *Isador's* deck to climb aboard.

"Get off!"

He made a negative sound.

I flashed the light onto his hands. "Get off that boat, or I'll put a hole in you."

He removed his hands at once from the deck and sat down. I kept the light on his hands which he held very carefully before him, hanging them out over his knees in plain sight.

He spoke again in a considerably altered voice. "I wouldn't pull a gun on a fellow for just getting on my boat."

"You know the rule of the river. No strangers aboard after dark."

"Well, we've been having a lot of hard times down here. People always watchin' us and comin' after us. My name's Elmer Heany,* an' I own a lot of land on both sides of the river. Who are you?"

Now it was my time to be silent.

"Who are you?" he asked.

Silence. I kept the light steadily on his hands.

"I told you my name," he whined, "and you didn't tell me yours." His boat was drifting away on the current.

I told him my name, adding that I spent the afternoon with the editor of his newspaper up in the town.

"What paper?"

"The *Republican*."

"That ain't our paper," he returned. "This side is Wisconsin. . . . Writin', are you? Well, you can put me in it."

"I don't know enough about you to put you in it. I'm minding my business. Mind yours."

There was nothing more. The darkness swallowed him. He spun his flywheel and went down the channel.

* This name has been changed.

But a hundred yards away the engine stopped—ominously—leaving us in some doubt as to where he was. Half an hour later, when I went out to bring in the motor, a strange whistle sounded from the island not far away.

Within the *Isador,* comfort had fled. We went to bed in our clothes, with the curtains of the windows wide open, to see what we could in our circle of moonlight. The wind which had died down, came up again. The bumping of the spud pole and the swish of overhanging branches against the roof made sounds incredibly human. They sounded like men breaking their way stealthily through the thicket; there even seemed to be the thud of feet on the deck.

Before dawn, while the white moon staggered drunkenly among the flying clouds, two men did pass again in the same boat driven by its all too familiar engine; but they kept well over on the other side of the channel and played their flash light hurriedly on us as they passed. They talked continuously and their voices had the high, plaintive note of men who wanted to let some one else know that they were near.

There is not the slightest doubt but that Elmer Heany will see this book. People, even as far away as China, always discover themselves in books. If he will write me the story of his grievances against society, I shall be glad to add it here as a footnote in the next edition (always hoping that there may be one.)

2

A few miles below the Pretzel Islands the river ran out into Lake Pepin—a glacial trough for catching the north wind, thirty miles long by two and a half miles wide, with a steep, harborless shoreline between rugged hills. Pete had warned us against Lake Pepin. It rose with remarkable suddenness, and had claimed many lives. A steamer named the *Sea Wing* had been overturned there and a hundred and thirty people drowned. (But who takes advice when he can learn by experience?)

The wind was blowing a little when we came out from between the islands at the head of the lake; nevertheless, we set out for the south. The wind made for the south too. It made better time than we did. (That's quite all right, Wind. Go right ahead. We won't try to keep up with you. . . .) Soon it was a gale. The *Isador* rose high and pitched dizzily. The waves lashed up into a surprisingly high sea. Pans slid from the stove, plates crashed on the floor. The mate discontinued her breakfast in order to hold on with both hands. The motor rose on high, spinning furiously, then sank into the depths.

It choked, coughed, sputtered, and went on again, the electrical connections soaked with water. Twice it stopped, leaving us wallowing perilously in the trough. I succeeded in starting it; the *Isador* went careening on its way.

The wind changed. To go directly down the lake was now no longer possible. We must steer diagonally for the right shore half a mile away, or the boat would go over.

Waves were breaking and surging on a rocky shore ahead. We could make out a short strip of sandy beach under some cottonwood trees. Would there be rocks there too? We would know in a few moments. Speaking objectively, the lake was beautiful. The forest-covered hills rose up steeply from the rocky shore.

We were within twenty feet. *Now!* The mate

dropped the spud pole and I jumped into the surf, ran up the beach, tied to a cottonwood tree, and ran back. At that moment the skiff—which, by the way, was one of the stupidest little boats ever built by man, swung around the back deck and whanged the motor a dastardly blow on the gasoline tank. Then, as I leaned down beside the mate to detach the motor and take it inside, a good-sized wave smote us hip and thigh and back of the neck, and, dashing over us, went ravening like the lion into the cabin.

Somehow, we got the motor in and the door shut; but the *Isador* had dragged the anchor pole so that while the waves continued breaking over the stern, the nose kept banging against the none too genial shore. I took up a section of the floor and pumped ten buckets out of the bottom, but the water ran in through the tiller holes nearly as fast as I pumped it out. We were hitting against submerged rocks. Again I jumped into the surf, and instead of pushing the *Isador* off the rocks, I dug the rocks out from under the *Isador*.

Now the pounding grew so thunderous and the boat squirmed so much in all its joints that we decided to take it to a slightly sheltered depression farther down the shore. So, while my completely saturated friend held a rope from the shore to the boat, I waded out again and held it off shore while the wind carried it two hundred yards down the lake to a more desirable spot below.

Unfortunately for her who held the rope, several large groups of willows grew at the water's edge, preventing her from carrying the line down the shore unhampered. Rather than leave me to my fate, she went resolutely out into the mid-October surf, made her way around the willows and came to the shore again—still holding the rope.

The waves were smaller here but the wind was still veering around to the west. The slight shelter we had found was at best only temporary, but it allowed time to get into some moderately dry clothes. We reconnoitered down the shore. Half a mile to the south, a point jutted out into the lake with a buttress of rocks at its prow. Behind the point was a bay, and in the bay, comparatively smooth water. We got the *Isador* off the beach again, and somehow started the motor; then while the mate ran along the shore (for there was no use in our both getting wet again), I took the reeling, careening houseboat down before the wind to the new haven.

It came into port as thankfully as the Mayflower, and apparently not much less battered. The cupboard had come open during the last scramble, and, besides the earlier wreckage of pans, cutlery, and plates, food

of the most unaesthetic nature, like stewed corn and
applesauce, diagrammed the floor. When the mess was
cleared away and another ten pails of water pumped
out, we found by degrees that the ship was not wrecked
completely. But when I looked with the electric flashlight at the bottom, I found that near the water line at
the back, one of the planks of the boat's bottom had
lost a chip an inch long and an inch thick. Taking a
pocket knife as Pete had done, I pushed it into the two-
inch plank. It ran right in a full inch and a half as
easily as though it had been cutting cheese, and only
stopped then because the blade was no longer! That
left a half inch of wood between ourselves and the
Mississippi. Rotten wood? I did not know. A longer
knife blade might have gone right through. Where the
ends of the plank joined the sides of the boat it was
spongy too. If you pressed hard with your thumb, you
left an indentation on the wood. How had Pete happened to miss a thing like that? Perhaps he had thought
that putting in a plank at the front was work enough.

At any rate, from that time on, we knew that nothing must hit the back of the *Isador* at the water line;
and there was no chance of forgetting it, because now
the boat leaked two good pails a day.

"YOU'LL TIE UP—"

CHAPTER XI

I

No longer having the shantyboat to bullyrag, the wind died down. As twilight came on we considered Pete's further advice about navigating the lake at night. Certainly the wind was now only a breeze, and Pepin itself had lost the power behind its rollers. We lit the ship's lantern; then, guided by government lights on the Wisconsin side and the pier light of a little town across the way, we started down the lake.

To the right Point-no-Point lay like the profile of a huge stranded whale, cut out of blackness against the moon. We trotted on for an hour, but the whale-like profile did not change—for the very good reason that the headland was not a point at all, but an enormous, semi-circular mound with a constant silhouette that held unremittingly to its original shape for a distance of several miles. At last, the whale grew a wen on his nose, the wen developed into a complete facial breakdown, and beyond the whale's wrecked visage, twinkled the lights of the little village of Frontenac where the French first settled in this north country.

On through the night went the *Isador,* down mile-long streaks of foam made by the storm of the day, on past rows of *coulees,* or half-hills, standing like stark, beheaded mountains of the moon against the moon's own light, and throwing black, headless reflections of themselves into the lake's dark mirror. Here was Point Ausable, where, Pete had told us, the Indians had once kept the whites out on the land's end and they had sobbed and shivered all night,—hence Point Au-*sobble!* In a roundabout way there may have been some truth in the story, for Point Ausable, of course, means the black point.

At two in the morning, just as the moon dropped behind the *coulees,* the encircling hills closed in, forming a black portal where the lake again became the river. Flowing in from the left as though to compensate the Mississippi for its temporary loss of identity, was the first considerable tributary—the Chippewa River. We moored to some half-submerged willows in the high water at its mouth. The sky was calm and clear, but at dawn a cold wind came blustering up from the south, and my heroine of yesterday added a woolen bathing suit to her other protective coverings. Dante Alighieri, but it was *cold!* It would not do now to steer with the front door open. We stopped at a bedraggled little water-side village called Read's Landing, and a man who was said to be a pretty good carpenter essayed to put a window in the front door so we could stand inside the cabin and steer. Very shortly, it became evident that instead of fingers he had thumbs, five to each hand. He cut the hole too big and broke one piece of glass, then cut another too small. But he realized his own infirmities, for when he had finished, he gave me his decrepit glass cutter, arguing, rightly enough, that if he didn't have it, he couldn't put any more windows in. But since it was neither useful nor ornamental I threw it into the river. The front door looked like the devil, with the window stuck on like a misplaced postage stamp.

An old man of the village told me that in the old days there never was a time when you couldn't see at least one steamer coming around the point. They weren't little freight-pushers either, but three deckers, side and stern wheelers, costing from twenty to forty thousand dollars each. Their average life was about five years, for they almost inevitably blew up, burned up, or snagged. During the great days *every* boat had made money, he said. The larger the boat, the better the profits. A boat would sometimes more than pay for itself in a single season. In the one year of 1857, six hundred and twenty-five steamers had registered during the season at St. Paul.

St. Paul was right tough in those days, he added, but Read's Landing had been worse. Indeed, it had

been one of the toughest places on the Mississippi
above St. Louis. In the heliotrope 90's, there had been
nineteen so-called hotels and just as many saloons
there. He had seen as many as seven hundred river
men and raft men gather there of a Saturday night.
The Mississippi men would fight the Chippewa men,
and there had been many killings right before his own
eyes. But all that was past and gone now. Read's Landing had shrunk to a harmless little village. The only
foul play we saw was what happened to the window
in our front door.

Filling the gasoline can, we coaxed the motor into
action and went on. But it was thankless work. Again
we pitched and tossed. The wind came blustering about
the boat, driving it toward the wing dams, first on
one side, then on the other. More than once, the *Isador*,
tugging like a refractory calf-elephant on the end of
a rope, shook off all control, and I had to turn it in a
complete circle before I could lead it on down-stream.

After a particularly austere half-mile of wing dams,
wind, and chopping water, came the town of Wabasha.
"Look!" said the mate. There—like a ghost of sixty
years ago—rising white and tall, its shining black
smokestacks standing side by side, its paddle wheel in
the stern, its hull glistening fresh and new, was the
first river steamer we had seen on the Mississippi.

The intrigued *Isador* anchored under its bow. We

came out on deck and looked at the great boat long and silently. *Altair of the Port of Minneapolis*. The glamour of the old days was about her. Almost we could see travelers with carpet bags and colored frock coats bustling up the stage plank; immaculate gamblers in gaudy vests and light strapped trousers watching for suckers to come aboard; ladies in flowered poplin with lace gloves and tiny parasols. The color of the old days came vividly back—the cries of porters, the clang of bells, the voices of laughing negroes, a sweat, a stench of life, a maggot vitality rising up from the river.

I went ashore and talked with a grim, solitary old man who was fastening some brass-work along the gunwale. The *Altair* was not a passenger boat after all, but a freighter. It had just been completed, and there had only been enough fire in the boiler to "turn the engines over." There were eight cabins with double-decker beds for the crew, a cabin for the captain, and another for the owner. The pistons had a six foot stroke, and a twelve inch bore. There was power behind them, and lots of it.

A new eighty foot barge lay moored at the shipyard just beyond. Would the *Altair* tow three barges like that, I asked. Three? She'd tow a dozen of them up stream against the swiftest current the river had. These river boats had power. He went on to say that once he had come from Louisiana, Missouri, to Hudson, Wisconsin, with a dredge that had pulled twenty quarter boats and barges up stream after it. We came out on deck and looked at the *Isador*. "I saw you out there, cutting circles and trying to keep off the dams," he said. "What have you got on the back to make it go, an egg-beater?"

"Something like that," I answered. "Anyway, we are hoping it will take us to New Orleans."

"You'll never get there."

"No?"

"No, sir. You'll tie up to the bank. I've been a long time on the river, and seen 'em start before. You'll never get there."

I thanked him and went back to the *Isador*, not particularly impressed. But if his prediction was wrong, at least it was not useless, for there were several times on the lower river when the expedition needed just some such impetus as the memory of that grim old man saying, "You'll tie up to the bank. You'll never get there."

Several days of much-needed calm followed, in which to repair our somewhat battered constitutions. It was good to find a strip of quiet water beside a wing dam in the evening, and good to lie long in the morning, debating the question, "Shall we attempt to raise our bruises and lumbago and rheumatism and broken backs from the bed, or shall we not?"—the vote being unanimously in the negative. Or perhaps we might consider rising if we only had a block-and-tackle fastened overhead, or a rope hanging to the ceiling with an iron ring on it. It was pleasant to lie there, battered and lame, and to think of the other swinging nimbly on an iron ring. If the motor went back on us, we might even rig a sort of squirrel cage (squirrel rhyming with Cyril)—a squirrel cage, and take turns running in it and so propelling the *Isador* down the Mississippi.

Then up and to breakfast and again on our way, watching what was taking place on the Wisconsin side of the river. The partly submerged groves and thickets gradually gave place to lofty, scrub-covered buttresses of rocks that veered vertically up like the palisades of the Hudson. Now they jutted ruggedly over the river, now drew back like retreating Titans into the blue distance, making a landscape as magnificent and mighty as the *Battle Hymn of the Republic.*

Ducks were flying south with their heavy twinkling flight; wild geese, too. No more practice flights now, with uncertain wheelings and pivotings. The great urge had come—that swift, deep impetus driving them relentlessly southward to the waiting guns of the hunters. One night as we sat at dinner, there came a sharp metallic *crack* from the back deck. Going out, we found one of our graniteware kettles with a bullet hole through it. But rifles are not used for ducks and geese. Perhaps some one had taken a pot shot at us "just for luck."

2

At La Crosse, Wisconsin, between the left end of the big bridge and certain factories farther down the shore, there is an eddy. The eddy has dug itself a hollow in the bank. It revolves smoothly and slowly, repelling by its rotation, any waves that attempt to enter it from the river. Such an eddy, of which there are numbers on the river, often makes a good place to anchor. We anchored.

There was another river-dwelling at its edge—a strangely-assembled little mouse-trap of a house, half over the water, half over the land. After we had passed back and forth up the bank to the town a few times, a little old gnome of a man with a totally bald head came out of the house, and beckoned to me.

"I'll tell ye something," he whispered. "Two hundred yards down the bank there is a carload of creosoted blocks, dumped there by the city. They make fine fuel. I thought maybe ye'd like to know."

But we had already had our hour with creosote; so I said, "We use an oil stove, thanks. Doesn't the creosote come out of the blocks and ruin you?"

"Only on the roof. Before I started using them, it

leaked in a couple of places. Now it doesn't leak at all."

He took me inside his house. The single room which looked as though it had been salvaged piecemeal from the city dump, was strangely neat. The stove seemed a little blackened at the joints, but there was no stray soot on the ceiling. An enclosed observation porch extended out over the river.

"You are very snug here."

"There isn't a finer mooring place from the Falls of St. Anthony to New Orleans, and I'll tell ye why. Right there is the bridge on the great highway between San Francisco and New York. There is the tourist park across the river, and over there beside it, the city bathing beach. I've got neighbors all around—but none too close."

"You don't like them close?"

"Well, since my wife died ten years ago, I've been living alone. I could go live with my children, but I like my little nip once in a while. People don't like to have ye around drinkin'. You know how it is. Besides, I've been a long time on the river; indeed, I've been living on the Wisconsin side for fifty years. My people left Chicago at the time of the fire. They came away while the fire was still burning, and I'm glad they did, for I like the State of Wisconsin."

"I have some great friends in Milwaukee," I volunteered.

His eyes sparkled. "Milwaukee? That's a fine place! When I was a boy I was in the State Reformatory at Waupun, and I knew a lot of fellows from Milwaukee there. Did you ever meet any of that Reformatory bunch? Perhaps we might have some, now, mutual friends."

"I don't remember any at this minute—although most of mine should have gone there."

"That's right," he agreed, nodding his head gravely. "Everybody is alike. It's just a question of whether you get caught or not."

"Do you think we'll have much more cold weather going down the river?"

"Oh, you're all right," he encouraged. "As soon as ye get to St. Louis, it will be summer. But when you're on the lower river, I warn ye—keep your weasel eye open! Don't leave the boathouse empty. Always let one of you be home all the time. There's a lot of bad men on the river. What ye need is a little dog to give ye notice."

"But the cabin is only seven by fourteen."

"That's all right. Build 'im a little house on the deck. Put a couple of gunny sacks in it, and he'll be all right." I said good-by, and went back to the boat. A little dog-house on the deck. . . . There were possibilities in that.

SLOUGH, BIRD, MODEL

CHAPTER XII

I

ON the right bank, the long-enduring State of Minnesota had given way to Iowa. On the left was Wisconsin. The mighty corroded banks of that infinitely vaster river which had preceded the Mississippi now drew four or five miles apart, rising grandly aloof from the flat farmland and orchards of the bottoms between. The colors of autumn flamed across the valley, sweeping away into mauves and russet echoes on the palisades beyond. The river curled away like a twisted silver ribbon through the plain. On the ribbon, like a conscientious and highly determined bug, the *Isador* inched its solitary way. We had overtaken the autumn now. The days were a flashing complement of gold and blue. At times the river exhaled a faint purple mist. The nights were filled with stars and untroubled sleep. We anchored in the mouths of rivulets or sloughs under a mantle of trees. Then in the mornings, while the birds were at their matins, the mate would take the tiller line, and I would climb the roof and sweep the heaped-up leaves into the Mississippi.

It was not all so idyllic as that. We had for one thing, a moron in our midst. I refer to the small skiff which I got in trade for the canoe at St. Paul, and which was undoubtedly the dullest, most utterly ignorant boat ever made by the hand of man. No matter how or where we tied it up at night, we could depend upon hearing it come thump, thump, thump with its abject snoot against the delicate ribs of the houseboat. It did not leak, but it was always a quarter full of water. When we passed a river steamer, of which there were now a number, it would take fright and try to leap onto the back deck, usually missing its jump, and hitting the flywheel of the motor. There was only one name for that boat. We called it the *Abject Stupidity*.

The motor was no moron, but it was nervous and temperamental. With the help of the three-mile current, it carried the boat down stream at a speed of five or six miles an hour.* When the weather was rough, and the *Isador* began to mingle with the river, the motor would get a little water on its connections and faint dead away. Like a mid-Victorian heroine, it suffered from the vapors. It would up and faint almost any time, for the very good reason that it wanted to get away from something it considered unpleasant.

Then there were those small spicy incidents of

* In the lower river where the current was stronger, we occasionally reached a speed of seven miles an hour. One filling of the motor's gallon tank would last two hours, and nearly fifteen miles.

chance, which gave infinite variety to the journey. This
for example, is a day just south of Prairie du Chien:

We had spent the night up a slough or narrow channel of the river beyond a wooden railroad trestle which
just allowed the *Isador* to pass through. The sunrise
was beautiful, not a cloud anywhere. Good! We would
make at least thirty-five miles to-day. Breakfast then,
and an early start!

I spun the motor, and we went down the slough.
Suddenly there was a dull snap, the *Isador* staggered,
hesitated,—and went on. What was that? I stopped
and investigated. One of the mooring ropes had slipped
off the back deck, caught itself over a stump, and
broken off short. Starting the motor again, we went on
toward the trestle. No use trying to make it with the
motor going. We shut off the power and poled the boat
by hand under the narrow viaduct.

As we passed out from under the trestle, a little
breeze caught the *Abject Stupidity,* and swung it behind a post, stopping the *Isador.* More breeze puffed at
the houseboat and swung it into a patch of water
weeds. I tried to start the motor, but it caught its propeller in the weeds, sighed, and fainted. Now the wind,
which had been waiting for just this *impasse,* sprang
at the *Isador,* making the boat quite uncontrollable
and pushing it farther into the weeds. We dropped the
anchor pole and considered. There was only one thing

to do: let the houseboat drift back against the trestle, hold it there cross-wise, revive the motor, and start off again.

I pulled up the spud, while the mate shoved us off with the pike pole. But the bottom of the slough was clay. As we got clear of the weeds, it seized the pole roughly out of the mate's hands and left it sticking upright while we drifted off unarmed toward the trestle.

To retrieve the pole, I jumped into the *Abject Stupidity,* gave a mighty pull at the oars—and one of the oarlocks ripped off! Meanwhile, the *Isador* was very close to the beams and piling of the trestle. I came aboard again, ran to that side of the houseboat which would strike first, put my back to the side of the cabin and my foot to the trestle, and—crack, splinter, *crash!* In went the thirty-six inch window glass behind my elbow.

At last we were at rest beside the trestle. We cleared out the glass, mopped the ever-present, mysterious mud from the decks, and again started on our way. But water from the mopping had accumulated in the hold so that the boat now rode lower in the water than before. A sunken dam at the mouth of the slough had not bothered us at all when we went in. But now, as we passed out, there was a scraping bang and we slid over the top of a submerged concrete block, doing Heaven only knew what, to the *Isador's* bottom. So we went on for a mile down the river, not knowing whether we would sink or swim, or both.

Now, thanks to the wind, the water was growing rough. It began to splash over the decks. We put in at the lower end of the slough, tied up, and ate a little food. Then I attached the motor to the *Stupidity* and went in the rain (for *that* had started) back to Prairie du Chien for a rope and a pane of glass. By the time the new glass was in the window, it was four in the afternoon. The rain stopped, the wind died down sufficiently to allow us to go on for an hour to anchorage in the mouth of the Wisconsin River. It was pleasant to know that at that point in 1673, Louis Joliet, Father Jacques Marquette, and their five voyageurs had floated wonderingly out through half-concealing mists onto the Father of Waters. But—coming down considerably farther in history—it was not quite so pleasant to remember that after a day of perfectly astonishing activity, the present discoverers had only done a very scant three miles out of their well-intentioned thirty-five!

2

The French, coming into the country both from Canada and the Gulf, quite as early as the English did on the east, claimed jurisdiction over the whole valley, even going up the Ohio River to the present site of Pittsburgh. "New France" included the whole territory between the Mississippi and the Alleghanies. New Orleans itself was part of the Roman Catholic bishopric of Quebec.

But the English, on the eastern seaboard, did not enjoy being so confined—hence the French and Indian Wars which lasted a hundred and fifty years, coming to an end with the fall of Quebec and the Treaty of Paris in 1763—a treaty which left France only "a hamlet in lower Louisiana."

3

The French have placed their indelible imprint on the upper river. La Crosse, the field where the Indians played their game; Prairie du Chien—not literally "prairie dog" but prairie of "The Dog"; a famous Indian chief; Frontenac, Trempeleau, Dubuque, Tete des Morts Creek, Pomme de Terre Prairie—these and many other names remain. In the Light List, which gives the names and numbers to fourteen hundred odd buoys, lights, and day marks, between St. Paul and St. Louis, there are also such vague appellations as "Frenchtown Buoy" and "Frenchtown Village Daymark" and again "Frenchtown Light," where the very names of the settlements seem to be lost, and their memory lingers on only in the generic designation given them by the early surveyors of the river.

These first surveys must have been grilling work, yet the young men who went out to measure the river had their fun, too. Pig Island, Vermilion Slough, Parsons Bar, Sourwine Bend, Beef Slough Buoy, Polly Towhead, Viola Daymark, Elsa Light, carry the possible overtones of merriment and laughter.

4

Something small and alive was floating in the mouth of the Wisconsin River. It made no particular effort to avoid us, so I ran the skiff alongside and picked it out of the water. In general effect, it was a small duck with the tail feathers shot off. The wings and back were a grayish brown; the waistcoat light tan, the bill long and sharp, and there was a huge pair of shovel feet, laid out in front like black snow shoes. There were three bad shot wounds in the head and neck.

We put the little fellow in a box by the stove where he would be as comfortable as possible; at first he kept twisting about and trying to get away from the pain. Finally he settled his head in the middle of his back, swelled himself up like a dingy powderpuff, and went to sleep.

The next morning no change was apparent in the

patient's condition. There was however, a change in the weather, with glare ice on the deck of the houseboat. Spurred on by that fact, and by the north wind behind us, we traveled that day fifty miles from the Wisconsin River to the excellent, rectangular harbor that had been cut out of the Iowa shore by the city of Dubuque.

We moored beside a row of boat-sheds. A man in hunting costume who was puttering around near by, told us that our wounded guest was not a duck but a hell-diver, very difficult to catch and nearly impossible to shoot. Hell-divers moved so fast in the water that they would dive between the time that a gun was fired and the charge could reach them. Our patient, he thought, had been shot by accident, for its kind migrated south with the ducks. Would he get well? The hunter thought not. He had never seen one caught before. If it were too sick to dive, it was more than likely too sick to live. Certainly it looked that way, twisting its head round and round in an epileptic manner until one almost expected to see that necessary appendage drop off onto the floor. We left water and weeds and wild rice beside it and went out to see the town.

There is in New York a now well-established publication called *The New Yorker*. It is modish, lighthearted, and very frequently clever. In its early adolescence it spoke of itself as being a magazine "for every one but the old lady from Dubuque." Thus we had come by the impression that not only "the old lady," but the town itself would be very solemn and stodgy. Dubuque, however, is neither. We found it to be a neat, prepossessing little city at the foot of a huge bluff, very lively and busy, with a very fair quota of "citizens of the world" in it. Indeed, with a jovial breadth of spirit, several of its news-stands sold *The New Yorker*. There was an idea in that! We would find an old lady and——

We found one, never mind how, up three rear flights of outside stairs, past and under a week's washing, in beyond a little kitchen full of washboards, steam, and babies.

"Grandma, some one to see you."

A beaming, fiery old lady with cap and cane thumped into the room.

"Come right in. You're just in time. Won't you sit down and have something to eat?"

Since the old lady had never heard of us before, and since we carried no letter of introduction, that, I opined, was hospitality *de luxe*. We thanked her, saying that we had had breakfast, and that my companion was making sketches of people along the Mississippi. Would she be willing to pose?

"Pose? Of course I'll pose! When we were in our boat, wasn't Pike Curtis always making pictures, and

Old lady of Dubuque reading The New Yorker.

didn't we black our faces and have our photos took!"

"On your boat?"

"Why certainly. Come in and sit down. When I was a girl my father had a side-wheeler eighty feet long and two decks high, on the river. There were eleven of us on it—Ed Groom and his wife to make photographs, and Pike Curtis who did sketches in crayon and Indian ink, and my father who was a doctor up and down the Mississippi. Then of course there was my man and myself, and those who ran the boat. We traveled the river for years, then my father sold it, but my God, he didn't get what he gave for it. My man was a river pilot. Father took him on after we nearly got busted in a big storm—and I married him. . . . What do you want me to do, stand on my head, or sit? I'm great at sitting!"

I said that we would be in luck if every one was as willing to pose as that. She leaned over and slapped me familiarly on the knee. "Say, kid! I've been all over. That's why I can bring you in here and treat you like my own folks. I feel like I know you. Ethel, show him the baby." A young woman brought in a baby that was fairly popping with milk and health. A fine baby—the young woman's of course?

"No," said the latter, "I'm the grandmother." The little girl doing the washing was the mother, it seemed, and she of the cap and cane was the great-grandmother, having qualified as a grandmother at the age of thirty-seven. The young woman began playing with the baby. "Our ma is a great old ma," she said. "What are we going to do with her if she lives much longer?"

"Har!" laughed the beldame. "A year from now I may be on a boat again going down the Mississippi. You're not a river man, are you?" she asked me.

"No, he's a writer," explained my mate. "He's writing about the river." The other looked up with admiring eyes. "Say! I'll bet you make more money than a feller who works for his living!"

Eventually she settled down and posed for the sketch on the opposite page, in the meantime, reading a copy of *The New Yorker* that we had given her. When the sketch was done, we asked her whether she liked the magazine.

"My God, it's fine!" she said.

So, as we returned to the boat, we decided that it must have been quite a different old lady from Dubuque that *The New Yorker* meant.

CITIES

CHAPTER XIII

I

MEANWHILE the hell-diver was becoming restless. He deserted the box by the stove, wobbled to the end of the boat and stood there ready to leap into the abyss between the floor and the planks below. The mate returned him to his box and held a saucer of water up before him. He drank, but more frequently he put his bill down beside him on the sack. No doubt, having spent most of his life afloat, it was his habit merely to lean down and take a drink! He moved around uneasily, but as soon as we started the motor and left Dubuque harbor, he settled down again to a state of apparent content. Perhaps that sixth sense in which birds are infinitely superior to man, told him that he was going south.

The tawny water of the river seemed perfectly still. Again, the landscape had that rare decorative quality which we had sometimes seen far to the north—massed, billowy tree groups and the rich unctuous vistas of Watteau and Boucher. It seemed possible that behind those trees might be a little grassy hill with a white marble belvedere on it, and a dozen slightly shopworn shepherdesses in rich brocade and lace playing with lambs on the grass, while a bored monarch sat yawning in the shade. Lovely islands rose from the river, the channels between opening to blue hills and idyllic farm land.

Then came a dark smudge of smoke on the sky, and under it, the squalid manufacturing city of Clinton made a dismal smirch over the landscape where the Lincoln highway crosses the Mississippi. We spent the night in a stinking creek that was filled with strange, unpleasant excretions of a dozen factories, feeling a certain annoyance at an industrialization which, in its fever after profits, forces men to work out their lives in such sordid surroundings.

We went on, anchoring the next night at the mouth of a small inlet. The hell-diver's health seemed considerably improved. He would quack mildly; sometimes he would get out of his box and wobble about the floor. But he had eaten nothing for four days. Perhaps that was for the best. When one was used to standing on one's head and pulling grass from the bottom of the river, Quaker Oats on a plate would probably be a severe shock. We realized a little sadly that we should have to let him go.

In the morning we carried him to the weeds at the edge of the inlet and set him in the water. He looked around, drank twice, paddled out a little way, took a good stance, and dove, reappearing again a few feet beyond. Excitement came into his manner; apparently he realized that he was home. He pushed out a little farther, and again went under. Only a ripple along the surface of the water showed the direction he had taken. Up again, with still greater animation.

"He has forgotten us already," said the mate.

"He never bothered very much with us, even in the beginning," said I.

He was half way across the inlet now, shaking his head gayly, twisting himself this way and that. We watched him a moment; then, *flip,* and he was gone for good.

"He was a fine little chap," she said.

"I thought he was a bit petulant."

"He was a lot pleasanter than most people with three bullet holes in them would be."

We went back to the *Isador.* It was strangely empty. What we needed, we agreed, was a dog.

Wisconsin on the left, Iowa on the right. Before us is the head of the Rock Island Rapids, and running along beside them, a canal with a government lock at the southern end. This is to be our first lock with the *Isador.* Ahoy, and heave ho! Let's be very shipshape and nautical! Overhaul the clew lines, mate, let the portcullis fall. When I say "Avast," shut the engine off to half speed.

Here is the lock ahead. We chug down the canal and approach the lock. "Avast there, my hearty. *Avast—shiver my timbers!*"

The black gates open before us, and we sail majestically in. I signal the mate again; she shuts off the engine, and we draw up to the side of the lock. There are rows of strong iron hooks along the concrete walls. The lock keeper looks down and from above tells us to fasten to the hooks while the water goes down. Very good. I take a trim coil of rope from the back deck and carry it to the front; dropping it, I try to find one of the ends. The ends have both disappeared into the rope. I remember Pete's advice, "Take your time, but be on time." The rope rolls itself into an orgy of loops. Out, damned knot! I work away, but it is as obstinate in its coils as a boa constrictor. The lock keeper gives up hope and begins to let the water out of the lock. Holding on to one of the iron locks with one hand, as the *Isador* goes down inch by inch, I labor feverishly at the pile of rope with the other. But I might as well spare myself the trouble. Now we have dropped the required six feet, and the doors at the lower end of the lock are opening wide. I know from the map that across from Moline, five or six miles down the river, there are more rapids.

"Shall we take the river, or the lock?" I inquired.

"If you take the river, you'll swim," answers the lock keeper laconically. I'm afraid he has not appreciated our seamanship.

2

On the Iowa bank the factories of Davenport began; on the Illinois side, were the first houses of Moline. We traversed the canal, dropped down another six feet through a lock, skirted the lower end of the beautiful two and a half mile island that carries the Rock Island Arsenal, turned back between the island and the mainland in a slough that is known as "Sylvan Water," and came to rest in a marshy overflow of the river beyond the Rock Island railroad station.

Davenport, Rock Island, Moline. Three cities at grips with industrialism. To the passer-by, they appear to have come considerably farther in understanding than Clinton up the river. No doubt their advantages are greater. They appear to be well on the way toward making industry sufficiently human to provide material comfort for its workers. I did not see a great deal of Rock Island, even less of Moline. I was in Davenport only half an hour. Has a man who spends half an hour in a city a right to express an opinion of that city?

I think so, provided he makes it very clear that it is a half hour opinion. If he has wandered considerably over the face of the world, giving full play to his receptive faculties, there is a possibility that he may have developed a certain intuitive accuracy in regard to the personalities of towns and cities—a hunch that resembles, in a way, the sense of smell. I should like to try out my hunch about Davenport. If it isn't right, somebody will undoubtedly tell me.

Without having talked to anyone about it, I think that Davenport is a little bumptious. I think it may be inclined to bully Rock Island and Moline on the other side of the river. I think it is trying very hard to be a large city—heaven knows just why. A hundred years from now, when we have ceased in a degree to measure values by bulk, Davenport, like our other large cities, will no doubt be fighting just as strenuously to reduce—and the sloughing-off process may not be so very pleasant, either. I think that in Davenport there may be too much "boosting," too many men of vision whose vision ends at the top of skyscrapers and factory chimneys.

In other words, I think that Davenport is very much like any other American manufacturing city. Imagine going into a manufacturing town and saying to an average American manufacturer, "Beyond the factory chimneys are the stars, which make a vaster music than the whir of your greatest machinery." The next music to be heard would probably be the rythmic intervals of some one being kicked down a long flight of stairs! An American manufacturer, somewhat better than the average, might, if the above quotation were called to his attention, feel a little uncomfortable or a little annoyed. He might be sentimentally silent for a moment, but almost inevitably a protest would rise in his mind. "Yes—I know all that," he might say, "but I have to haul in just so many thousand dollars a year or know the reason why. I help support the art society and the municipal orchestra. But I haven't any time to fuss about the stars. Besides, I don't want to. It might make me different from the rest of the crowd, and it's hard enough to keep in with 'em now." *

The fact is that neither Davenport nor the rest of industrial America has any time for contemplation. Our philosophy is frankly industrial, finding its reward in mechanical achievement. Its worst feature is its intolerance of the ideals of others. Aside from that, there is nothing greatly wrong with it—although it may not entirely please those of us who do not enjoy being members of this or that standardized group. Pessimists to the contrary, out of this intensive industrialism may come more time for leisure and such

---

* An American manufacturer—an actual person—submits this: "You can't look at the stars without food in your belly—and we provide food."

new arts—the new architecture, for example—as will take firm root in our vigorous, enthusiastic soil.*

But now, under a fusillade of discarded machine parts from the factories of Davenport, and tomatoes unfit for its canneries, let us return to the comparative safety of the river.

A century or more ago, Ma-ka-tai-mi-she-kia, or more familiarly, Black Hawk, was a name of importance in this country. Lieutenant Zebulon Pike, whose trail we crossed several hundred miles to the north, came ashore on August 9, 1805, and talked with Black Hawk at the mouth of the Rock River, two miles below the present city of Rock Island. After a friendly speech, Pike requested the Indians, who were waving British flags, to wave the American flag instead and to give up the medals which had been presented to them by agents of the Great Father in England, adding that he would send them medals from the Great Father in Washington. Black Hawk, who had "one of the finest heads that heaven ever let fall on the shoulders of an Indian," decided that under the circumstances it would be a good thing to have medals from both the Great Fathers!

His medals did him no good, however. Years later, expatriated and broken, he addressed his conquerors in

* "The sculptors of the future are the engineers," says a modern artist. This is heresy—but invigorating heresy.

a few words of profound pathos and dignity, saying. "This was a beautiful country. I liked my towns, my corn-fields, and the home of my people. I fought for it; it is now yours."

3

We approached Burlington, Iowa, just as darkness fell precipitately over the river. Like many of the cities on the Mississippi, it displays an armored water front of cobble-stones sloping down to the water. We avoided this dangerous incline, and picked a spot just back of a large Naval Reserve barrack, thinking that there, at least, the anchorage would be good.

I took a line ashore; but there was a slight breeze blowing—just enough to send the *Isador* crashing against a large submerged building block of unknown purpose but very definite position. Feeling about with the pike pole, I came upon several similar blocks. That was no mooring place, in spite of the proximity of the Naval Reserve barracks. So up anchor, and in rope, and down against the wind through the darkness to the mouth of what proved to be the Burlington sewer, where a slight indentation in the shore line gave a little protection against the wind. There, we thought, was rest. But the wind pushed us toward the bank, the oars hit on shallow mud, and I called to the mate to drop the anchor pole before we ran so badly ashore that we could not get away. A slim, square-shouldered old man who looked like an ancient knight came out of an amply built houseboat on the shore and directed us to a narrow mooring place between two launches. Finally we made it, hands numb with cold, feet soaked, clothes daubed with unattractive mud off the ropes. The old man had long since gone indoors. There was no one in sight. But the next day, the Burlington Press announced our arrival as follows:

"A small but immaculate houseboat drifted up to the levee as darkness fell upon Burlington last night. A man dressed in khaki trousers, a khaki shirt and high leather boots, guided the boat to her moorage, made her fast as easily as the best boatman on the river, and then gazed upon the bluffs of Burlington. . . ."

I shall keep that clipping. If I keep it long enough, I may be able to persuade the mate that that was what really happened.

For thirty-seven years, the knightly old fellow had been a diver. Eugene Farris was his name, Captain Eugene Farris, and he was not inclined to talk. But I persevered; and presently, walking on before, like an old-time warrior in his armory, he showed me his forge, and his well-equipped tool shop, then his diving suits with their bulging insect eyes, their valves and water-tight wrist bands and ponderous-soled shoes, explaining that the belts he wore with his under-water outfit, ranged from seventy-five to a hundred and fifty pounds in weight, depending on the depth at which he was working.

Then, as talking was not so unpleasant after one had made a beginning, he told about the numerous family of river folk to which he belonged, most of whom were now gone. At one time, twenty-five men in the family were licensed captains, mates and engineers, but they had passed with the great days of the river. He himself, so far as he knew, was the oldest deep-sea diver in the United States—now that Jobin and DeWitt and Folick were gone. How old was he? "Sixty-seven years; *just* sixty-seven on the twelfth of October," he added with care.

"Of course you don't do under-water work any more?"

"Oh yes, I finished a job on an intake just two weeks ago." An intake job sounded prosaic enough, but, with that fine simplicity so often apparent in men whose lives have been spent facing danger, he went on to tell about the intake valve where at different times three divers had been killed. He had approached as warily as though the thing were a crafty enemy, finally subduing it with an inside valve which he had invented himself.

Once, in fifty feet of water, he had removed one hundred and sixty-nine bodies from a sunken packet. At another time he had taken one hundred and thirty from a steamboat that had turned turtle—the very *Sea Wing,* of which we had heard before at Lake Pepin. He had been a steamship captain himself in the days of the great steamboat lines—the Northern Packet, the Red Collar, and the Diamond Joe. No wing dams in those days, but plenty of sand bars. He had seen as many as three steamers at once aground on a sand bar off Plum Point, sitting there like turtles and working the mud soft with their paddle wheels until they slid off again into the river.

"You ought to write your story," I said.

"No, I don't care for that."

"Do you ever wish you were on the river again?"

"Well, I have thought of it. I have the timbers for a new barge—but I guess I'll never get around to it. I'm all alone now, you see."

"You have your children," I said, for he had spoken of them.

"They're all away."

"But you said your grandchildren write to you?"

His face lighted up. "Yes, they do. Here, I'll show you—" He hurried off and came back with a letter from his small grandson. "He has the same name as mine—Eugene." Then he brought me the photograph

*An old knight of the river—still a deep-water diver
at sixty-seven.*

of a comely-looking woman, a woman with a motherly expression, and tranquil, understanding eyes.

"*She* has been gone two years," he said. With that, the memory of his solitariness came flooding back; and the old knight of the river, stalwart and fine, but with the deep, pathetic grief of a lonely little boy, turned away his head.

MORMONS

CHAPTER XIV

I

WHEN we pulled in toward the levee at the city of Ft. Madison, we did not expect to see a woman waiting for us on the grassy bank; even less did we imagine that she would wave a welcoming hand; and least of all did we expect the figure to take on the lineaments of a tried and trusted friend.

We approached, one of us mingling exclamations of joy with thanks to heaven that the dishes were washed, the other, divided in his mind between pleasure and wondering if any other man had ever come so strangely upon his mother-in-law!

She would not come aboard at the time, however; so at her hotel we learned how she had arrived. Knowing when we would be on this section of the river, she had come from visiting friends in a nearby state to Rock Island, only to find that we had left that city two days earlier. She had followed, then preceded us, by train, trolley and bus, through Davenport, Muscatine and Burlington, to Ft. Madison, always getting word of us from those along the river, but never quite catching sight of the *Isador*. An hour or two earlier, she had

been a little in doubt as to our whereabouts, because
the evening paper reported that we had "gone down
the Mississippi past Ft. Madison on our way to New
Orleans." But the complaisant host of the hotel had
notified the police and, unless I am mistaken, the fire
department; so that when we came under the bridge
above the city, the news was brought to her at once.

Next day, we carried her from Ft. Madison to Nauvoo, Illinois, past mile after mile of strange dead forest whose blackened limbs rose starkly up out of the
flooded waters. The weather, praise God, was all that
it should have been; so when she took the train at
Montrose that evening and expressed herself as being
fully satisfied with the boat and its crew, I could see
that she would visualize us as sailing down the river
through a paradise of calm and idyllic days. Indeed,
she will not really know into what an Odyssean voyage I had led her daughter until she reads this book;
and by that time the journey will be so many months in
retrospect, that I hope I shall be forgiven anyway.

The present Nauvoo rises from the meadows and
woodland a mile from the river. We had without knowing it, anchored beside the oldest house in the vicinity.
It had been a good house of roughly squared lime-
stone, but now it was half submerged by the back-
water of the dam at Keokuk a dozen miles to the south.
When Lincoln pleaded his cases in that house before

the judge of the Circuit Court, it had been several hundred yards from the edge of the Mississippi.

Going up from the river along the dirt road that leads past cornfields and orchards and isolated houses of red brick, one is impressed by the fact that the entire meadow land below the pinnacled hill of the town was at some time in the past laid out into city streets. These old man-made "improvements" have been so changed by the ebb and flow of the seasons that now their straight outlines are nearly obliterated under a lovely garment of meadow-grass, wild asters and goldenrod.

Here and there, within nodding distance of each other, are the substantial red brick houses, all of an earlier time and distinctly of the same period. At the top of the hill stands the pleasant, ordinary little town, with its schools, its banks, its newspaper. But what is the meaning of the grass-grown streets below?

When Chicago was only a hamlet, Nauvoo, now a village of a few hundred, was the thriving capital of the Mormons. Driven out of Missouri with his followers, Joseph Smith, the prophet and founder of Mormonism, came in 1839 to this beautiful stretch of valley and river. In a few years the town became a hive of commercial activity. Between 1840 and 1850 the population rose nearly to fifty thousand. Unfortunately, the prophet found it impossible to leave politics alone, thereby bringing down on himself the dislike of both Whigs and Democrats. The Mormon city and its leader became very unpopular in the state. In addition —or perhaps because of that fact—there was much murder and outlawry in the vicinity. Horse-thieves and cattle rustlers had the unpleasant habit of driving their stolen stock in the direction of Nauvoo so that the Mormons would be blamed for their outrages. The city became a rendezvous for criminals. The political activities of the Mormons brought on a conflict with their neighbors. In 1849 Joseph Smith and his brother Hyrum were shot to death in the county jail at Carthage, Illinois, where they had been taken under the alleged protection of state troops. Two years later most of the Mormons were driven from Illinois. After severe hardships, a small percentage under the leadership of Brigham Young, reached Utah. Here were included hundreds of women whose husbands had been killed in the recent disturbances, and who certainly, in those rough days, needed protection. Polygamous marriage followed. But those Mormons who remained in the Middle West, never engaged in polygamy, nor in certain other early malignant policies of the Utah faction.

After the Mormon evacuation, other settlers came in to occupy the deserted houses. An old building near the ferry, bearing the name upon it of Johann Georg Kaufmann, carried this inscription under its rooftree:

"Dies Haus ist mein und doch nicht Mein,
Wer nach Mir kommt wird's auch so sein.
Ich bin hier gewesen;
Wer das wird lesen, der is auch hier gewesen." *

2

When I went in to the local barbershop, *The Chicago Tribune,* which functions under the blushing title of "The World's Greatest Newspaper," had just arrived carrying an article on Nauvoo, entitled, "The Weirdest Place in Chicagoland." If one were to judge by the remarks of the group of citizens about the stove, the world's greatest newspaper was badly out of order.

"Chicagoland, my eye!" said a stout red-faced citizen, casting a dark look down the offending column.

"They send a guy down here to write us up, and all he does is to turn over the old bones."

"Yeah," said a short young man in leather puttees, "You'd think we were just a cemetery for preserving the remains. Where does he get that 'weird' stuff, anyway?"

"They have to have something to write about," said the first speaker, "and they don't give a damn what it is as long as it's what they call 'news.'"

---

* This house, though mine, is not mine, too.
Who follows next, will find that's true.
　Still I have been here; who reads this
Will also have been here, I wis.

"Yeah, that's right. It wouldn't be news if they should tell 'em we had deposits for a couple of millions in the banks or the best schools in Hancock County. It wouldn't be news to tell 'em we shipped a hundred and fifty carloads of grapes out of here last season."

"All they care about is the murders, and ole Joe Smith with the gold tablets in front of him."

"What is that story about the tablets, friend?" asked another, apparently a traveler.

"Why, Joe Smith said he found them when he was monkeying around in a cave, but it's funny nobody saw them before him. He used to put a chunk of nephrite up before one eye and a chunk of something else up before the other, and a sheet over his head, and read the tablets by the hour. Oh, he was smart, Joseph Smith. I knew his wife, old Emma, and she was a kind old lady. I don't know how much she believed in him herself, but she wouldn't say anything. *The New York Herald* sent a man out here to interview her one time, but she only told him that the Mormons never preached polygamy here, and that was right, too."

"Do the red brick houses down the hill date from the Mormon time?" I asked.

"That's right," said the young man with the puttees. "Have you seen Joseph Smith's house?" When he found I had not, he added, "I'd be glad to take you around in my car." So he showed me the landmarks of the town—Joseph Smith's mansion, with its secret chamber and the chimney, the site of the Mormon temple, Brigham Young's house, the Nauvoo House built as a tavern by the prophet, and the homes of several of the present elders of the church. A friendly old lady took us through the house where Joseph Smith had lived. Next to the fire-place in his room was a secret closet, with still another closet leading from it and a ladder going up into the darkness of the loft above. I found the Mormons to be a pleasant, simple-mannered people, living plainly but well, like the Society of Friends. They were not, I found, expecting Joseph Smith's return from the dead as some one had told us. The dwelling places of the early Saints were only being kept in repair out of veneration for the founders of their sect.

"There's one thing more to see," the young man said, "and that is the oldest house in Nauvoo. Lincoln and Douglas used to plead their cases there."

Thus, automatically, he returned me to the *Isador*.

3

Ducks again by the thousand, spraying out into wisps and smoky tendrils high above the water. Wild geese too, curving and cavorting, whirling and spinning—undecided, perhaps, whether to stop with their lesser kindred or to carry on down another hundred miles to the south. Some left, some stayed. The latter settled down in wide circles about the houseboat. They had learned several lessons since leaving the north, one of the most essential of these being the necessity for resting at night in open water as far as possible from the shore and the islands, which held sudden, crashing death.

The number of duck hunters in Illinois alone during the season was extraordinary. Perhaps in one day we might see eighty or a hundred. We passed thousands of decoy ducks, some sitting calmly on the water because they were wood, others flapping their wings because they were bored. Sometimes it seemed as though there were more decoys than wild ducks.

The river broadened again into a lake. Neat farms and orchards, beautiful bluffs and rolling fields,—the best of middle western farm country—appeared distantly on either side. Twelve miles below Nauvoo the river pulled up short before the Keokuk dam.

Its concrete mass is thrown across the entire width of the river. At the Iowa side, forming an L below the dam, is a power station of immense proportions, and beside it a lock one-third greater than any in the Panama Canal. If you should walk from Illinois across

the dam, then through the power house, and across
the lock to the Iowa shore, you would have traveled
two miles. High steel towers carry the current away
to various cities, including St. Louis, one hundred and
forty-four miles down the Mississippi.

We were told higher up the river that there had
been a slight but cumulative mistake on the part of
the engineers who had figured the water power at the
dam. We were advised (with an accompanying nudge)
to look carefully at the fifteen electrical generators,
for we would see only seven of them turning at one
time. However, let it be stated that when we walked
down the length of the power house, all fifteen were
turning with a pleasant, steady hum. Thus the serpent
is crushed by the advancing heel, and truth goes stag-
gering on.

4

The trouble with the advancing heel on a journey
like this, is however, that it advances too fast. In my
note book I find only the following entry for the town
of Keokuk: "Pop. 14,483. Excellent up-to-date library,
run by two charming ladies. Best-smelling town on the
Mississippi."

5

To the left Illinois; to the right, the slightly draggletailed border between Iowa and Missouri. Behind us, above Keokuk, rose a parachute of smoke, composed perhaps, of the aroma of its candy factories, bakeries and coffee roasting establishments. The river stretched straight before us, freed from many curves by the speed of its current. Up to this time it had been rising; now it began to fall a little, exposing along the banks several feet of dusky mud. Sandbars too, began to appear. Sometimes we ran into them, but we always managed to back off again.

Now, out of a pother of sandbars and islands, Quincy, Illinois, appeared. Quincy is a pleasant, slightly mussed, solid-looking town, full, I should judge, of citizens of not too Attic temperaments. "We are the kind of people," one of them told me, "who never take a chance. We would rather sit tight on three per cent. than gamble on anything." Of its 35,974 inhabitants, it is represented in *Who's Who in America,* only by four. There is not much excuse for that low average on the basis of an invasion by poor foreigners. It is a purely American town to which foreigners have not been drawn by high prices for cheap labor.

There is a cordon of very pleasant parks about Quincy, with Indian mounds of great archeological interest. Washington Square, in the center of the town, has more squirrels to the peanut and more pigeons to the bread-crumb, than any other park I have ever seen. On the water front is an old-time Mississippi store run by Mr. C. L. Adams, where you can buy anything from an anchor or a pound of oakum, to a bunch of carrots and a box of talcum powder. The public library is fine. The people of Quincy were friendly. The local papers made agreeable comments on our journey. I have only the most kindly feelings toward the city; nevertheless, I have something unpleasant to say.

After nearly thirty centuries of progressive civilization which include the teachings of Christ, Plato, and Gautama Buddha, the awakening of pity, the sculpture of Rodin and Praxiteles, the unceasing effort of messiahs and poets and philosophers to attempt to shape and lift the world's vision to their own vision, a city of thirty-five thousand souls in the center of a nation which prides itself on being in the van of civilization proudly brings forward as one of its leading civic achievements, the following: "Quincy is the largest producer and forwarder of railroad tonnage per capita in the State of Illinois."

That quotation will either mean something to you, or it will not. To me, it seems the most pitiful, ant-like negation of human values that we found on the entire Mississippi.

BECKY AND IGNITION

CHAPTER XV

I

THE water front of Hannibal, Missouri, was desolate with the desolation of rain and a falling river which left a thirty-foot smear of maltese mud along the cobble-stoned jetty. We coasted along its edge seeking a harbor, but there was none. Was that a creek ahead? *Good!* We turned into it through the fog and rain, only to find—shade of Marat—that the creek was not a creek after all.

Up stream again and into a cup-like depression in the mud bank under the straddling legs of a red freight house that overhung the water. Poor shelter this for facing the mile wide stretch of water. As we tied to the pier fore and aft, up out of the prevailing grayness came a bellowing monster of the Mississippi, the first three-deck packet boat we had seen, snorting and thundering, and blowing hoarsely for the bridge to open for it. Partly because it loomed so huge in the river, partly because its waves would shortly send us rollicking like a Chinese junk, it seemed greater than the mightiest ocean liner.

This captured leviathan passed up stream, leaving to the rear of its stern wheel a series of six-foot waves like spines on the back of a dragon. I read on its stern *Cape Girardeau of New Orleans,* but read no more, for in a moment we were jigging between our wooden posts like something unhappy at the end of a hangman's line.

River beast

In time the river composed itself again, and the rain came down as it had before the *Cape Girardeau* interrupted it. We went up through the dingy, dripping city and bought a copy of *Huckleberry Finn.* A man in Keokuk had told me that people in Hannibal were queer, for if you stopped one of them on the street and asked him where Mark Twain's house was, he would unfailingly direct you to the Mark Twain Hotel. We tried it several times, but since man, woman and child invariably gave us the right information, I suspect that the man from Keokuk had inquired, "Where is the Mark Twain house?" And since "house" is often used with a hotel's name, like "Parker House" or "Palmer House," the people he questioned naturally thought he meant the Mark Twain Hotel.

One ancient man in that hostelry said he remembered Samuel Clemens himself, and that Sam was a rotten pilot.* Sam had bumped the snoot of many a good ship on a sandbar; at least, that was the reputation he had had. Besides, a good pilot, one who liked his job, would never have given it up just to be a writer. There weren't many people left who knew Sam from the old days—but the girl who was Becky Thatcher in *Tom Sawyer,* now nearly ninety years old, was living seven or eight miles out of town at the old Ritchie farm.

"Do you think she would pose for a sketch?" I asked.

"Sketch? That's easy. Call up her son, Ed Frazer."

So I called Mr. Frazer on the telephone and stated my case and credentials. Would the lady who was Becky Thatcher pose for a sketch to-morrow?

"I suppose so," he said, a little wearily. "What time would you like to come out?"

* Mr. Archibald Henderson in "Mark Twain" states otherwise.

"Would ten o'clock be all right?"

It would.

2

She sat in her chair, very sedate and still as my companion began drawing. She seemed to feel upon her the necessity for silence. Was she thinking of the early days, when a little beribboned girl of six, and a slim, slouchy little boy of seven attended Mrs. Horr's school together?

I essayed a question. "Do you remember much about Mark Twain, Mrs. Frazer?"

"Yes, I remember a great deal about him," she said, in a quiet, grave little voice, which immediately hurried back into silence. Was she thinking about the little boy doing cartwheels in front of her house, and walking to school with her? Or did she have, perhaps, the memory of another more dramatic period in her mind —a series of events which began when General John McNeil of the Federal Army had been invited out of the rain into the house of a young girl for lunch. The young girl's husband, a Southern sympathizer, was not at home, for the very good reason that he was in hiding.

Appreciating her hospitality, General McNeil informed her that her husband Dr. Frazer, might come home without fear. So he returned, but was arrested soon after and held in the military prison at Hannibal.

Shortly after that General McNeil, as a measure of war retaliation, ordered the execution of ten Southern prisoners. The girl, desperately anxious, went to Palmyra to beg for the life of her husband, but was given no hope. She hurried to the Hannibal prison. Dr. Frazer, unaware of the impending tragedy, greeted her tenderly. A few minutes later, the doors opened, and a Provost Marshal entered with two lists. "Becky Thatcher" listened, her arms about the young physician who was still ignorant of the grim game of life and death that was taking place.

"Dr. Frazer," read the Provost Marshal, "to be transferred to St. Louis."

She took rooms near the prison in St. Louis. After ceaseless effort, she succeeded in bringing about her husband's release.

That's the kind of girl Becky Thatcher was. Samuel Clemens, it seemed, had chosen accurately and well when, long before, he picked her for his first heroine.

"Will you tell us some of the things you remember about Mark Twain?"

"Well, Mr. Clemens and I went to the same school, you know. We girls didn't bother much about the boys. (Of course not, Becky Thatcher!) Samuel was just an ordinary boy, very average, and didn't show much ability of any kind. He had a habit of telling stories in a slow, drawling voice that somehow made you listen. They weren't very good stories. If any one else had told them, they wouldn't have amounted to anything; but when Samuel told them, they usually sounded quite funny. He had no gift of writing, as far as any of us knew. He used to get into scrapes quite a lot, and he often played hookey from school, but he was a nice boy and used to divide his candy and oranges with me. Like a great many other American boys, he had his pockets filled with queer things to trade."

"And you first met him as he tells about it in *Tom Sawyer?*"

"Yes. Pretty much that way. The first meeting was when Samuel turned hand-springs in front of our house, and accidentally struck me on the head. He inquired about whether I was hurt,—but I wasn't. Then we became acquainted and soon were very good friends. A great many years later, he invited my granddaughter and me to his home in Connecticut. It was a fine visit. Mr. Clemens said he was just going to be a farmer. He didn't know whether he would raise turnips on trees, or what. My granddaughter took a photograph of us, and he called the photograph, 'Tom and Becky.' "

She had another photograph to show us too, one of Mark Twain taken not long before his death, on which

Mrs Laura H Frazer
I am Becky Thatcher

Becky Thatcher, Mark Twain's first sweetheart. "Everything is true except about our being lost in the cave together. Mr. Clemens made a mistake about that."

was written, "To Laura Frazer, from her earliest sweetheart." She lapsed into silence again, and would not be persuaded from it.

Now the portrait sketch was finished. "There is just one more thing I should like to ask," I said, as we rose to leave. "Did you get lost in the cave as it is described in *Tom Sawyer?*"

Her face grew serious. "No; we went there often on picnics, but always with a party of friends, and we *always* had a guide," she said. "I was never lost in the cave, and I never went in alone with any one. . . . Mr. Clemens was mistaken about that."

3

Tossing and bumping against the mud bank, with the freight house on one side, and the river on the other, the *Isador* passed a cold, benightmared night, groaning as though in terrible pain. We rose to find Hannibal in the act of crossing the Alps, with half an inch of snow on the *Isador's* roof and the water keg frozen nearly solid. Fortunately, there were one or two pilgrimages to be made in the town. Certainly it was no day for going down the river.

Since Mark Twain's time, Hannibal has moved to the south and west, leaving the writer's little old house in a drab back-water of the city, surrounded by second-hand dealers, cheap restaurants, pool-rooms and pawn shops. The Planters' Hotel, a few yards away, furnishes dinner for thirty-five cents; "Room and Board, Seven Dollars a Week," says a sign on a shabby house across the way.

The house itself is a two-story wooden structure, utterly plain, utterly commonplace, and decidedly ugly. Next to the house there is a broad magenta fence, with no Tom Sawyer to keep it white. That is probably just as well, for the railroads and factories of the rather ugly little river city are no better than they should be. In looking at that squalid house one has the feeling that it was a very good thing the river pilot came away. There's no great need for sentiment about the treatment Mark Twain received at the hands of early Hannibal. He was ignored for years; only when he became famous did they make much of him, and even then the praise came for the most part from a newer and more appreciative generation.

But certainly the Hannibal of to-day sincerely venerates the memory of her most distinguished son. There is an excellent group of Tom Sawyer and Huckleberry Finn at the foot of Cardiff Hill. When, after ten minutes of stiff climbing, one arrives at the top of the hill, one finds a proper setting for the spirit that rose from the squalid little house below. There, facing twenty miles of river, stands a bronze figure of the great-hearted writer himself. If, when no one is about, he should turn a little to the south as he undoubtedly does, he would see another twenty miles of river, curling majestically away among his beloved islands and hills. (Turn a little more, Mark Twain. Now! Don't you see that fine old farmhouse out there, of yellow brick, with the figure of some one standing at the door? Can't you see her without getting down? Well, it won't be the first time you have gotten down off your pedestal to see—Becky Thatcher!

We returned to the houseboat and stood watching it from the frozen bank as it pitched and tossed in the waves, butting into the bank with surprising vigor. Even while we had been away up the hill, the temperature had dropped another two points to twenty above zero. If we watched much longer, the north wind would freeze the very marrow in our bones. Two minds with but a single thought, we retreated to the steam-heated luxury of the Mark Twain Hotel.

4

Morning is cold again. On the deck of the *Isador* is ice; on the roof, icicles. But the wind has died down and the sun, off over the Illinois shore, is nerving himself for the day's work. I chop the houseboat loose from the frozen ropes, pole it out into the river, put on the motor, press up the carburetor caps, push down the choke, rock the fly-wheel a few times, and bump it against compression.

No answer. I bump it again. Still no answer. I rock it and bump it; I look at my spark plugs; I fiddle with the timer; I blow into the gas tank. Meanwhile we are drifting down the river. I rock the wheel fourteen times. No reply! I bump and rock, and rock and bump, a suspicion rising in my mind. The motor gives every indication of *rigor mortis*.

The current is with us, and the wind too. A wing dam is approaching fast. The mate takes an oar from the *Stupidity* and paddles from the front of the house-boat. We avoid the wing dam; but here is a light-buoy, a privately-owned buoy set out by the Portland Cement Company which has a factory on the hills south of the city. Evidently the *Isador* does not like privately-owned buoys. The river is nearly a mile wide here, but the boat comes right up to the buoy and attempts to hit it on the nose. I prevent this discourtesy only by running to the front deck and kicking off the buoy myself. I return to the motor.

Spin, bump; spin, bump. As often before, blood from my knuckles smears the top of the wheel a rusty red. I may as well stop my efforts. I am only tampering with a body from which the life has fled. The next thing to do is to tie up and consider. We are fairly near to the Illinois bank. We pick a spot just below the island where Tom Sawyer, Joe Harper and Huck Finn "looked their last" at civilization. I get into the *Stupidity*, and tow, but the current and wind are strong. Before we reach the bank, we have passed a second wing dam—an ugly one, all teeth—on our way down stream. (A lucky thing I did not impose my will against that of the river, for if I had we should probably be sitting on the dam with a hole in the ship's bottom.)

As it is, we make the bank just above the second dam. I take a few more ghoulish turns at the dead motor, but no use. Gloom settles down upon the entire party. When will the river freeze over, we wonder, and lock us within its rigid embrace? I go inside and thaw out my fingers.

There is only one thing to do. I must take the motor, together with its tools and a can of mixed oil and gasoline, and row back to Hannibal. But Hannibal is now four miles up stream. Up stream against that wind is an impossibility. In the skiff I find that the best I can do is to reach the other shore without going down river. A man and a few boys are tinkering with an old row boat on the bank. The man is in shabby overalls, and wears a week's beard on his face. His leathery features look as though they were retreating into the underbrush. I inquire how I can best go the four miles to Hannibal with the motor.

"Now that's a right hard question. There's no car here and no train stopping except the Polak at three this afternoon. But there's a store down the road a piece where they have a truck. They might take a man to town if he had to go."

"How far would you say the store is?"

"Well, I reckon it is a good quarter mile."

"Will the boat be all right here?"

"Sure! No one will touch it."

I take pains to explain that the five gallon can I am leaving in the boat contains a mixture of oil and gasoline, not suitable for running an automobile. Then I lift the motor to my back, take the small valise with the tools in it—old General Ketchall, in fact—and start off toward the road.

The first few hundred yards are enough to bring a vivid realization that an outboard motor is not designed to be carried. It has more gadgets and knobs than Perseus and the Gorgon's Head cast in bronze. I shift the position a little, pressing inadvertently on the carburetor valve, and instantly receive a generous libation of oil and gasoline down my neck. I shift my burden again. Gurgle, gurgle, gurgle. The warmth of my body has affected the motor. Shade of Emma Bovary, a brown, unknown liquid emerges from the pump's mouth and runs down the housing. I stagger on at least half a mile. Where the hell is that store? The man behind the beard, trying no doubt to encourage me, has made the distance shorter by two-thirds than it is.

I feel as though I have been walking with the motor on my back for days, and that I shall have to walk many days more. I can note quite objectively the poison of exhaustion creeping into the muscle fibers. The motor is like an old man of the sea astride my back. How long must this keep up? Where is the store? Fatigue no longer passive takes command. I'm done! I stop, lean down and set the thing gently on its heel. It overbalances my outraged muscles and we go over. I keep it from hitting the ground, but it pushes me over onto my back and lies on me. I am prepared to be a little annoyed at that, but I get over it at once, remembering that the motor, poor thing, is dead.

So I stand the deceased by a fence, and go on a quarter mile to a farm-house, where the farmer says that the store is another quarter mile beyond. In the store there is a comely Russian woman who is the wife of a Czecho-Slav, who in turn, is away hunting. The woman, out of the goodness of her Muscovite heart, offers to telephone to town for a taxicab. The address she gives the taxi-man is, Monkey-Run-by-the-Cement-Works. In spite of that peculiar address, the taxicab gets there.

In Hannibal I take the motor to a scholarly-looking man who resembles Woodrow Wilson. He has a boat house and repair shop on the water front filled with the customary quota of large, husky, warmly dressed gentlemen who sit about the stove and occasionally condescend to feed it with a morsel of the scholarly man's wood. The latter, who is mending a cracked cylinder head, pauses to look at the motor and says, "I'll be with you directly." Soon he is taking it apart and inquiring, "That is a Katwater-Ent ignition system isn't it?"

"Yes."

"I never did like that Katwater ignition," he continues, tickling the trigger with a doubtful screwdriver. It occurs to me that perhaps the reason he doesn't like it is because he doesn't understand it. Attaching the batteries, he twiddles the timer a little, and then a little more. Presently it snaps out a spark or two.

"Ouch, I got it," he cries. "There's a short in the stop-button." Taking the timer to his bench he comes back with a washer so thin that one can hardly feel it between finger and thumb. "You better keep this, you may need it," he says. I drop it into a vest pocket, saying, "Yes," very intelligently, just as though I knew what it was for. He claps the top on the timer before the spirit escapes; then we fasten the motor to a board, prime it, rock the fly-wheel, and—*bang!* The thing barks back to life with a vitality more intense than before. I get into the taxi, and with the motor in my arms, bounce back over hill and dale toward the house-boat, grateful indeed that we shall not have to winter at Monkey-Run-by-the-Cement-Works. And I feel so carefree after the suspense of the day that when we pass a sign which says, "This way to Mark Twain's cave," I ask the chauffeur how much he will charge for waiting while I go through the cave, and he replies, "Six bits." In a small house near by, we find Mr. Cameron, who owns the cave (and while he is lighting his gasoline lantern, we'll slip unnoticed back into the past tense).

5

He threw open a narrow door and we walked down the dark, much-traveled passage. Sometime far in the past, the long, tortuous galleries were cut through the rock by the action of water. Various strata were etched and eaten away into fantastic formations along the walls. All about us, in the irregular seams and folds of lime-stone, strange shapes appeared—the Eagle, the Monitor, Adam's Foot, the Devil's Backbone—all the old metaphors to be found the world over when man, through some trick of nature, is forced for once to have a good look at his surroundings.

On the walls and ceiling thousands of names had been scratched into sooty smears made by the wicks of closely applied candles. Here was the signature of Admiral Coontz, there the names of two privates in the Army—more interesting, too, than the Admiral's, for the date that followed them was 1863. Nearby, some one had drawn a small round-stomached hieroglyph of a man hanging by the nape of the neck from a gallows and had scrawled underneath it, "Jeff Davis." Some one else—obviously another artist, for the technique is quite different,—had drawn another long figure hanging beside the first, this one bearing the title, "Abe Lincoln."

Here was Becky Thatcher's own rounded signature —not actually "Becky Thatcher," nor "Laura Frazer," but Laura Hawkins,* her maiden name—bearing the date, 1855, and under it the signature of some old time admirer of hers. The chirography of the name "Laura" seemed to be identical with that which appears under the sketch at page 178. As I examined her autograph on the cave wall, an impression came to me from somewhere, that very probably Samuel Clemens and he of the name that stood next to hers, had shared the privilege of admiring the young lady with a good many more.

* Mark Twain used the name "Laura Hawkins" in *The Gilded Age.*

Mr. Cameron proceeded down the irregular, twisting tunnels; plainly, it would be easy enough to get lost there. He himself had once been astray in the cave for three hours. Once a member of a party had roamed away from the guide and had stayed in the place all night. Small bats, clinging head downward from the ceiling, glared evilly at us.

"One man asked me if they were alive," remarked Mr. Cameron.

"I told him that if they weren't, they wouldn't be hanging there for long. They'd rot and drop down on him." He laughed a hollow, macabre laugh, which has probably brought thrills of terror and delight to the small boys of the neighborhood whom he brings into the cave quite often. Here indeed, was a hole in one side of the passage, where an urchin could climb along twenty or thirty yards through the darkness, and come up into the gallery again—a hero.

As we passed back to the entrance, I asked my guide if he had known Mark Twain. He replied no, that he had only seen him once distantly, when the writer had returned in his latter years to Hannibal on a visit. He had all of Mark Twain's books though—all that come in the set. However, a lady he had been taking through the cave recently, told him about another book that Mark Twain had written. Had I heard anything about it?

"Do you mean that it wasn't the kind of book that is published in the set?" I asked.

He looked at me scandalized. "Mark Twain never wrote any kind of a book that couldn't come in a set."

"No?"

"No."

"Oh." *

6

The taxicab stopped within a hundred yards of the spot where the *Abject Stupidity* was lying. I carried the motor down to the river. The man with the beard came along, and said, "Did you get it fixed?"

"Yes, I think so. By the way—what was that train you called the Polak?"

"Oh, that's just the local train," he said blushing pinkly above the rim of his beard. "It's an engine with two cars that runs down here from the town loaded with Hunkies who work in the cement mills."

I got the motor started, said good-by, and took stock of what was or was not in the boat. The five gallon can had not been touched. I had done wrong to be suspicious. There was nothing gone at all—that is, nothing except the pair of copper tips that had been fastened to the ends of the oars.

* For the sake of verities, I refer Mr. Cameron to page 185 of Van Wyk Brook's, "The Ordeal of Mark Twain."

THE SMOKY SAINT

CHAPTER XVI

I

FOR twelve days of savage wind from the south, we went on in a running fight down the river, now creeping along close to the shore, now dashing across an open stretch of water, now getting caught unawares in a tossing channel where the wind and the opposing currents made battle. Often, as we turned a point or came around an island, the motor, hardly recovered from its last illness, or suffering a relapse in the presence of the wind, would cough and spin and go dead. Then the waves would heave the *Isador* into their trough and try to swamp us there, until with groans and grunts and elbow grease, and the generous application of gasoline, I would revive the failing carburator, and we would totter on. Those twelve days were not very happy; sometimes we would be forced to lie for hours at a time behind wing dams or small islands or in the mouths of sloughs, watching for that uncertain moment in which to cross the river.

The rudder acted badly too. One cold day I found

that the housing had sagged, taking quarter-inch bites out of the blades of the propeller. There was too much play between the rudder and the frame that held it. Washers were needed on the upper and lower rudder bearings. I leaned out over the motor. In my interest I put my hand on the tipped-up horizontal rudder bearing. Forgetting that the motor was not solid I leaned out a little far. Splash! Down head first into the frigid water—but not for long, however. Before the mate had got to the door of the houseboat I was back on deck. Indeed, the return from the depths had been accomplished with such splendid zeal that there were spaces on my clothing that were not entirely wet!

There was, I am sure, landscape along this section of the Mississippi, but it was of quite secondary interest to the wind.* Once, at dusk, as we completed a desperate passage across the river to a protected point of land, two large steamers came panting up the stream, heading directly for the same point. A white channel guide stood on the bank. The steamers were well within their rights to follow the channel; in fact, if they had not followed it, they might have run aground. There was only one thing for the *Isador*

---

*If I have not devoted the maximum of space here to the landscape I must beg for clemency in the words of a vigorous friend who read the manuscript: "If the mechanics of the voyage was a drag on you sometimes, it would have been a futile fake to rhapsodize about the scenery when you really were wringing bilgewater out of your socks."

to do, and that was to head out into the river again. Darkness was coming on, and with it more wind. As we floundered toward the opposite shore, I thought I heard some one hailing us from the first of the two stern-wheelers, but the message was lost in the wind. Somehow we succeeded in making a slough; but when we moored under a sheltering bank, I found that the *Abject Stupidity* was gone. At some time during that passage, it had snapped its chain off short and had left for parts unknown. To go out after it with the houseboat into the darkness and wind was impossible.

Perhaps the skiff was not so stupid as we had thought. When it left it took its oars with it. We never saw it again.

2

A small freight steamer passed us bearing the name *Genevieve of the Port of Hamburgill*. We went on, wondering where on the face of the earth Hamburgill might be. Certainly it was not on any map that we carried; but a few miles farther on, we came to the village of Hamburg, Ill.! Hamburg was the center of the apple district. I went ashore there for gasoline and water over mounds of crushed apples and apple skins. A scent of apple juice, and better, filled the air. Large men in high laced boots and hunting costumes stood around looking at me suspiciously. There was a sense of mystery about the place that was not relieved by any fulsome pretense toward hospitality.

"You ain't from Hamburg, air ye?" an old shopkeeper inquired.

"No, that's my boat down there. We are on our way south as fast as we can go."

"Well—you've got more sense than the wild ducks, ain't ye?" he said grinning.

"Do you mean that some of them stay around Hamburg—and get shot?"

He winked a bleary eye and laughed uproariously. "A feller's all right here if he minds his business," he said.

So, with the large men still eyeing me suspiciously, I made my way down over the mounds of crushed apples to the boat, leaving Hamburg at ease again, in her virtue or iniquity, as the case might be.

3

There was something ominous about the river now. Its power was increasing, and the power was malignant. I felt its force, myself, and I could see its effect in the mate's face. Those arduous days had gradually broken down the strength of her resistance. There was dread in her eyes when we had to cross the river.

We were approaching the great joining of waters, the place where the power of the Mississippi combines with the power of the Missouri; and now we had no small boat in which to get away in case of trouble.

Mist drove up from the south, half hiding the shore and changing the trees and the high bluffs into paintings on a Japanese screen. We passed to the right of an island that hid the mouth of the Illinois River, and came to a wide expanse of the Mississippi that ended abruptly to the south in a strange band of white lying along the surface. The white streak came rolling up through the mist. We made for the shore, but it rose and enveloped it. We passed out of the world into a no-man's land of grayish white space, with the heavy, wet fog sweeping silently, mysteriously, to the north. We went on, listening apprehensively for the sound of a steamer's horn, or for a bell, straining our eyes for a glimpse of a buoy, red or black, in the nothingness about us.

Now a red buoy glided past close on our left. Good; we were still in the channel. I let the *Isador* take its own way. An hour later the tops of cliffs appeared on the Illinois shore. Beyond, out of the fog appeared colossal steel frames—similar to those we had seen in

Keokuk, one hundred and sixty miles to the north. These, like the others, were carrying electrical power over their inch thick cables to St. Louis.

The city of Alton rose up out of the emptiness. We tried to buy a skiff there, but no skiffs were for sale. We got fuel, and went on. The river had quieted down under the fingers of the fog, but the island at Alton Slough where we expected to spend the night, had disappeared under high water. The river was vastly different from the map we carried. Nosing back of a narrow sandbar, we found shelter beside a thick edge of weeds, the lights of the city twinkling beyond the foliage like fiery flowers.

At five we rose. The morning was calm, but as we started on our way, our old enemy came up the river to oppose us. No wonder early man believed that the winds and the currents were malevolent deities! I think that we too half believed there was some malign influence standing across the river trying to bar our way to St. Louis, twenty miles farther on. We were a little doubtful about St. Louis anyway; where on the vast stretch of municipal docks and water front would we be able to find a mooring place for the *Isador?*

The channel led along the left bank, the edge of which had been rip-rapped, or roughly paved with broken stone into a sloping, formidable bulwark. The waves were high,—not high from the standpoint of

ocean traffic, you understand,—but high for a houseboat. The water took on a muddy, reddish hue which we
had not seen before. On the left we passed the mouth
of a small creek that was pouring sticks, branches and
froth out into the river. The waves went higher; in a
moment the motor would submerge and stop. The mate
stood looking at me from the back deck. Watching my
chance, I turned the *Isador* around and tried to make
the mouth of the creek, but the turbulent water rushing past the stone embankment was too swift. We
hung for five minutes in exactly the same spot below
the creek's mouth, the motor chugging feebly against
the current. What to do next?

Far across the river, I saw a sandbar with what
seemed to be an inlet below it.

"We'll have to cross;" I said.

"No—no!"

But there was no other way. The waves in the center
were huge—as large as they had been on Lake Pepin.
They rose up in patches where the wind wrestled with
the current. The motor doused under and stopped but
I started it again while loose objects crashed to the
floor. Tossing wildly, we approached the sandbar, and
found ourselves opposed by another current of the reddish water which appeared to be pouring from behind
the bar. It traveled along in streaks, quite independent
of the olive-drab water of the Mississippi. The sand-

bar, we found, was an island. I steered in slowly toward that bank of the reddish stream which lay below the bar.

As the boat, contesting every inch, was forced slowly backward by the new current, we watched tensely. I eased the left tiller rope a little. Slowly now! Not too much of a turn, or the current would seize us and twist our bow down stream. We sidled in slowly toward the bank. Now we had stopped losing ground; we remained stationary in the rushing water, the lashing propeller just holding its own. A little closer in shore! Tension . . . Then, no faster than the crawl of a snail, trees on the bank began to move past. *We were going ahead.* Now we had gained an inch on the bank, two inches, a foot, a yard. Ten minutes later we slipped into quiet water beside the shelving bank, cut off the power, and dropped the spud.

What was this reddish tide that came pouring into the Mississippi? Was it a chute of the river coming in around Maple Island, tinged by the waters of the Illinois? We looked at the nearly useless map. No, that must have been Maple Island where we anchored last night—and that was Mobile Island over there. Then this—we looked at each other with a strange surprise. Then this——

We had in fact, without knowing it, fled for protection into the tawny mouth of that mighty brother of the Mississippi—the Missouri.

4

Up before dawn.

A quiet river again; and again, just before sunrise, the freshening breeze making the sixteenth day of wind from the south. Even now it was not too late for the sullen gods standing astride the river to do with us what they chose; for St. Louis was still seventeen miles distant. But perhaps they would relent. Such a small houseboat, after all! So, with uncertainty upon us, we went on past the long, jagged embankment, down past the two high mid-river castles from which St. Louis gets its water supply, carefully past the dangerous "chain of rocks," that have bitten holes in the bottom of many a boat, and then past the large squalid-looking houseboat colonies, the quays, the bridges, the mills, factories, docks, and steamboats, to the fog that is St. Louis. In the heart of the city just above the Eads Bridge, we found a cozy floating dock with quiet water inside, also a gang-plank to walk upon, and the best accommodations that we had seen for the *Isador* on the Mississippi.

If we arrived there in spite of the wind, it was partly

luck and partly because we knew no better; for we
learned that tug-boats and barges ten times our size—
the *Ghost,* and the *Silas Buck,* and the *Old Bill*—which
should have made St. Louis from up the river long before us, were still wind bound far to the north. We had
covered nearly five hundred miles by canoe, and nearly
seven hundred by houseboat from St. Paul to St. Louis.
We had navigated what is known as the Upper River.
The Lower River was still before us—and a distance of
thirteen hundred miles.

5

A fine, worn old city is St. Louis, rich in achievement
and in memories. A city not at all worried about what
New York or any other metropolis is doing; a city not
self-conscious and jumpy like Chicago, a city standing
firmly on its own precedent, with no hint of the *gauche*
or *nouveau riche* about it, like Minneapolis. Cities, like
individuals, often benefit in manners by having a few
generations of breeding back of them. If St. Louis ever
went through any period of crass adolescence, that has
been left many years behind. The young city's religious
training was long and excellent, the first mass having
been celebrated there in 1764.

The pride of every true St. Louisian's heart is the
old courthouse, on the east steps of which, in early

Slaves were sold from the steps of this fine old court house in St. Louis.

days, a slave market was regularly held. Certain factions have suggested plans for remodeling the fine old Doric edifice, but the city springs at once to protect the landmark against any such desecration. "It may not be what you call a handsome courthouse," said one citizen to me, "—but just try an' tear it down!"

St. Louis calls the Mississippi "The Big Muddy," and pays very little attention to it. Indeed, the city has more or less turned its back on the river. But in Forest Park, the site of the World's Fair, there is a little creek. After a heavy rain, the creek sometimes rises up quite harmlessly, and fills its channel with rushing water. Then you will find automobiles parked wheel to wheel for a mile while their occupants, in some excitement, watch the little thing bubbling along in its infant rage.

Statue of Saint Louis in the city's oldest church.

During our days in St. Louis there was snow—the heaviest November snow on the government record; snow that broke down countless wires and fifty telegraph poles in the city, giving the out-door statue of Saint Louis a garment of ermine and transforming the park into a land of exquisite unreality, where very real, runny-nosed little children, both poor and rich, enjoyed themselves to their possible, under the silent indulgence of the guardian snow-clad trees.

The city, marshalling its hundreds of workers, its trucks and tractors, moves majestically along through the smoothly geared cycle of its snow-removal problem. While I, having several fewer gears to my domestic economy, climbed on top of the *Isador* with a dust-pan and shoveled off the roof.

My companion enjoyed St. Louis, too. Her first observation was a delighted, "How well-dressed the women are here!" Her last was expressed in a final sigh of regret when at the last possible moment she left the splendid Union Market, with its white enamel, marble, and plate-glass, and its remarkable concentration of the finest fruits, meats and vegetables to be found on the Mississippi. She liked the city's art galleries, its old churches, its parks, its monuments and its people. So did I. If during the week we anchored in that hospitable harbor, we took aboard enough soot to alter the appearance of the houseboat for several hundred miles, we accepted it with a certain equanimity. For when we left St. Louis, we carried with us the conviction that its interest in the art of life extended to planes that were untouched by the soot of its factories.

At the office of the Mississippi River Commission, I procured thirty-seven sheets of maps, at the scale of one inch to the mile, for that section of river between St. Louis and the Gulf; but I returned them for I found that on twenty-three of the sheets, the channel was not marked at all. Instead of these, I was forced to buy a book containing maps one-half inch to the mile, which were published thirty-five years ago. Apparently they were printed at that time too, for the paper was so brittle with age that it immediately broke to pieces under the fingers.

As far as being a guide to the present river was concerned, this book, we found, was nearly worthless. Towns marked on it had disappeared; others had grown where none were designated. Great bends in the river had become solid land; chutes had opened; islands had disappeared; the channel of the river itself had shifted so far from its marked course, that for miles the country was not recognizable. True, Cairo, Thebes and Memphis still flourished on their ancient sites, but if we had not been provided with the up-to-date and reliable list of channel marks from the Light House Service, we should have been adrift indeed.

5

Much time was occupied in trying to find a row-boat. I combed the St. Louis water front from the

Eads Bridge forty blocks north to the water-works and the shantyboat colonies—which, by the way, seemed to contain a very high percentage of sullen people and bad tempered dogs. Then I went south from the bridge for another forty blocks, past factories and municipal plants and gas tanks, coming at last on the water front to the house of a furious-looking, but affable little old man with red eyes very near together, who kept bees and ran a launch to a truck farmers' island across the river. At first, like the others, he said there were no boats to be had.

"People don't build row-boats around here any more," he said, "they steal 'em." But he bethought himself of a man, a farmer from the island, who might have a row-boat, adding that the man was inside his house at that very minute. He called out a rotund, energetic Jew to see me, saying to him, "Here's a man who'll buy that boat of yours that got away and that I tied up down at the Point."

"All right, by golly; that's obsolutely the fines' boat you could get, strong built and everythink. The only think is—is she still there?"

"Sure, she's there. I tied her up with a piece of wire. She's there and sunk and full of mud."

"The mud I can get out with a shovel."

"Does the boat leak?" I asked.

"Not! If she leaks a drop, I'll buy her back for double."

"How old is it?" He did not know exactly; he got it along with his farm on the island, and he had had the farm for seven years.

"What is it worth?"

"Twelve dollars."

The up-shot of it was that we took the launch and went down two miles against a bitter wind to the other side of the river. Near the bank the gunwale of a boat appeared above the water. The Jew, who had hip boots on, jumped in and shoveled out the mud, bailing out the water until a large, ungainly shovel-nosed craft, all full of ribs and with no seat, rose above the surface. It did not look very prepossessing, but since it could not be stupider than the *Stupidity,* and since there was nothing else to be had, I bought it, and took it back across the river, and tied it up beside the old man's launch against the time when we should leave St. Louis.

At the Eagle Boat Store where the New Orleans packets come in, I bought some oars, at twenty cents a foot. Then we filled the *Isador* with provisions to the place where the scuppers ought to have been, shoveled a little more new-laid snow from the roof, cracked the ice off the ropes, filled the water keg and sputtered off down the river. At which time, I regret to state, the south wind again sprang upon us. The water too, was rough because of many packets and freight boats and ferries. While I steered as well as I could through the mangled and choppy wakes of the greater boats, the mate stood silently on the back deck. When I glanced at her in an unexpected moment, her face had the look of a child who had been hurt, and who awaits the same hurt again; and I thought to myself, are we going to *hate* the river? Shall we, like Charles Dickens, "never hope to see the Mississippi again except in troubled nightmares and dreams?" Instead of this being a pleasantly rigorous adventure, will her—our—dread of the savage power of the river increase as we go on, until that dread over-balances the element of pleasure, and the journey becomes only something to be remembered as a long, painful dream?

We picked up the skiff beyond the gas tank and, with the old tension on us, went on past ten miles of factories, into a country of low, beetling hills lying foliage-clad and swarthy under the snow. As the afternoon progressed, the wind slunk away; reality returned to the scene; the river flattened its glittering folds and the sun descended slowly into a cloud-hung chamber of copper-rose and green. We took heart again, finding anchorage in the quiet mouth of a slough. The waters, slashed with short, vertical reflections of the stars, became a mirror for the night. In spite of the week's rest in St. Louis, we slept the profound sleep that usually follows exhaustion.

LAND OF EGYPT

CHAPTER XVII

I

WHEN we rose, there was plenty of water in the skiff, also plenty of mud, and a two-inch layer of ice. It leaked, of course; but we could not sell it back to the Jewish farmer for double the price as he had suggested, because we were twenty miles away. Poor man! How bad he would have felt if he had known!

The day before, when we had stopped for the skiff, the old man had not been at home, but his wife was there; so while I put on the oarlocks she invited the mate into the kitchen to get warm. She was a fat, brisk, rosy-cheeked woman, with a background of clean linoleum. For seven years she had lived on the island where the Jew now lived, sending her three young boys over the river every day to school. Always for the boy who was littlest, she had a big covered wooden box with a folded quilt in the bottom. She would put him inside, lower the cover, and wrap a tarpaulin over the box. Then her husband would carry it down to the boat, motor across the river, open the

box and take the little fellow out—dry. She had done
this with three boys in succession. The neighbors used
to laugh, but each of her three sons went his eight
years to school, never missing a day.

Never missing a day wasn't so much, of course; but
when she herself had been young, she was the only
girl in the family, and as a result, when "anything
happened," she had had to stay home. Once when her
father was sick, she had been kept out of school for
nine weeks, and as a result, "got put down." She
vowed afterward, that if she ever had any children,
they should never have to miss school. No doubt when
once the little lads got their mother's ideal firmly fixed
in their minds, they themselves were mainly responsible for that three-times-eight-is-twenty-four-year-
record; and no doubt their daily task of crossing the
river, rain or shine, made them not a whit less excellent men.

Again the wind hounded us all day, running us at
last onto a sandbar, from which we managed to escape by a liberal application of the pike pole and good
luck. Late in the afternoon, we found a little slough
or chute, separated from the river proper by a narrow
strip of sand at a sharp bend, near Cinq l'homme
Light. During the early part of the night, five packets
went laboring and snorting around the bend, making

a wake that hissed on the sandbar like a storm at sea, but leaving us snug and quiet in our chute a few feet away. When we arose at three-thirty and lit the lamp to prepare for an early start, another huge three-decked river beast came blowing and panting around the bend. On stepping inside the cabin after looking at it, I found that the mate had turned the light down. When I inquired the reason, she said that she didn't want the monster to see us, for it might get some queer ideas, and come wallowing and splashing in behind our sandbar!

Rowing in the skiff to the mouth of the chute, I found the narrow channel clear, with a swift current flowing out between willow thickets into the river. A few moments later, with the motor purring good-naturedly in the damp air, we swung down the chute and into the composite, many-toned darkness of sky, and hills and water. There was an indescribable sweetness about the night air; only a faint breath from the south came into our faces. Shore signal lights, a mile or two apart, lay before and behind us, those down the river coming into sight one by one, as those behind disappeared back of points of land and invisible groups of trees.

One could imagine the lights carrying on and on—infinitely fragile links of security—a thousand miles southward to the Gulf. The moon, peering out from behind the mottled doorways of cloud, lent the glamor of its sorrowful, mildly-demented presence to the scene.

Almost imperceptibly, the east began to awake. Now a faint gray thread of light lay along the horizon, as though a painter, spreading broad stripes of cool color with his palette knife, had got a speck of flake-white on the knife blade and had drawn it across the canvas with the

Government shore light

rest. The stars lost their sight, the moon faded; the hills emerged from their garments of blackness. We seemed to be looking through a blue screen of slightly frosted glass on which the channel lights and the infrequent lamps of early-rising farmers were pricked out in a naïve, golden pattern. Soon, even the blue dissolved. Silver radiance filtered out between the eastern clouds. The sky and river turned to hand-wrought silver. Then the sun rose, embossing the landscape with the sharp splendor of his newly-burnished gold.

All day we traveled down vast open vistas of the river, dodging twice around islands to avoid trafficking with bawdy river steamers that seemed to smell out our frail craft with rare persistence. The surface of the Mississippi lay like quick-silver under a warm, quiet sky. We sat on our camp chairs on the front deck, and steered idyllically down stream for a distance of nearly seventy miles. "This," we said to each other, "is the sort of thing our friends meant when they said, 'How we envy you that *glorious* journey down the Mississippi!'" But the next day——

The next day started with a little breeze from the usual direction. However, Cairo, Illinois, where the Ohio River flows into the Mississippi, was only twenty-three miles away. Perhaps we could reach it and find some sort of shelter there. On turning a bend, we were shut off near the left bank by rough waves. Ahead of us a semi-solid breakwater of drifted trees that had been roughly cabled together, jutted out from a high bank into the river. Immediately above the breakwater, the river, forming an eddy, had eaten a fifty-foot semi-circle out of the bank. Here, at last, was temporary protection. We ran into the eddy, let down the spud, and tied the front of the boat to the breakwater.

But as the minutes passed, an oblique wind blowing toward us from down across the mile-wide river, keyed itself to a higher and still higher velocity. Gradually the small area of quiet water about us decreased and disappeared. The *Isador* was filled with emotion. The spud pole began ripping open a larger hole for itself in the deck. I moored with four ropes forward to the breakwater, and took the anchor, with fifty feet of rope, to the shore on the opposite side of the eddy so that our stern would not swing against the bank. The wind became furious. The houseboat reared and bucked like a horse with a burr under his saddle.

Holding on to the walls, we prepared a little food, but the cavorting was too much even for our well-seasoned stabilities. My light o' love wore a strangely sad and preoccupied expression, as though she were listening pensively to an inner voice. We crawled wanly over the tree trunks of the breakwater to the shore. At the top of the fifteen foot bank, spreading away to a sycamore grove, was a field of stiff, brown pods topped with a thousand white puffs of cotton. We sat down on the bank and watched the lightly jumping *Isador* and the rheumatic old skiff which was gradually filling with water beside the mud bank. The wind still came roaring and howling over the river. One thing was certain: there was no more possibility of sleeping aboard the *Isador* than on the dasher of a washing-machine. So I clambered out over the logs again, put bread and honey and stewed pears in a basket, found a rubber sheet and raincoats and a poncho, and returned over the raging waves to the shore.

The mate had collected a huge pile of dry grass and put it in the middle of a little thicket. There we rigged a shelter tent—the poncho below, the rubber sheet sloping up from the ground away from the wind—and fastened it at the ends to a pair of small trees. At the edge of the cotton field a few hundred yards away, there was a solitary negro hut. I went to it and knocked. A bulgy negress came to the door.

"My wife and I have a boat on the river, but we can't sleep on it because of the wind. We have put up a tent in the thicket over there. I'm telling you so you won't be frightened if you see a light."

"Oh, no, sah! We wouldn't be afraid," she said, her eyes rolling at the mere thought of a light in the thicket; "we wouldn't be afraid!"

I returned and we climbed into our snuggery. The wind howled over our heads but did not penetrate the underbrush. Any native mosquitoes were now blown miles away. We ate our supper, settled down and slept—man superior to nature.

2

A vivid flash of lightning woke us. The storm was bringing up its artillery from the southeast. Who cared? The careening *Isador* was not bumping anything, and we were snug enough in our shelter. The voice of the gale rose to a howl carrying with it the spatter of rain. Being on the side nearer the storm, I held down the lower edge of the rubber sheet that protected us. That was easy enough, there was no great pressure of wind on it. Then the howl became a yell. Rain crashed across the river. The lightning, almost venomous in its white intensity, left the eyes blinded before the shattering report of the thunder. We shrank back into the smallest dimensions possible. The mate, who had been getting a little damp from water splashing up from the grass, removed a small forked stick at the end of the rubber sheet, unintentionally replacing it in such a manner that the sheet made an efficient reservoir for collecting a goodly supply of rain above us. In spite of the fury of the storm, a great calmness came over me.

"Man superior to nature," I said aloud.

She giggled.

"Why do you laugh, my simple friend?"

"Man superior to nature—but his wife has to wear rubber boots to bed!"

A moment or two later the improvised tent sagged down against my nose. It had a strange, bulbous feeling. "A lot of water has collected up there. Wait a moment—I'll raise it up and let it run out."

Unfortunately the poncho that was under us had curled up outside the tent against some saplings; so that when I pushed upon the reservoir above, allowing the water to rush down the rubber sheet, the current turned inward and it seemed for a moment as though the bank had given way and we were in the Mississippi. We rose moistly enough, gathered our possessions together and crawled out over the tree trunks to the *Isador*. The rain grew less, the wind died down a little, allowing us an hour or two of sleep. But at five A. M., it came blustering up again, blowing furiously until the boat hopped about like a wild thing. Once more we dragged our harassed carcasses to the frost-covered shore again, each with his boots on, each carrying a pair of shoes, swearing not to return until the river should regain its poise. And as we came to the land, we saw that the waves had eaten five feet into the solid bank beside the houseboat.

3

Cairo could not be many miles away. We plodded inland, across the black, semi-liquid fields. As each foot went up and down, it gathered to itself more and more of the sticky, viscous mud. The mate struggled on ahead, her feet apparently encased in two large black valises, which stuck out stiffly in several different directions. Suddenly she turned with animation in her eyes.

"Boppo, do you know what day yesterday was?"

"No," I answered weakly, "what day was yesterday?"

"It was—*Thanksgiving!*"

Thanksgiving Day for some people, I said, but not Thanksgiving Day for me; and I went on to add that if any one ever told me that I should have been thankful on that day, I would punch him in the eye and call him a bad name as well. Then, as we plodded along, we came to the first growing persimmon tree that either of us had ever seen. I hurled a club at the persimmons, and they came down,—thump, thump, thump,—in the mud and water. But the mud made no difference, for we found that unless one has eaten persimmons before breakfast on a cold frosty morning as they fall directly from the tree, he has never really eaten persimmons at all. My friend looked at me and laughed, saying:

"Who would have thought that I should ever see you standing at six o'clock on a frosty morning, where Illinois and Kentucky meet, eating persimmons and mud!" Though she laughed gayly, she looked pale and tired. I hated to see her so played out; and as we went on through the muck toward the road to Cairo, I evolved what I thought was a fine plan.

"How's this: When we get to Cairo, you will stay at the hotel, then take the train on to Memphis and wait for me to come with the boat. You can rest there four or five days, and when I arrive with the *Isador,* you'll be ready to re-join as mate."

But she said, "I'm afraid you can't manage it alone."

"Oh, yes, I can. I'll string a wire through the throttle to shut off the power from the front of the boat. As far as food goes, I can throw some bacon and eggs on the stove any time. There are plenty of canned things, and vegetables, and bread. Don't you think it is a good idea?"

"Well—perhaps——"

But as I went on enlarging on the plan, I saw that it did not "take." There was something else in her mind, something besides her comfort in the hotels at Cairo and Memphis, something beyond the fact that I should have to prepare my own food; and then it came to me quite clearly that in spite of her weariness she was thinking of the houseboat in a storm with one man alone on it.

"No, I won't go to Memphis," she said.

Of course, a man's mate is supposed to stand by him—at least, that frequently seems to be the original intention. Nevertheless . . . And I went on through the cotton wondering—despite Mr. Mencken and the rest—just how I had managed to stagger along down my own muddy field, through so many years of single

cussedness. . . . Then trudging silently, we reached
the road. A farm truck came along and took us into
Cairo.

4

Fifty years ago Cairo, lying on a low point formed
by the juncture of the Ohio and Mississippi, was by
no means what it is to-day. Mr. Charles Dickens
passed that way twice in a rage; once in a rage coming down the Ohio on his way to St. Louis, and once
in a rage on his way back.

"At that juncture of the two rivers," he wrote, "on
ground so flat and low and marshy, that at certain
seasons of the year it is inundated to the housetops, lies
a breeding place of fever, ague, and death . . . a dismal swamp on which the half-built houses rot away;
cleared here and there for a space of a few yards; and
teeming then, with rank unwholesome vegetation, in
whose baleful shade the wretched wanderers who are
tempted hither droop and die, and lay their bones; the
hateful Mississippi circling and eddying before it, and
turning off upon its southern course, a slimy monster
hideous to behold. A hot-bed of disease, an ugly sepul-
cher, a grave *uncheered by any gleam of promise;* a
place without one quality in earth or air or water to
commend it, such is this dismal Cairo."

Lest all this apparent venom remain upon the early
Cairo, let us quote part of a letter written by Dickens

to his brother-in-law three weeks earlier—a letter in which he shows the real reason for his distaste for the American scene:

"Is it not a horrible thing that scoundrel book-sellers should grow rich here from publishing books, the authors of which do not reap one farthing from their issue, by scores of thousands; and that every vile blackguard and detestable newspaper, so filthy and bestial that no honest man would admit one into his house for a scullery door-mat, should be able to publish these same writings side by side, cheek by jowl, with the coarsest and most obscene companions. . . . I vow before high Heaven that my blood so boils at these enormities that when I speak about them I seem to grow twenty feet high and to swell out in proportion."

This holy rage, like many other holy rages, was purely economic. Dickens was notably choleric about royalties. The American publishers at the time were breaking no international copyright law because there was none to break. In any event, the "gleam of promise" that the great novelist failed to see, has developed Cairo into one of the most attractive and well-kept of the smaller cities of the Mississippi Valley.

It lies in that part of Illinois called Egypt, where the great alluvial delta begins. The name Egypt dates from a year when the corn crop failed in central Illinois and the inhabitants came down into the land of Egypt to get corn. Not far away are Thebes and Karnak, and the county itself is Alexander; but that comes very near to being a bore unless the early settlers were moved by a sense of humor, which I somehow doubt.

No doubt the early Cairo was not too attractive. A wilderness city at the juncture of great rivers is likely to collect much more disagreeable drift than merely logs and mud. But Cairo to-day has a statue by George Grey Barnard in the center of its square. It has a fountain by Janet Scudder before the public library. Within that attractive building there is a portrait by William M. Chase. Perhaps the happiest and the most remarkable feature of the little city, "uncheered by any gleam of promise," is that while the population is sixteen thousand, its public library during the last year, issued one hundred and ten thousand books.

It was in the newspaper file of the same public library that we read:

"Little Rock, Ark.—An eccentric tornado or series of tornadoes traveling northwest, killed at least fifteen people last night in three Arkansas counties. In Brownsville, Mo., three are dead."

No wonder the *Isador* had jumped.

HERE'S DIXIE

CHAPTER XVIII

By this time we had learned the very important lesson that when there was a moon, night traveling, on the whole, was better than day traveling, for the river was usually calm at night. So, at two-thirty A. M. under a moon washed clean of rain, we left the doubtful protection of the eddy and went on to the mouth of the Ohio. Two miles up that river glowed the white street lights of Cairo. These, casting their reflections in the seemingly motionless water, blazed like a double row of brilliants along the shore. In their center flashed the magnificent, intermittently-appearing ruby of the harbor light.

Here, Illinois gave way to Kentucky, while Missouri carried darkly on down the right bank. After dawn I went ashore at a little Kentucky town named Hickman for gasoline. As I walked up the street, the world seemed to have become a place with more courtesy in it. When one finds a town where a filling station man stops his work to carry five gallons of gasoline

down to a boat, where a venerable druggist goes
around the block to change a ten dollar bill for a
stranger, where an unknown old gentleman standing
near a soda fountain says to you, "Have a drink, suh!"
then you may believe without the slightest doubt that
the frost and cold weather will not bother you much
longer, for you are getting near the South.

On that day, tra-
veling from two-
thirty in the morn-
ing till four in the af-
ternoon, the house-
boat made its record
run of ninety-five
miles. Nearly forty
of those miles were
spent in a vast double
loop where the river
turned due north to-
ward the town of

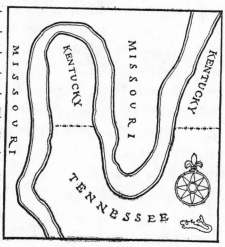

Kentucky irredenta

New Madrid. A crow—just an ordinary crow, or even
a crow that was slightly sub-normal—wishing to get
south, would have reduced that journey by exactly
twenty-five miles. On the other hand, he might have
failed to be impressed by the very interesting geograph-
ical fact that for ten miles a section of the State of
Kentucky lies *west* of the Mississippi.

The havoc caused in and about New Madrid by the great spring flood of 1927 was not the first rough treatment this country has had. The low ground has not only been swept by previous floods, but it is also a region of small earthquakes. In the early days of the white men, some of the fissures, which generally ran north and south, were so bad that "the settlers felled trees east and west, building their cabins on them so they would not be swallowed up."

As we passed Caruthersville, Missouri, we saw that the river had begun a flanking movement against the town. A numerous government fleet had gathered there —tugs, dredges, hundred-foot barges filled with stone and willow saplings for revetments, quarter boats with their laborers and engineers—all the paraphernalia that has been mobilized to prevent the depredations of the ever-changing river.

From Cairo on, the Mississippi—to quote one of the engineers I talked to—"is just simply hell on wheels." Obviously it cannot be driven; it must be persuaded to behave. The basic difficulty rests in the fact that the river, which formerly in high water spread over an area of fifty to a hundred miles in width, is now confined by levees to an average width of not more than a mile and a half. Thus thousands of square miles are reclaimed for agriculture, but occasionally the river takes back its own—as we have recently seen.

Both Mr. Hoover and Mr. Harris Dickson describe the dangerous part of the river as a rough trough extending from Cairo to the Gulf. But if I had not seen the river itself, that description would not be adequate unless it were explained to me that the river is not like a trough *in* the ground, but like a wooden trough standing *on* the ground's surface, with raised sides not of wood, but of reënforced dirt. These sides, of course, are the levees; and unfortunately, the dirt of which they are mainly composed is alluvial dirt of the kind into which a stream of water can eat with great ease.

In high water, there are certain places in its course where the river backs up into vast, temporary lakes. When these lakes once get away, all that man has made goes out before them. Apparently the difficulty does not rest in the fact that the river bottom has been raised up by alluvium dropping on it, as was previously thought, but in the fact that the river is compressed by artificial bulwarks that are neither strong enough nor high enough to guide it on its way. Higher and stronger dikes will, no doubt, be built. The matter is in the hands of the country's greatest engineers—but it is also in the laps of the gods. After a thousand miles on the Mississippi, one begins to realize that the gods are powerful gentlemen.

2

Kentucky had turned its river front over to Tennessee. Across the way, Missouri had capitulated to Arkansas. Flat lands folded away on both sides. There were few farms; distant sandbars and more distant banks were covered with timber. We passed down the river in sunlight. It was an enormous river now, nearly three miles wide, stretching out lazily in the heat, uncoiling its huge folds good-naturedly.

We found the entrance of a chute * at the right, and turned into it. The day was perfect. Reflected in the chute before the trotting *Isador,* was the blue sky with white clouds in it. At the sides, there were low willow thickets—brown with rose-colored tops—and giant, white-trunked cottonwood trees shining out against a haze of purple underbrush beyond. Above, as below, like the completing line of a triolet—the blue sky again, with white clouds in it.

Here is an unpainted ramshackle little group of farm buildings, lending the tonal beautitude of their gray to the bright color about them. A man with a dull, hopeless face, is standing immovable in his doorway

---

* A chute is a small or large channel that leaves the main waterway for a time, rejoining it again farther down stream. It may go many miles through forest and field before coming again to the river. Here one travels intimately through the countryside, and finds relief from the vastness of the great river.

watching us. Perhaps he was born in that house, or perhaps he was brought there when he was very young and has grown up there, and has married there, and will die there on the bank of the chute without ever having had a view of the river beyond the island. As I look at him, I feel for a moment, as though not he, but I were standing heavily there. The impression is so vivid that the very color of the landscape, which I am sure he does not see, goes out of the day as though a cloud has passed over. A strange, slight dread comes over me, and the necessity for escape. Escape from what? I do not know. A remembered sentence comes to my mind— "They did not complain because in all their lives they had never known anything else." Perhaps I want to escape from the uncomplaint in the man's eyes.

3

Here was the village of Luxora, a study in chocolate mud from the recent cyclonic storm, with roads axle deep in mire and no one to repair them. Soon the mud would be gone, though. The sun was hot—*hot*—for the first time since the far-distant days of the canoe. The man who occasionally sold gasoline at the river bank had gone fishing. I walked up over the levee and down into the town beyond. When I looked into the little stores, no white faces shone out through the windows. Here was the Black Diamond Barbershop, certainly with action inside; yet only the barber's white

Down shimmering miles

coat was visible. There was no head above it, nor any other heads, only a feeling of darkness and richness, like ebony. In front of the Luxora Five and Ten, clustered a dozen dusky men of infinite leisure, from whom rose the sound of slow, lazy laughter. And when I returned through the hot, steaming mud to the boat, my friend said, "Oh, Boppo—do you hear the little insects singing in the trees again? I'd like to live always where we can hear the little bugs singing."

We went on drowsily through the day, down shimmering miles of the ever-growing river past distant points and promontories and islands, set far, far away to the right and left in a vastness of space that was awe-inspiring. Whole sections of the country were under water. Channels had become lakes. Bends had straightened themselves out by flooding their banks, only to become segments of still greater bends which faded away beyond the flat horizon.

Then came a faint breeze and a ripple, breaking the tawny, blown-glass surface. When we had crossed the next wide area of water with its sandbar and willows and mighty cottonwood trees, we were glad to take shelter in a winding chute, set off by willows and sedge. We tied to the willows and stayed there all day. The wind came down upon us but the waves could never be very large. They played against our bow with a few distinct, silvery tones like the often repeated notes of a primitive xylophone. As night came on, we shut the doors, but the tinkling of the waves against the bow grew clearer still, resolving itself into a monotonous little tune, warranted to produce sleep:

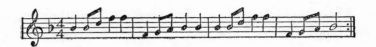

4

No towns on the river now. No more, indeed, until Memphis. Here are a few houses compositely called Osceola. Fill up the gasoline cans, for Memphis is sixty miles away. What a river it is, and how different from the map! Where is island No. 35? Where is Bateman's Bend? Is that Beef Island Chute, or is it the Amazon? The shore across the river lies below the blue horizon line. Perhaps this is the sixty-five mile wide Yangtze-Kiang. Keep your eye open for a pagoda or two.

A pair of minute government patrol boats, like nearsighted water-bugs, come nosing up the shore a few yards apart. They are watching the bank with meticulous care, looking for any of the great trees that may be about to fall with the caving bank and become a menace to passing steamers; watching the river eat into the levees to find a lower channel to the Gulf; observing the twisting currents and eddies, which in the course of a few days, may cut hundreds of feet into the soft alluvium, leaving the tag-end of a cotton field sliced off sharply like the upturned, scalloped blade of a cake knife.

Now twisting to the east beyond Yankee Bar, the river narrowed to a quarter mile, rushing past a forty foot bluff and returning again in a series of whirl-pools, which, cutting into the high, eroded bank, had thrown down a hundred large trees. They lay like symbols of destruction scattered down the red clay slope.

This great mound of earth was the first of the Chickasaw Bluffs. In May, 1541, either from these bluffs, or from others somewhat farther to the south, Hernando De Soto first saw the Mississippi River. No doubt his legend lingered long among the Indians as the symbol of something decidedly unpleasant. DeSoto had learned a few things about handling natives with Pizarro in Peru. This time, among other accessories, he brought with him a pack of Irish greyhounds.

Landing near Tampa, Florida, he immediately struck inland across the swamps of what is now Georgia and Mississippi, attempting "the conquest of Florida." But since the whole country was Florida to him, conquering it was a large order. He had his troubles. In one encounter with the Indians, one hundred forty-five of his men are said to have received a total of six hundred eighty-eight arrow wounds. The booming of guns then; the shrieks of the stricken horses; the groans of

sick and dying; the sound of hammers pounding together the quickly-constructed barges; the tumult of
passage to the western side; the noise dying away into
the wilderness out of which De Soto never returned.
The red men saw no more white faces for one hundred
and thirty-two years, not indeed, until Louis Joliet and
the restless Jesuit priest passed the bluffs on their way
down stream in 1673.

Nine years later, René Robert Cavelier, Sieur de
La Salle, with twenty-three Frenchmen and some Indians, came out of the mouth of the Illinois River and
proceeded down the Mississippi. Of the hundred miles
below the Ohio and the present site of Cairo, his chron-
icler notes: "From the mouth of this river you must
advance forty-two leagues without stopping, because
the banks are low and marshy and full of thick foam,
rushes, and walnut trees." Forty-two French leagues
are equal to one hundred and forty-five miles—just
the distance from Cairo to the first Chickasaw bluff.

Reaching the lower end of the Mississippi where the
river divides itself into three channels, La Salle erected
a column which bore the French coat-of-arms and the
inscription: "Louis le Grande Reigne; Roi de France
et de Navarre, Le Neuvième Avril, 1682." Hence the
name, Louisiana.

A little later, two other Frenchmen, Bienville and
Iberville, ascended the river, founding settlements here

and there. But in time, what was French became Spanish. Finally, the new government of the United States claimed land on the east bank of the river. A fort rose on the lower Chickasaw bluffs, and Memphis began.

Below the upper bluffs, not far from Beef Island Chute, occurred what is probably the worst single marine disaster on record. One day, in the spring of 1864, the steamer *Sultana* went up the river from Memphis with two thousand four hundred people aboard. When she reached a group of small islands called Paddy's Hens and Chickens, her entire battery of five boilers blew up at the same time. The boat burned to the water's edge and sank on a sandbar near Bradley's Landing. Two thousand lives were lost.

A narrow rivulet appeared to the left of Beef Island Chute. We went into it gratefully. The sun was shining. Birds were singing in the meadow grass. The waterway, only a few feet wide, wound among trees and underbrush that had felt no touch of frost. It joined with another little river, and ambled peacefully on. A factory appeared to the left. The dual rivulet joined still another; then, winding down past houseboat colonies, boat works, tugs, barges and ancient hulks through a mile more of the most picturesque flotsam and jetsam imaginable, it led us to the base of the high bluff on which rises the city of Memphis, Tennessee.

As we came up to a private dock, a young fellow with bronzed skin, red cheeks and long, blonde sunburned hair flying out like Medusa's locks all over his head, pulled alongside in a row-boat and asked us whether we didn't want to tie up to the bank across the way. One could tie up for nothing there, he said. Was he "on the river?" we asked. Yes. He and another chap had drifted, in that yellow houseboat over there, all the way from Iowa.

Later, they came aboard the *Isador*. They had just finished college, and were making their way down the river to New Orleans, where they wanted to tie up to the bank and become writers. They resembled each other only in the fact that they both wanted to write. MacGovren, the first who had greeted us, was a small blonde god, full of earnestness and nervous energy. He could not always find words to express the subtlety of his ideas, and so he made slow, clutching gestures with his two hands as though he would seize his syllables out of the air. Rork, the other, was a black haired, blue-eyed Irishman with a bump on his nose, a very quiet manner, and a rare sense of humor. Their solidly-built boat, a little larger than the *Isador,* was always in a great mess because they were young and didn't care. We were to see them again and again on the river.

OFF DUTY

The old "Patonia" at Memphis, Tenn., has carried her last gay party of gentlemen in brocaded waistcoats and ladies in crinoline.

5

Memphis was captured by the Federal forces early in the Civil War, and was held under a number of commanders, including Grant and Sherman. One of the most pronounced characteristics of the city at that time, seems to have been its mud. An English war correspondent went so far as to write:

"I wonder that they gave it such a name of old renown, This dreary, dismal, muddy melancholy town?"

But Memphis, high on its bluff overlooking the little Wolf River and the Mississippi beyond, has become a very attractive city. After the manner of Tennessee its theaters and moving pictures are closed on the Sabbath. A few months preceding our arrival, it had been impossible to buy gasoline there on Sunday. On the other hand, alcohol was at all times to be had. The islands across from the city were "jammed with stills." No one in Memphis would rent a boat to a government prohibition agent, for very shortly the boat would be sunk or disappear. I had it direct from several newspaper men, who always tell the exact truth when they are not speaking officially, that the holiday supply had flooded the market with corn whiskey until it could be had at the still—or F. O. B., if you had a boat—for $2.25 a gallon. Transporters who formerly worked on a fifty cent margin had been forced to drop to twenty-five cents. A decent man could not live on a stipend like that!

The newspapers reported that George White's *Scandals* would be "forced to undergo a searching investigation by the Protestant Ministers' Association of Memphis on the opening night," and that the average annual fall of soot in the city was "six hundred and sixteen tons to the square mile."(!) In other words, Memphis is an interesting and lively American city in an age that may some day be known as the Transition Period.

There are pretty girls in Memphis. The southern flapper resembles her northern sister in everything except that she is a little more wobbly. Her legs wobble a little more when she walks; her body wobbles too. I think she is clever enough to wish to give the impression that her brain wobbles (which in most cases, it doesn't), but that is a matter of technique. Possibly in this walkless age, flappers' legs are generally weak and wobbly. But certainly the terrific array of limbs one has to observe on Fifth Avenue, leaves no such impression of shakiness as those seen on the lower Mississippi. Perhaps where man is so gallant, woman becomes more dependent. It is strange to think that these delicate, wobbly little creatures may one day become

solid, square-rigged, resourceful young matrons, looking out at the world with the shrewd, understanding
eye, telling their husbands just exactly what is what,
and what is not. Strange, and a little sad.

Memphis has by no means turned its back on the
Mississippi. The river, in fact, does not permit it to.
For one thing, the city promenade by the post office is
on the bluff facing the river. For another thing, the
parking space for Memphis automobiles is located halfway down the wide slope of the bluff. For still another,
the island across from Memphis that is formed by the
narrow channel of the Wolf River on the near side and
the Mississippi on the far side, is gradually getting so
long that it may make trouble for the shipping. Then
too, just a week before we got to Memphis, a plot of
land half a block from the river, nearly six hundred
feet long by one hundred and fifty feet wide, with several buildings on it, had sunk slowly, deliberately
down, like an elevator, eighty feet—so straight down
in fact, that some of the structures on it were not disturbed at all. This phenomenon was probably due to
the washing-out of a stratum of sand by a subterra-
nean channel of the river. And finally—so Memphis
might not forget the river—there was the matter of the
Thanksgiving Day storm, which played havoc with the
houseboats and shipping in plain sight of the bluff.

A thirty-ton stern-wheeler, that of the only "show

boat" man whom we saw on the entire river, was tied near the *Isador*. The showman had lost a sixty foot barge containing his tents, four hundred seats, and all his scenery and properties in that storm. Later, his troupe of seven had broken up, leaving himself and his wife stranded for the winter in Memphis, where he was making the best of it by taking a small part in a local stock company.

We found Padriac Colum, the good Irish poet, in Memphis, lecturing; and in his honor, the mate submitted chicken à la Maryland with baked yams and cranberry jelly, and a dessert that melted in the mouth. But he ate sparingly, as becomes one whose hunger is primarily intellectual; so that I, who enjoy my food, was hard put to it not to suffer by comparison, and still get enough to eat.

During the long afternoon, he lay talking among the gay cushions on the couch, starting up occasionally under the impetus of an idea; and the small cabin of the *Isador* was filled with the color of his thoughts shining in the rare matrix of such simple and beautiful Gaelic English that it would be an injustice for me to attempt to re-capture his ideas in my own words.

"What have you learned from your journey down the river?" he asked at last.

(What *haven't* we learned, sweet friend!) "Well,

for one thing, we have learned that the girls in the five and ten cent stores from Bemidji to Memphis, should take a special course in wrapping up packages."

Immediately he became very solemn. "Is that really so, now? Isn't it fearful! Oh Lord—books come to me at home; people sending books and saying, 'I've had so much joy out of this book—would you please inscribe it and send it back?' Oh—the paper and the string! It's that that makes it such a trial. Do you know, that is one reason I stay with MacMillan for a publisher. Sometimes I am in town with my arms full of bundles, with the string coming off all of them; and I go to MacMillan's, and there is a wee girl there who will wrap them for me."

But now he must be going. He had his lecture to give that evening, and he must prepare it. I accompanied him to his hotel, and came back alone through the busy, well-lighted streets. A pleasant town, Memphis, combining southern hospitality with northern activity. On its streets were amiable people, well and comfortably dressed. That reminded me that I needed a new pair of shoes—a good pair of shoes, well mated and efficient, that would take me on in my confirmed pedestrian way. Here on Main Street, was a shoe store with an illuminated sign over head. I read it and stood transfixed:

BANNISTER
SHOES
COOK & LOVE

For such highly talented foot wear I had not hoped!
When you go to Memphis, you can read the good news
for yourself.

ALONG THE LEVEES

CHAPTER XIX

I

Now the land is constantly guarded by levees. Some of them rise directly at the water's edge, others cut inland out of sight beyond the forest to head off the river in case of flood. The small river towns have taken shelter behind their formidable sod-covered fortifications. Only a few wisps of smoke and the tops of their chimneys are visible from the river.

Below Memphis, it rolls magnificently along past distant yellow sandbars. Low willow thickets lie like a red miasmic haze against the mauve background of ragged forest. In spite of the prevailing presence of high, massive timber, the landscape is broad and horizontal. Only when we approach the bank do the trees loom up before us like the giants they are. Some, slipping into the water, clutch with enormous roots at the crumbling edge of the bank in their last grim battle with the river. Sometimes the edge gives way and they go down with a mighty crash, sending a small tidal wave out into the Mississippi.

The town of Friar's Point passes us beyond its levee.

There are nine negroes to one white man in this particular county. The river, Heaven be praised, is narrowing just a little, pulling in its banks, so that it does not appear to spread quite from the Alleghenies on one side to the Rockies on the other, as it did above Memphis. We can see details on both shores at the same time. On one side a government dredge with tugs and quarter boats is repairing the levee; opposite is a tented logging camp where negroes cut the condemned trees at the edge of the bank and drag them to safety with powerful horses before the hungry river swallows them.

We jab the anchor pole for the night into a sandbar where the tracks of wild water-fowl have made an intricate tracery in the wet alluvium. As twilight sifts down over the sedge, a low-lying black-hulled freight boat of the Mississippi-Warrior Line comes panting gently up the river, pushing three immense barges.* Wild geese, disturbed by this caravan, fly toward our sandbar. On seeing the *Isador,* they change their minds and wheel away, making small noises of wistful complaint. Darkness comes. Other geese settle on the bar, and talk to each other in tones almost human. But soon they fly off, and only the QUACK QUACK-QUACK-QUACK of ducks on an inland puddle disturbs the silence. Gradually they too settle to rest. A few dogs at dis-

---

* A towboat recently conveyed barges carrying 224,000 barrels of oil from Lake Providence to Baton Rouge; that is as much oil as 25 trams of 40 carloads each could carry.

tantly removed farm-houses, bark out to each other the uneventful news of the day. No big head-lines evidently; just the usual routine of rabbits and fence posts and kicks. Now they are silent too.

I go out and look at the depth gauge that I have made by sticking a notched sapling down into the sandy river bottom. An hour and a half ago, the water was just at the notch. Now it is an inch lower. That is too much of a drop for our present shallow mooring-place. If we do not move, by morning we shall be stuck on the sandbar. In the slow current I pull the boat around the end of the bar, holding when necessary to a hook on the outside of the cabin. *Clip!* Out comes the hook. I lose my balance on the narrow runway, waver for an instant, then leap for the bar hoping it is not quick-sand. Excellent! I light firmly in a foot of water.

My ribulet, hearing the splash, comes running out; and, perhaps a little relieved to find me standing there, cries, "Now your shoes are all wet."

"The hook came out."

"Of course it did! It has been loose for a month! For Heaven's sake, how many times are you going to fall into the river, anyway?"

So with chastened spirits I climbed aboard. But the next day—dear reader, how can I make you believe it was actually the next day? I can't. You'll have to write and ask the mate.

The next day, as my companion, the before-mentioned mate of the *Isador,* was leaning out to grasp some willow branches when we were about to anchor beside a towhead for lunch, something happened. Afterward she explained the technique exactly—how she had reached for the willow, how it had broken off, how she walked three steps along the runway and reached for another; and how, missing it, she had lost her balance and—*splash!* Whatever it was that happened, the mate was gone.

I ran back along the runway. The willows, growing up out of the water, were within three feet of the boat's side. There was only one possible place where she could re-appear. I waited, in the fullest, most terrific meaning of that passive word. How long? Long enough. Then, breaking up through the tawny water, like something necessary and promised and inevitable, came that dear, dark head.

"It wasn't very c-cold," she said. "It wasn't very c-cold. . . ."

2

"What were you thinking about when you went down?" I inquired, after the morbid manner of my kind.

"I was thinking," she said, "about—yesterday."

"You mean, when I——?"

"Yes."

And at dinner that evening my favorite pudding appeared—of pears, apples, cinnamon, and sugar, all baked to a delicious brown; with super-dumplings so light and excellent that they were not dumplings in the usual sense of the word at all.

3

On the Arkansas side, we stopped in a little creek of clear water with some fishermen who, after their kindly manner gave us fish and wished that we could stay longer. Their wives told the mate how lonely it was. No doubt that was true, for whereas the men managed to get away sometimes to the town in their power boats with loads of fish, the women saw the same faces and landscape every day. And though the landscape and faces too were changed from time to time under seasonal foliage, the women were not content with that.

"Nature is wonderful—but what are you going to do about it?" seems to be their attitude. The men, however, busy and satisfied with their active work, do nothing about it. So the women grow old quickly, sometimes so much more quickly than the men that they appear to be of an older generation.

As recently as fifteen years ago, the river was a

highway for a large number of houseboat vagabonds. They built their houseboats in the fall, and, trapping and shooting on the way, drifted down to New Orleans. Then they sold their boats and the skins they had collected; and, buying a lower deck ticket on one of the packets, they returned to some spot suitable for growing a few rows of corn and cabbage until the next fall, when the journey would be made again.

Now, however, the river people for the most part settle either in colonies near the towns where the men can find work in the factories, or locate in near-by chutes or bayous from which they can take their fish to market in their shovel-nosed john-boats. On the wooded shores of the creeks they build huts for their chickens and ducks and pigs. Sometimes they own cows. When the water rises, all must come aboard until, on some local Mount Ararat, when the disembarking begins again, they give notice of their tenancy, perhaps, by putting up a sign like this one, which we saw in a chute in Arkansas:

NOTICEA
NO HOUTEN
& CHUTEN

They waste no time in superfluous English. "Noticea" means, I believe, "Notice here." A little farther
down the river was a houseboat bearing the terse message: Keep out or get shot.

4

So far, we had had no animals aboard except the
hell-diver. With ice on the deck at St. Louis, the idea
of having a dog had gradually fallen into disfavor.
But somewhere in Arkansas, we took aboard a ship's
mouse.

At first, beside a few incursions into the sweet potatoes, and the rustling of paper bags, he made no
trouble at all. But one night I was awakened by something crawling slowly up my spine between my pajamas and my back. The human frame is so constructed that it is difficult to seize with any great pre-
cision an object moving along between the shoulder
blades. Besides, the idea occurred to me that it might
be a large spider, and a spider as roughly shod as that
one was should by no means be tapped into eternity
against one's epidermis.

I awakened the mate and asked her for the flashlight. She, half asleep, but sensing some imminent peril,
advanced the light with such right good will through
the darkness that she thumped me a wicked blow over

the eye with it. In the ensuing illumination, I saw the ship's mouse, (who by that time had left my company), scuttle down the companionway, round the chart-room, and disappear into the galley. Now belay me with a marlinespike! That wouldn't do at all. A ship's mouse should know its place.

The following night he crawled over my ear. I announced the fact.

"Oh, no, no! It's your imagination!" But the next moment came a squeak that was not from the mouse. This was too much. We decided to be rid of him.

But that was not so easy. All the next day we trailed him into his haunts—under portfolios, into the pantry, among our shoes, between the motor tools under the table. The poor creature was really very unhappy; he had nowhere to go. Once I saw him disappear under the floor. So, taking the flashlight, I illuminated the murky, dripping space between the flooring and the boat's bottom just in time to see him picking his way nervously across the flat, wet boards, raising each foot very high like a fussy old maid with galoshes in a flooded sub-basement.

The poor little devil looked so unhappy that we unset our traps. But that night he crawled on us again. Why didn't he keep out of bed? That was really the only thing we held against him. We steeled our hearts, set the traps again, this time with bacon. And while we

were reading in a week-old newspaper about things
that had happened in the far-distant United States,
there came a sharp click, and the mouse had gone on
his way. Whereas a soldier might wish to die with his
boots on, or a miser counting his gold, or a holy man
on his knees, what more could a mouse wish than that
he be let die instantly with his mouth full of certified
and government-inspected bacon?

5

So on to Caulk's Point—which the maps of 1892
called Cork's Point—and on through the pleasantest of
weather to a bend in the river where a sawmill stood
smoking and roaring on the top of the levee. On the left
hand the river ran around a sandbar; on the right was
another sandbar under an impenetrable growth of
young willows. A village called Arkansas City should
be back of it. As we drew near the mill, a narrow channel appeared through the thicket. We plowed into it,
got stuck, freed ourselves, followed its devious, jungle-
like windings, finally coming out into a strip of open
water with the bar on one side and the levee on the
other. As usual, beyond the levee, was the town.

To be a true exponent of pathos, the bearer of that
quality must not be aware of its presence. Arkansas
City is one of the most pathetic places I have ever

seen. On the main street, a few two story buildings with high wooden verandas facing the still higher levee contain the stores of the town. Back of the main street the rickety houses fray out to the edge of town in a sea of mud. The levee is by far the highest point on the landscape. The town's fifteen hundred inhabitants live in constant hazard of the slightest whim of the river. In spite of the poverty of the place, apples— bananas, even—were sixty cents a dozen. Canned food on which the unhealthy-looking citizens lived, was higher than at any other place on the river. Supplies from New Orleans were shipped first to Kansas City or St. Louis, and then back by a branch railway to the town.

Without exception, the people with whom we came in contact, were friendly and generous. They were entirely unaware that I was taking notes on the river. It was enough for them to know that I was a stranger. A hardware merchant gave me several bolts for the motor, which had been gradually strewing its parts down the Mississippi. A machine shop mechanic turned a rudder nut for me on his lathe, and refused payment. A colored man carried the gasoline cans to the top of the levee. The feeling of the poor little place was amicable and kindly. Yet I have never heard nor read anything but ill of Arkansas City.

In April, June and July, 1927, the town suffered

three distinct floods which swept away nearly two hundred houses, ruined one hundred and twenty-four more, spoiled three attempted crops and forced the inhabitants to live for weeks at a time on the levee top. As far as I can find out, these misfortunes have been met with a rare and courageous fortitude.

South of Arkansas City, our previously-employed imaginary crow, flying as crows generally fly, would have had less opinion of our intelligence than ever; for while the river, in vast serpentine coils, led us a tortuous forty miles, the crow would have flown eleven. We saw the smoke of a steamboat a mile away across a neck of land, but we had to travel fifteen miles before finding out that it was a Mississippi-Warrior tugboat, with its underwater paddle-wheel and its common-sense wake—not a huge confrère of the *Cape Girardeau,* sending back a succession of bed waves each of which might be considerably higher than the *Isador* itself.

Greenville, Mississippi, and the fifteenth of December arrived simultaneously. We moored in a pocket which already housed six or eight small yachts and motor-boats. The water sweeping up stream close to the bank and down stream beyond, gave us a harbor immune from waves.

So much for our location—but what about the fifteenth of December? You can't hide from the Christmas spirit in a pocket of the Mississippi! Indeed, you don't want to. But some way or other, river mud and white tissue paper with holly ribbon, don't synchronize at all. You can't wrap up your gifts and spread them out in the next room, when the next room is seventy feet deep and full of catfish. What to do? Come, dear friend, use that excellent brain of yours. Mine has all oozed out long ago fighting the wind and the rain on this everlasting river. Give us an idea for a Christmas greeting.

She did. She went into Greenville and bought one square foot of linoleum from an astonished household furnisher; she bought two chisels; then in the afternoon she traced a drawing I had meanwhile made, upon the linoleum and began to cut out the background with the chisels and a pocket-knife. She worked eight hours one day and nine hours the next. How pleasant it was to see her swift, accurate progress, particularly when I was doing nothing. But by the third afternoon the effort was beginning to tell on her. Making a linoleum cut is interesting work, but the worst part of it is that you must not make a mistake, for a mistake cannot be repaired. The least I could do was to get supper. Was I capable of doing that? Yes, I thought so. I opened a can of soup and seasoned it and set it proudly alongside some lesser viands on the table, but unfortunately the top had come off the pepper shaker. I retrieved it out of the soup with a large spoon, but not all the pepper. She tasted it, and looked at me with a strange, contemplative eye.

"What did you do to it?"

"To the soup? Oh, it's pepper—I just seasoned it."

"I should think so!"

"What, don't you like pepper?"

"Well not quite as much as that."

"I'll fix it." So I took her soup away, opened another can, heated its contents and brought it to her.

"Aren't you going to have some of this, too?" she inquired.

"I? Oh no! I liked it the other way. That's the way the Mexicans eat it." I admit that I made the remark out of pride; but as I ate, I saw her looking at me quite amused, and that was very good, for it relaxed her nerves and she could work so much better when she was happy. Besides, one must make sacrifices to the Christmas spirit. But the going with the well-peppered soup was terrible. Before I got well into it, my forehead broke out in a cloud of mist and my larnyx began working like a hysterical caterpillar. By the time I reached the bottom of the plate, I was suffering from acute arson; the Christmas spirit was a total loss, and I was thinking in terms of hairless dogs, *haciendas,* barracuda fish and *libertad.*

By the end of the third day, the background was cut,

leaving the drawing in relief. We got some red paper and printed it by rolling printer's ink onto the linoleum with a rolling pin, then putting the inked linoleum face downward on the paper and stepping on it, thereby getting a result like the little sketch on the title page of this book, but larger. Then, when we had sent off prints with a blessing, I went out to find the man whose presence had led us to stop at Greenville.

COLOR OF THE SOUTH

CHAPTER XX

I

WILLIAM ALEXANDER PERCY sat in his private room of a law office in the rather musty old building that is occupied by the town's attorneys, judges, and insurance men. He was young, small, slightly built, with steady blue eyes, sun-tanned face and hair that was nearly white. I was unknown to him, but he greeted me with a friendliness and a courtesy so instinctive that I doubt whether he himself was aware of the rareness of its quality. My first impression told me of fineness and breeding; my second assured me that the first impression was right. Indeed, at the time I could not bring myself to speak about his poetry. We talked instead of a number of incidental things, and finally, about the river.

He told me how, for months and years at a time, the river sweeps untroubled and untroubling past the Greenville dikes. Life in the beautiful little town of fifteen thousand goes quietly on under the shade of its broad-leaved oaks and cypresses and magnolias. The out-lying estates and cotton plantations quietly raise the great cotton crops for which the district is famous. But at last, inevitably, comes the time when the Mississippi rises to the high-water mark. Interest focuses itself on the river. As the waters advance past the flood stage, excitement in the town rises to a higher and higher pitch of intensity. The swirling tide rises up the side of the dikes. Now comes the ceremony known as "guarding the levees." There is an old fiction, or perhaps a distant truth, that at times dwellers on one bank of the river have cut the levees on the opposite bank to lessen the pressure on their own. Not that people in Greenville, for example, actually remember when their Arkansas neighbors cut the levees—however, it is well to be on guard; and at any rate the river is rising and must be observed.

The town's entire male population pours out for a distance of seventy-five miles along the county's water front, "guarding the levees." Negro workers from the cotton fields concentrate in camps along the river. Sometimes at night they sing together in that strange, barbaric rhythm and harmony which gets into the blood of listening white men, and makes the pulse beat faster. One very valid object of guarding the embankments is to watch for "boils." Boils occur when the water of the river, eating under a levee, rises like a small geyser on the inside. This, if not stopped at once, becomes larger and larger, gnawing at the intervening levee until the rampart goes down and the river rushes in. It does no good to try to block the boil with dirt. A well of sandbags must be built around it. The water gradually rises in the well. When it reaches the level of the water outside the levee, the boil ceases to boil. For the time, the danger is over.

While he was telling me things, I suppose we had been taking stock of each other. I asked him to pot-luck with us on the *Isador;* he invited us to meet some of his friends at tea and to dine with him so that we might meet his mother.

So for several days we felt the presence of an elusive evanescent gayety different in type from that to be found in the North; we perceived about us a freedom of spirit, a rare appreciation of the art of living; we noted that here people were not all of a pattern, not all turned out of the same mold. Why not? Perhaps because the senses had not been dulled and dominated and possessed *ad nauseam* by an urge toward standardized prosperity.

I talked again and again to the young lawyer, who is one of the South's authentic poets. There was a gayety about him and a flashing humor that is not to be found in his poems, for they are the consummation of his finest thought and they carry their clear starlike beauty beyond the place of laughter. His first two books, *In April Once* and *Sappho in Levkas* contain passages of that rare loveliness which the name of Keats evokes for us as perhaps no other name can—that beauty, which, because of its infinite delicacy, may easily turn brittle in lesser hands. I said, "Considering the fragility of your verse, what seems strange to me and what I do not quite understand, is the apparent balance that you have found between the reality of life and the reality of the dream. Coleridge fused the two with opium; Poe had his alcohol; Milton his blindness; Edna St. Vincent Millay her quest for the Carthaginian rose——"

"And I," he said, laughing, "am a lawyer."

But that was not enough. The law, might give one some necessary unfulfillment, might be a compensating enough balance to make a man produce verse of considerable lyric beauty; still, in his third volume, *Enzio's Kingdom*, there was, along with its beauty, a newly-found power which transcended even such a negation as a law practice. As we talked, I came by degrees a little way through the surface barrier, so subtle yet so strong, which a poet, whether he wishes it or not, carries with him as an armadillo its shell. He told me how Greenville had fought the Ku-Klux-Klan and had defeated it, but that it had been a terribly bitter experience, more bitter and disillusioning than the war. He had not known before what hatred was, what it was to hate and to be hated. For months he had gone

Poet of the Delta

armed; for weeks he had not permitted his father, who was leading the fight, to go out alone.

Their house, which had never been locked before, was now locked at all times. One night during a storm there came a knock at the door. A stranger was there saying that his automobile had broken down and that his two sisters were waiting in the rain some distance away. The response was, of course, immediate. But as the motor was being brought around the house, the sheriff of the county happened to come up the walk. The stranger, whom the sheriff recognized as a particularly cold-blooded gunman, disappeared into the darkness.

Now the young poet would have no more of seriousness, but must roll up the barrier of laughter before him, telling how, after a talk he had given on poetry in New York City a strange woman had come up to him and had said, "I love your soul!" And how a less strange man had said, "Damned if I know what your poetry is all about." We agreed that of the two, we much preferred the man, for he, at least, was honest; whereas if a woman really loved your soul, she wouldn't say so in just that way.

Farther down the river, we heard of this young man as a lawyer, both from white people and from black. Perhaps his most famous colored case occurred not

long ago, when news came to Greenville of a black
prophet who had found a spring of healing water a few
miles away in a white man's cotton field. A great number of cures had been made among the colored people.
The halt, the lame and the blind, to say nothing of those
with angina pectoris, hay fever, St. Vitus dance and
hair-lip, flocked to the little pool of ditchwater in such
overwhelming numbers that the white planter's cotton-
field was ruined. (However, no law suit arose over that,
for the planter put a fence around the field, charged
ten cents admission; and made three times the value
of his cotton crop!) At first the prophet baptized his
patients *in toto,* but as the water in the mudhole got
low, he only sprinkled them; still, the cures went on.

Certain members of the medical profession, on
whose practice the prophet had made distinct inroads,
brought suit against him as a quack. The colored man
claimed no power himself, but said that whatever cures
took place, were the result of the Lord's will working
through him. When Will Percy arrived in court the
first morning of the trial, the yard was black with
negroes.

"Who are these?"

"They are them that is cured, suh."

He interrogated them.

"Yessuh, Ah was blind from mah childhood. Now
Ah can see."

"Ah couldn't walk, but now Ah kin."

"Mah a'm was sure nuff stiff, but now Ah can bend it double."

In his argument, however, he did not use them as witnesses, but based his plea on the contention that the man himself was not a quack. The healer had made no misrepresentations. He baptized the people and they became well. If Christ were to come back to earth, he would be indicted as a charlatan too. Why should we not believe that this man healed by faith?

While he talked, the negroes in the audience were swaying back and forth, humming after their manner, and greeting each point with "Amen-brother!" "Yes, dat's so!" "Come on, little Jesus" (that was the lawyer); "The Holy Ghost done said a mouf full."

The case was won for the black prophet. His fame spread. Special trains were run to the cotton-field; ferries brought loads of pilgrims from across the river. Everything was serene, until a number of Arkansas contract labor negroes broke their contracts and came across the river to the healer. Their angry employers came after them, entered the enclosure and started to get the negroes out.

The prophet, probably not understanding the situation, disappeared into his tent, came out with a service revolver and began banging away, sending the white men tearing down the road and the colored brethren over the fence. That, of course, wouldn't do at all. So the prophet, like many another, was put away.

2

We started from Greenville, but had to put in at a willow-topped island three miles down the river because of wind. After the wind, came rain,—a torrential cloud-burst of astounding force. It lasted three hours and when it was over I bailed thirty-one gallons of water from the skiff. Then the motor failed to work. I took it apart and tinkered with it all afternoon; still it did not respond. There was nothing to do but row up stream to the town. However, that might leave the mate alone on the *Isador* for the night, a plan which was instantly vetoed in my mind because of the unsavory reputation of the island to which we were moored.

Not long before, two houseboats had been anchored near each other there, one occupied by a single man, the other by a friend of the first—a blonde, curly-haired fellow who was living with a girl. Word spread abroad one day that the light-haired man had been drowned. Two weeks later the Greenville police went down to investigate. They found that the single man was there, but that the girl and her companion had disappeared.

They dragged the waters near the island without result. As they were about to leave, some one pulled on a mooring rope to bring the two houseboats nearer the shore. Suddenly, coming up stark naked out of the river, there rose the ghastly cadaver of the light-haired man. The mooring rope had caught under his arm, and when it was pulled, the corpse had risen upright beside it. They found that his body had been ripped open and stuffed with sand to make it sink. The other man was tried, but there was no evidence, since the girl did not come back. Under the circumstances, I did not care to leave the mate alone on the houseboat.

We rose early and rowed three intolerable miles against the current to the town, passing a large government plant of floating barges where hundreds of negroes were making concrete slabs for revetments and piling them on other barges to be shipped to points where the river was devouring its banks. The negroes, who have little respect for river people, since the latter are frequently "poor white trash" of the trashiest, watched us rather insolently, but said nothing much amiss. That was perhaps due to the presence of government overseers, who in their turn gave us great and friendly assistance in getting the motor up over the barges and into the town. A few years ago when private contractors worked for the government, no woman who appeared to be of the river could have passed such an outfit without hearing a number of very unpleasant things.

This was the only time on shore or afloat when southern negroes showed the slightest tendency to be disagreeable. At our various stopping places, we talked to them frequently, went to their churches to hear their remarkable chanted sermons and singing, bought their garden wares, and at times anchored not far from their houseboats. We found no fault in them. In heart and mind their simplicity seemed very near to that of children. And they seemed happier to me than their fellows in the North.

Again southward, with a new battery and a rejuvenated motor. On the left, Mississippi, and on the right Louisiana. Over both banks there was fog. Only the right shore near which the *Isador* plodded like a slow, faithful turtle, showed its presence by the blue silhouette of its tree-tops rising out of the prevailing obscurity. A delicate but steady insistence on the part of the current against the left tiller line, showed that its direction was changing to the other side of the river. Should we follow it, losing ourselves again in that detached, mysterious world of gray space? The ayes won. I loosened my hold on the tiller, and let the boat go where it would. In a moment, the shore was gone.

The mate, who had been making the cabin ship-shape, threw a crumpled letter out into the river. We watched it disappear, a morsel in the mouth of the fog. A little breeze came up, ruffling the water and stirring the mist into vaporous shrouds. We chugged on for half an hour, straining our eyes for the trees and logs, which singly or in groups, float down the river, with their talon-like roots ready to pounce on shantyboats. A slight object, by no means a log, approached us on the water. It was the mate's letter. Like men lost in the woods, we had made a complete circle. We set off again, but at the end of twenty minutes, to our vast surprise, the letter reappeared, coming toward us on the same side as before! About us was the uncanny presence of the fog, with that bit of paper drifting past our bow.

We stopped the motor expecting to find out at once which way we were drifting. We could not tell! We had no way of knowing where the river itself was going. Certainly we were moving, but *which way?*

How was it possible to get lost on a river that had a current? It happened to us, and it had happened to many others. Couldn't we tell by the logs and floating sticks which way was down stream? No. Everything was floating in the direction we were. Besides, in a two-mile river like the Mississippi, the eddies sometimes carry everything up stream for a considerable distance.

If there is a slight change of the wind, and if the river itself alters its direction, attempting to find one's course is made more mystifying still.

We drifted on through the gossamer grayness, hearing only the gentle chuckling of the highly-amused waters. Then, very faintly, from the far distance came the sound of birds singing. After several starts and stops,

Shantyboaters sometimes lash their boats to floating logs, which keep in the current and aid progress down stream.

we made certain of their direction and came at last to an overhanging forest bank that was slowly shedding great trees into the river. Now the current seemed to be flowing up stream toward Bemidji, but when we had traveled with it for a time, our minds whirled suddenly around to the proper points of the compass, and we went on all day in the warm fog, hugging the bank, and avoiding sandbars with their eddies, and ramparts of beetling snags. Until, as we came around a towhead, some one hailed us out of the fog *a few feet away,* and the animated faces of Rork and MacGovren shown out of the door of their dilapidated houseboat! We tied up by them for the night; but the two collegians, who cooked with a wood stove, burned some sort of wet wood that had a vile, sweetish, sickening smell. The odor of it drifted into our cabin; and the wind blew the window shut after it; so that when we woke in the morning, we felt as though we had been embalmed by an undertaker who himself had long since crumbled into dust.

In a soft rain, we started down the river together. It was the day before Christmas, and the mate had promised us food that evening of great excellence. Rork, who was the collegiate engineer, sat in their old john-boat tinkering with their moribund one-cylinder motor and giving it occasional injections of gasoline, while their unwieldy yellow ark swung ponderously behind at the end of a rope.

Soon we had left them far out of sight around a two mile bend, so we shut off the power and drifted along in the rain until they came up with us. They brought the wind with them, and before we could start the motor, which, as usual, was sulking in the wet, we drove ashore between a fallen tree and a high bank. I got us out of that with the skiff, then went aboard and spun the fly-wheel into action. But the wind came in a gust and again sent us shoreward. I heard the mate cry out to me to stop, and at the same moment, a thunderous boom, bang, thud, sounded from under the ship's bottom. With a final bump, up from beneath the back deck, rose the end of a black cypress log two feet thick and as long as the *Isador*. It missed the motor by a fraction of an inch and sank down again into a trough in the waves, while the boat scurried nervously on.

Why hadn't the square-sawed end, with its scalloped cypress knobs, smashed in the old planks of the *Isador's* bow? For the reason that when it had arrived within striking distance the mate, throwing herself down on the front deck, with legs out over the water, had come down on it with both feet. The sharp end, suddenly submerged, had slid harmlessly under the boat's prow.

With only the loss of a slipper, we went blithely on our way. But after another mile or two, the collegiate engine, in spite of Rork's most concentrated efforts, sneezed a few times, again lost consciousness, and would not be revived. It had chosen a bad spot for its anesthesia. The wind was high, the river was swift, and ahead of us there was a decided veering of the current toward the right bank where water seemed to be disappearing into a ragged growth of heavy timber.

We tied the boats together in a sort of caravan—
first, the *Isador,* then the skiff, then the john-boat,
then the college houseboat—each fastened to its pred-
ecessor with a length of rope. While Rork worked
away at his engine, we traveled on—two skiffs and
two houseboats, shepherded down stream by an out-
board motor!

A forest-walled chute appeared to the right in the
center of a long bend. I tried for it, but the motor with
its unaccustomed load did not respond in time, and
we were swept on past the opening down the river into
the worst series of whirlpools we had met. The boats
twisted and sawed. The college shanty turned sideways
and plowed along at a dangerous angle with the water
banking up before it. The *Isador,* tugging this way
and that in the whirling eddies, refused to respond to
the rudder. We came nearer and nearer to the menac-
ing trees. In the forest beyond them we could now see
and hear the water rushing down a three foot drop,
and roaring in among the great trunks beyond. It
looked as though our whole outfit would be dashed
against the trees and held there.

Suddenly we noticed that the rope pulling the other
boats had slipped over to the *Isador's* right side; no
wonder that the rudder failed to respond with all that
weight dragging it toward the bank! In a moment we
had it off and re-fastened it to the opposite cleat. The

boat swung out of the current, whipping the others perilously near the trees. MacGovren came out on his deck trying to look unconcerned. Rork worked steadily at his defunct engine. For a few moments it was only touch and go as to whether or not we would be drawn by the rushing waters into the forest. Then the motor took the current between its teeth and carried the cortège out into the river.

3

An hour later, we moored side by side in a kindly chute. The danger being over, now for the dinner! MacGovren mended his ragged clothes; Rork slicked down his black Irish hair. Soon they were sitting at our table, rosy and cub-like, eating slowly and with the calm certainty of men who have before them a rare and unescapable pleasure. As the good food warmed them, they told about their voyage down the Mississippi, first in a leaky launch which had sunk with them in four feet of water while they slept; then in their dismal houseboat, with the cranky engine to help them out when it would. It was plain that for both of them, this was a magnificent adventure. Rork was quiet and composed, MacGovren talkative. When his thoughts became too much for him, he threw back his head, clutching, after his fashion, huge unexpressed ideas out of the air with grasping fingers, and saying no more than, "I don't know . . . it's wonderful. We've been cramped up in college for four years. . . . Now we're free! It's like . . . I don't know. . . . In Europe, after college they have a *Wanderjahr*. Well, this is a *Wanderjahr*. It's . . . wonderful!"

A man as inarticulate as that, wishing to become a writer? Certainly! A young writer shouldn't begin by being too sure. A little uncertainty to begin with is likely to allow him invaluable years of thought-freedom beyond the age of fifty, when the brains of most of his contemporaries have become as impervious to new ideas as though they were made of zinc.

Their adventure was a strange and rare experience. Indeed, for men just out of college, I don't think there is another journey in the United States to compare with a voyage down the Mississippi. The only thing they could possibly lose would be their lives; and if they played into luck they wouldn't do that.

So there we were, on Christmas Eve in the security of a good chute, enjoying the best of cheer, which included chicken, and small, dark squashes baked with butter on the half shell, and sweet potatoes, and carrots, and tomato jelly, and corn bread, and the already admired apple-and-pear pudding which is made into something transcendental by being allowed to stick a little in the pan. How the mate produced these things on a two cylinder Perfection oil-burner would be a little difficult to explain; but certainly she played sweeter chimes on our ribs than many a gustatory St. Cecelia attended by damsels and a five-manual white porcelain stove. Being well-fed to a degree almost mediæval, we gathered together such lutes, dulcimers, and hautboys as the two vessels afforded, and pooled our harmonious efforts with such right good will that before we knew it, Christmas Eve was gone, and it was Christmas.

Rising early, we went down the high-swollen river to Vicksburg on its serrated bluffs, a mile up the Yazoo River. And as we passed into the Yazoo's mouth, we received the most thorough and elegant trouncing from a ferry-boat that we had so far known on the entire journey.

BUGLE ECHO

CHAPTER XXI

I

VICKSBURG has what is probably the largest house-boat colony on the river. The boats lie for a mile or more along the narrow Yazoo, tied against the abrupt side of the levee. As the water rises, the houseboat people drive their stakes higher and higher up the bank, until in flood water they find themselves looking over the railroad track onto the lower ends of the streets which run abruptly up a steep hill beyond.

Shantyboats of all kinds and sizes line the levee, these ranging from tiny craft like the *Isador* to sixty foot houses with many rooms. We tied in the lee of a floating ship-yard. On one side of us rose a large three-room boat with a woman and children aboard. On the other, a diminutive home for two was occupied by a recently-mated pair, themselves not much older than children. A large trunk stood self-consciously on the back deck. The trousseau, we thought. But on the following morning, which was Sunday, the young husband wandering opulently in slippers about his maritime estate, raised the lid; and out came the inquiring nose of a small black pig.

"Fine mawnin'," said the young man to me.

"Very fine."

He reached down and lifted up the pig, who exploded into a rare cacophony of groans and squeals.

Fine mawnin'

"What you doin', Robert?" called a pleasant-looking woman from the larger boat beyond us.

"Ah'm turnin' mah hog loose, Mis' Bee."

He dropped the pig among the cans and bedsprings and logs on the side of the levee. A stumpy, tough-looking "river rat," with a friendly scowl and a seamed face, came out beside the woman on the deck of the large boat and greeted me.

"I noticed you anchorin' last night. . . . Come on over." The houseboat was clean and spacious, with two little children and a dog playing on the hardwood floor.

"My name's Bee, honey or stinger, the way I happen to feel. This is Mrs. Bee, and these are the kids."

"You have a fine house. Do you belong on the river?"

"Yes; I'm just a river rat. I've been off it five or six times, but I get somewheres where I can see it, and I'm on again."

A shriveled old colored woman, with a face like a ripe olive, came aboard over the well-built gang-plank. The stumpy man turned to her. "Well, Annie! What you doin' here this time of day? I declare you're getting more triflin' every minute. I guess you've been makin' up with some good-lookin' brown skin, that's all."

"Hee . . . hee . . . hee . . ." came the other's slow, lazy laughter. She went into the house to mind the children.

"Are you a river man?" he inquired of me.

"No, we're just on our way to New Orleans. There aren't many towns along the river down here, are there?"

"No, you've pretty near got to get out your gatlin' gun and take out a search warrant to find some of the little towns back of the levees. Just you and your missus, traveling down?"

"That's all."

"Bring her over!"

So I brought her over, and they took us into their houseboat and made us at home with generous and hearty simplicity, lavishing on us oranges and cake and candy for the holiday. Bee was an expert ship-builder;

he worked on the floating ship-yard, and traveled with it up and down the river. He knew the lower river like a book, but liked best to tie up at Vicksburg.

What did he think of Memphis? Memphis was all right in high water, he said, but when the Mississippi was low, Wolf River beside the town was nothing but a sewer. The stench from it was terrible.

"Baton Rouge? I wouldn't tie up there fifteen minutes. When the wind comes up stream, the river splits wide open. It's the same at New Orleans, too. Nowhere in the city to anchor. Big docks and ocean-going ships all over the place. Of course, when you're young, it's different. When I was a punk, I and another fellow pushed off from Pittsburgh in a boat like yours without even an oar. We went wherever the wind took us. We didn't care. We didn't even have a line to tie up with. If we got stuck on a sandbar, we'd wallow 'er off with a pole and go on. When I got married, I changed and began putting a few groceries away. Vicksburg's the best town. These are the most congenial people on the river. When you go into a store, the merchants are fine to you. No cash payments, no C. O. D. They deliver the groceries right at your boat."

In the meantime, the women had been looking over the house together. They stopped near us. "I hired her last year," the river wife was saying; "then she left and went to messin' around in the cotton fields, but she came back without a cent. I was sorry for her, and said any time she wanted a meal she could come around. I bought her a pair of stockings for Christmas, and put a dollar bill in one of them, and she was like to die, wasn't she, *Harold?*"

I looked up suddenly. The river rat, who was very alert, saw me. "Is your name Harold, too?" he inquired.

"Yes."

He rubbed his nut-like face, and laughed with unholy glee. "We look like a coupla Harolds, don't we?"

"Harold is all right when you are young," said I, "but I keep thinking about a venerable old man, all bent over, with a cane and a long white beard, and his hand on the small of his back, and some one saying, 'There goes Harold!'"

He laughed again. "I don't figure on havin' a long white beard."

2

Later in the day, Rork and MacGovren came walking up the levee. They had not arrived at Vicksburg earlier because the night before at the great eddy they had run out of gasoline, and had been forced to put ashore on a sandbar where the Vicksburg ferries, some of which are said to carry forty freight cars, rocked them violently until midnight.

They did not seem on particularly good terms with each other. When Rork went back to clean up their boat, I asked MacGovren if they had had any trouble.

He looked at me a moment, then burst out, "No, no trouble! We're very good friends. But it's the darndest thing—there seems to be something in the air. We never say anything, but sometimes I think I'll have to bust out."

I went back to the *Isador,* considering. Here were two young men, both writers, living together for three months, in a cell nine feet by fourteen, eating, sleeping, thinking, writing in that cell. What surprised me was their fortitude in not having punched each other's heads long ago. Two painters might live together like that more or less amiably, for they could work on different subjects. But two writers, both too young to understand the futility of their first jealousy, each probably afraid to leave the other very long for fear that the other would be getting some good "material" —no! They might squeak through on the river where there was constant action, but when once they settled in New Orleans, that single cell life wouldn't do.

I conferred with my shipmate. We agreed that if the *Isador* survived to New Orleans, it should be theirs. Then each would have a small place of his own. Having

some sort of a den to crawl into where you can be alone
with your thoughts, is one way to begin being a writer.

3

Vicksburg sits rather stodgily astride its ridge, high
above the Yazoo and the Mississippi. It is bounded on
three sides by a vast complicated fabric of hills and
ravines, which bear the well-preserved and carefully
marked Confederate and Federal lines of investiture
and defense. Let us go, if our feet still function, and
spend the day on the battlefield. Have no fear, however, about our wanting to "do" the entire thirty-two
miles of battlefields!

We begin at the National Cemetery where men of
the North and South and East and West lie together
under linden and sycamore and yew—Arthur Dolan,
Illinois; Jacob Koch, Missouri; John Cromwell, Maine;
—thirty thousand men who have sometime been very
weary but who sleep soundly now beyond the sound
of Maxim or Vickers or howitzer. Then we go up to the
Union lines, where Farragut stands squarely against
the wind, and down a lovely valley between the two
lines, past little negro houses and fields to three small
bridges that cross the road. Beyond these, to the right,
a half-hidden path winds across a field, leading over
a rivulet of sweet water. If we are not beyond the

swarming age, we can swarm up the grassy hillside under the fine trees, in the footsteps of Thayer's brigade, which once strove desperately to take the top of the knoll from some men of the 26th Louisiana Regiment.

Now, on the hill's crest, we turn to the right, past Baldwin's Brigade and the station of more men of the Louisiana 4th and the 46th Mississippi. "Look! That howitzer was trained over there so that it would not be enfiladed by any one in that ravine. I'll bet there was a damned good row here!" And I stamp around a bit, and smell again the smell of gun-powder. But my companion says, "See—there's an oriole's nest!" And, "Isn't it strange how the mistletoe grows up out of the branches of that oak tree. . . ."

Here's the well-modeled bust of one, John Adams, Brigadier-General. I stop and read his record:

Cadet U. S. Military Academy,	1841
2nd Lt. U. S. Army Dec. 6,	1846
First Lieutenant Oct. 9	1851
Captain November 30	1856
Resigned May 31, 1861	(Resigned like a gentleman, no doubt, to join the Army of the Confederacy)
to rank from March 16	1861
Colonel	1862
Brig. General Dec. 29	1862
Killed in battle Nov. 30	1864

There's a soldier for you! What a fine face. High open forehead, well cut nose, firm chin under his wide growing mustaches. The face of a patriot. *Killed in battle, November 30, 1864.* Well, perhaps he would rather have died.

But some one interrupts me, saying, "Look—the maple leaves are turning from vermilion to crimson. And see that little house in the hollow with the white fence around it. And all the little clothes hanging on the fence. There's a tiny baby in there."

So we go on, a man and a woman, thinking our different thoughts, past grim field-pieces which represent batteries, and stone markers showing where advance attacks were thrown back, and statues and bas-reliefs and bronze tablets telling of the work of companies and brigades and corps.

The various states have different types of markers which can be recognized at a glance. Many have raised fine memorials to their men, not with a blare of trumpets, but with impressive feeling. The greatest of these is that of Illinois, where under a beautiful dome of shining marble are the names of thirty-nine thousand Illinois men who engaged in the siege of Vicksburg.

We reach the edge of the bluff above the wooded plain just as the sun is setting. Centennial Lake rides below, an enormous silver crescent on a carpet of translucent rose. Looking to the left, miles away, the

Mississippi coils and uncoils its serpentine folds into obscurity. Veils of blue mist drift down turning the rose of the plain below to mauve, to lavender, to violet, to ultra-marine. Behind us the sun's rays linger in a nar-

Shantyboats at Vicksburg

rowing band of brilliant orange-green across the tops of the trees. We watch the slow, lovely weaving of colors before us until there will be absolutely no excuse for us if we sprain an ankle in the dark descent. Then we hurry down between two spurs of the bluff to the valley. We reach the houseboat, only by stumbling a mile through the darkness along the railroad track. Night comes quickly in December, anywhere along the Mississippi.

MEMORY LANE

CHAPTER XXII

I

SIXTY miles below Vicksburg is Natchez—but there are a number of things between, including Race Track Bar, Diamond Bend, Jennie Campbell Light, Cannon Point, Ship Bayou, and Hard Times Bend. Hard Times Bend was the despair of the old barge men, who in pre-steamship days strained and sweated at their long oars or sweeps, working their cargo-laden barges up and down stream against wind or current— perhaps only to be raided by river pirates at the mouth of the Arkansas or Red River. Enough curses have been dropped overboard in the long arduous curve of Hard Times Bend to have warmed thoroughly a lesser stream than the Mississippi. Besides adverse currents, the wind rises consistently at ten in the morning and blows until four in the afternoon. No matter which way the voyageur may be going, the wind seems always to be against him as he crosses the broad loop.

Occasional gray, negro houses appeared among the prevailing forest of cypress and gum and live oak. Some of their foundations rose only a foot or two

above the water. A few days more and the occupants
would have to move inland, or remain to be picked
up when the relief boats came along.

Just as a reminder to us that it was Hard Times
Bend, the nut jumped off the top of the motor, leaving
the fly-wheel ramming around on its shaft and apparently about to follow the nut into the river. We found
some copper wire and, winding up the projecting end
of the shaft like a sore toe, we hobbled on our way. But
the motor thundered and rumbled and clattered, and
we learned from our book of directions that at any moment the crank-shaft might be damaged or the fly-
wheel hub cracked. Then along came the mustard-
colored ark of the college men. Fortunately, they had
with them a dozen long iron bolts which they had
picked up somewhere as loot, and on the bolts were
nuts with threads that nearly matched the fly-wheel
hub. So we went on to Natchez, stopping and starting
and popping one nut after another into the river to
join the imposing assemblage of articles that we had
already sacrificed. These included one good maple paddle, one paint scraper, one rifle, one hatchet, one skip-
per and mate (both salvaged), combs, brushes, tooth
paste, funnels, cake pans, a sweater, shoes—and on,
ad infinitum. The only way to prevent casualties like
that, is to be born on the houseboat yourself. After
you have lost a favorite doll or lollipop in the river at

One of the last of the river showmen. He had recently lost his tent, four hundred chairs, his "properties," and a sixty-foot barge in the tail of an Arkansas twister.

the age of three, there is every good reason to believe that you will arrange your future affairs to stay where you put them.

Natchez rises two hundred feet of breath-destroying climb on a mighty billow of land high above the river. Across the way the flat-lying village of Vidalia peeps out over the levee. We came down the Vidalia side past a snorting dredge to a meadow near the ferry landing, where the water was lipping the fine, cattle-cropped grass. Normally there would be no good mooring place there at all, but the rising river had run into a pretty, stocking-shaped depression in the meadow beside the levee. At the edge of the grass, under some splendid elms, an old colored man with kinky white hair was caulking a dilapidated shantyboat.

"This isn't the mooring place of some other ship, is it, uncle?"

"No, suh, Cap'n. Come right in. Ain't no one occupyin' that harbor. Proceed, Cap'n, proceed." We poled in gladly, secure in the knowledge of grass on three sides of us and underneath as well.

The mayor of the village lived with his family in a ramshackle house a quarter-mile beyond us on the meadow. The water rising higher day after day in our grass pocket, ran down a depression beside the levee, and shut his house off from the town, making it necessary for his children on their way to school, to cross and re-cross near the *Isador,* where their skiff was tied. Sometimes returning home after dark, one of the boys from the house would find that their boat was already on the opposite side of the narrow inlet. In that case, he would take the skiff of some colored sawyers who lived near by, fastening it to the rope of the *Isador.* Later, in the darkness, a plaintive voice would sound from the other side:

RLW

"River sho' am risin', son."

"White folks? White folks?"

"Yes?" I would answer.

" 'Scuse me—but you seen mah skiff anywhere?"

"Yes. A young boy from the house tied it to our boat."

"All right. Thank *you,* Cap'n. I was afraid it done passed off in the night."

The chief out-door pastime of the dwellers of the village seemed to be to stand on the levee and observe the river. Indeed, below Memphis, interest in the levees was almost pathological. The water was rising fast. We could read the numbers on the gauge marker by the landing across the river at Natchez as they rose day by day—37½-R (rising), 38¼-R, 39½R.

Competitive ferry companies from Natchez sent their boats two by two across the river. One of the ferries was changing its landing-place. A dozen teams of mules followed each other in a wide circle along the meadow, tearing up scoopfuls of dirt and carrying them to a new level, while their black drivers cracked their lines and cried, "Come on, now, Mewl!" Old colored aunties with bright bandanna headcloths watched in the shade, or joked with the old shantyboat negro, until he said, " 'Scuse me, leddies; I've got to stuff mah boat wif cotton. High waters shoo gone catch me unless."

High water would shoo catch him unless! That was the middle of January, 1927. By the middle of April, the spring flood, coming down on the already exceptionally high river,* would drown out Greenville, put Arkansas City under ten feet of water, and turn Vidalia into a few visible house-tops and a strip of levee.

Natchez across the way was quite apart from Vidalia in character and history. First the home of the Natchez Indian, the precipitous ridge had in turn been French, British, Spanish, American Territorial, and Confederate, finally coming to political rest under the Stars and Stripes. The Spanish rule—1779 to 1797—has left its mark on Natchez in the form of two well-shaded squares which overlook the river. In one of these the Spanish citizens enjoyed the air, while in the other, such citizens as were not Spanish, took what air was left. On the whole, the Spaniards were bountiful gentlemen in those days; they scattered their largess lavishly, particularly in the matter of giving each other titles. There was, for example: Don Garcia Joseph Dabila Ponze de Leon Calderon de la Barca Fernandez de Hemestrosa y Borques, Cabalero de Orden de Santiago, Brigadier de los Reales Exercitos, Gobernador Militar y Politico de la Plaze de Veracruz, Intendente de su Provincia, Castellano de la Real Fortaleza de San Juan de Ulua, Subdelegado, de la Superinten-

---

* In reading considerable material about the Mississippi's greatest flood, —that of the Spring of 1927,—I have failed to find a single article stressing the importance of the fact that the river was already filled to capacity by excessively high water during the Winter. If the Winter level of the river had been normal, there might have been no such disaster in the Spring.

dencia general de Correros maritimo y terrestres, y
Juez de Matricula y Montres en te puerto y ambas Cos-
tas.

The Spanish governor was favorable to American
colonists and donated city lots to those in good standing who asked for
them. Finally, the
United States, not to
be outdone by its citi-
zens, asked for the
town itself, claiming
that the boundary
line between Spanish
and American terri-
tory was consider-
ably too far to the
north. So the Span-
iards marched out,

At Natchez

the Americans marched in, and Natchez became an
American city.

During the golden days of the river, when a dozen
packets a day stopped there, the landing far below the
town was a little roaring Babylon well-equipped with
the necessary properties of wine, song and women; but
high above, Natchez rose in aristocratic aloofness on
its bluff. Even now, as one walks along the well-shaded
streets, a little apart from the center of town, past old

mansions and older gardens, rich in camellias and vibernum, sweet-olive and magnolia, there comes again with that blossoming fragrance a nostalgia for the gallant days "before the War"; a strange vicarious longing for times that one has never known, and indeed shall never know.

2

"Angola, La." We read the name on the Light List, but it connoted nothing to either of us. It was, no doubt, a place where we could buy fuel. Except for its iron smokestacks, it hid itself like the others, beyond its dike. We stopped against a green bank below the railroad ferry, and I went ashore.

It was not a town, however, but a prison camp, with brick buildings and well-laid-out road-ways, flanked by barracks. The arrangement was that of a military headquarters. The setting sun shone yellow through a cloud of dust down the road. Many convicts, divided into small groups, were coming in, proceeded and followed by mounted guards, who wore broad-brimmed hats and who held their rifles out like scepters from their thighs as they rode.

The prisoners halted, stopping in a pathetic, sunken group. They did not stand upright, these de-socialized men, but leaned in toward each other, toward the center of the crowd—for comfort, perhaps, or for courage.

Some were tall, some short; some only hideous. In the front rank, a little man with a weasel face gnawed his thumb and glowered at me. Beside him, in the streaming yellow light, stood a tall, frail, flaxen-haired boy, with a chronic expression of blanched surprise, and features like a young archangel. An order was given They collected themselves, and started raggedly on their way, men suffering the undiscipline of defeat.

I went in to the superintendent, a man with frosty red cheeks and pleasant snapping black eyes—pleasant, no doubt, as long as you behaved yourself. Could I buy some gasoline, I asked, for a boat on the river? No, they couldn't sell any gasoline, they couldn't do that. This was state property, you see. There was a town three miles away, with an oil refinery near it.

"But the man hasn't a car, he has a boat,"—some one said.

"That's so. Um . . ." The superintendent rubbed his well-shaven chin, rose, and beckoned to me. We went outside. A tall, strapping chap of perhaps thirty, blue-eyed, clean-looking, was coming up the walk. I liked his appearance.

"Chief," said the superintendent, "how are you for gas?"

"Well, I haven't much on hand. I didn't get any yesterday."

"Here's a man going down the river who wants

enough to take him to the next town. Can you spare a few gallons?"

"Right," said the other.

"You go along with him," added the superintendent, "he'll fix you up."

I followed the tall man down the road, past a watch tower that looked like an enlarged birdhouse, to the oil shed. We talked together as he poured gasoline from a drum into a pail, and from the pail into my five gallon can. He had about him the buoyant air and manner of another eternally young man, named John Reed, who lies buried in Moscow in the Kremlin. Apparently they had good men in charge down here.

"Is this your section of the country?" I asked.

"No, I'm from California," he replied with a broad smile. I smiled back, I don't know why, unless it was in response to his own delighted grin as he pronounced the name of his homeland. "There's no place like California," he added, "that's where I'd like to be right now."

"It doesn't seem so bad here," I said.

"No, not so bad. Not so bad. *I've only got one more year to go.*"

3

The mouth of Bayou Sara is only a few feet wide. Coming down the river, one could miss it easily. Beyond its mouth, the creek itself—a narrow thread of water, but sometimes deep and high—runs far up into Louisiana. Louisiana, with its "parishes" instead of counties, is now on both sides of the river. The village of Bayou Sara consists only of a handful of broken-down houses. Once it was the largest shipping point between Baton Rouge and Natchez. In 1853, two thousand, two hundred white people lived in its parish, West Feliciana. These had ten thousand, two hundred ninety-eight slaves. The planters were all rich. They lived in a manner that has probably not again been equaled in rural community life in the United States. For the most part, they were people of brains and education. The young men were sent to Europe and to the best American colleges. The libraries that remain in the old houses give proof of excellent taste. These people had all the luxuries of a seaport, all the home necessities furnished by a country abounding in game, fish, fruits and garden produce, all the Athenian opportunity for cultural leisure. Many of the hospitable old mansions still remain, some with twenty or more bedrooms and their accompanying towers, balconies, ballrooms, and banqueting halls.

But the animated ladies in bonnets and pelisses, and the sport-loving gentlemen are gone. Only a few old people remain in the ancient homes, living on in their memories, true to the old blood of which they are so proud. Kindly people! Though we met the first of them only through the most casual of introductions, there was nothing else for it but that we must visit many plantations in turn, so that we might better understand the life that was led during the days of the old South's ascendancy.

Many of the grounds and parks, though suffering unavoidable neglect because one or two gardeners cannot take the place of twenty, have achieved a natural loveliness which many gardeners could not devise. Here is the exquisite ruin of a three-story hothouse where tropical fruits were grown and ripened. There, beyond a broken moss-covered rockery, is a grove of camellia trees, with a profusion of magnificent gardenia-like blossoms, pink and white and red. All about us are tulip trees and locusts, beach and magnolia,—and sweet-olive, from which one can break off a sprig that will be even more fragrant to-morrow.

On the five thousand acre estate of Mr. James Bowman, a remarkable gentleman of ninety-five, there is an avenue of massive live oaks; and in their green twilight, marble statues of the gods and goddesses point the way to the old manor-house. More than likely beyond an ancient arbor, you may find an ancestral negro warming himself in the sun, and he will say of the other old man in the house, "Yes, suh. We calls him

Marse Bowman, or Jimmie. We used to shoot marbles together when us was boys."

4

Here was a many-roomed house built in "flamboyant Tudor," so imposing of entrance with its half-mile avenue of oaks and its triple-arched gate, that during the Civil War, the Federal troops, thinking it was a government building and so not subject to looting, left it entirely unmolested. We walked through its rooms, delighted with its fine old furniture and the quaintly carved cypress decorations of its window casings and wainscotings. On the stained glass of a window leading to a balcony, some one in the long ago had scratched the name, "Ada Mead"; and below it, "Ada Mead, thy . . ." Probably at that point some one else had pushed the writer's hand.

"Ada Mead?" I said, half to myself.

"Yes," replied our host. "She was a belle of long ago. She is dead now, but her daughter sings in musical comedy and has taken her mother's name. She calls herself Ada Mead, too."

And in that moment there came to me a sudden vivid memory of a theater, and of a very young writer of music, with broad forehead and flashing dark eyes, sitting in the well-filled orchestra; and beside him another very young man who wrote verse—Heaven forgive him for some of it!—and there beyond the footlights, a sparkling girl, who made something very excellent of the words and melody; a girl named Ada Mead.

HOBO JUNGLE

CHAPTER XXIII

I.

A "HOBO JUNGLE" is a camping ground usually on the outskirts of some good-natured railroad city where hoboes from all over the country meet, exchange their views and information, share their food, wash their clothes, and find the impetus to go on. I knew that there was one to be found in Baton Rouge, and that it was called "The Willows." I put on old clothes, an easy job, and set out to find it.

True to its name, the "jungle" lay under a group of dusty, scrambled willows, where the south edge of the broad city dump bordered the Mississippi. Finding it had been fairly simple, for instinctively I had turned to the river. The first time along the bank I missed it, because the high dump hid the willows below it from view. Returning, I walked nearer the edge, and so came upon the semi-circle of trees at the river's edge. Men were scattered here and there through the thicket. They lay or sat in the weeds around several small fires.

Those in the group around the first fire nodded to me affably. I sat down and looked around. Southward, over the levee, rose an enormous metallic freight-shed with a covered runway through which cargoes might be taken dry from the ocean and river freighters. Above us, negro scavengers were at work on the dump. The thicket, a little denser to the north, showed other men and the smoke of two other fires. Before us was the river.

There were five men in the group I had joined; a tall, husky young chap called Chili—very alert and wearing his old suit of tweeds with a cosmopolitan air; an older man as tall as the first, very bronze, and with the manner of a marine from the Philippines; a ewe-necked, cat-hammed youth of twenty, called "Slim": a square bristle-headed man with a Dutch face; and a bobbing little old fellow whose red, knobbly features appeared above a long black raincoat that dragged on the ground and gave him the appearance of Santa Claus in a black nightgown. He was drying a pair of brown silk socks on top of a flat oven over the fire, turning them this way and that with great care.

"Did you stop at Angola, at the prison camp?" the bronze man asked the thin youth.

"Yeah, I worked for a week or so around the barbershop. I'm a barber on the inside."

"How was it?"

"Not too good. The captain up there sure was hell on the prisoners. I saw him lay onto one poor bastard with a strap. Every time he slapped him, you could see the smoke rise off the poor guy's butt. There was too much work in the barbershop, anyhow. Always three or four waitin' around. I got sick of it."

"We goin' to have some rain to-night," observed the old man in the raincoat.

"How do you know, Johnnie?"

"I can feel it in the ends of my fingers. Just the ends. I got 'em froze once up on the Columbia River. When we're goin' to have rain, they tingle like."

"Say, that's a great country, the Columbia River," said the bronze man. "I was salmon fishing up there one season. You hook horses to the seine fifty feet apart and pull them in. Then you load 'em into wagons with steel heads. They won't let you take any fish under twenty inches. I'd like to go back."

"Me, too. One thing I found out down here, they won't give a Northern man a chance. But now that I'm here, I hate to leave. I can't stand the cold. It puts the kidneys on the bum."

"Where are you headed for now, Johnnie?"

"I want to get to Oakdale forty miles out of New Orleans on the Great Northern. I've got a brother-in-law who'll stake me there. Where are you goin'?"

"I'll stay here for a while—as long as the town lasts."

"And I'm heading up into Texas," said the one in

tweeds, called Chili. "They tell me they need hands up there. But I'm afraid of that damn country."

"Look out for Beaumont. They'll give you hell in that town."

"I know it. I've never stopped there yet. My brother and me had a cave in VanBuren, Arkansas. We had money, to eat, but darned if we weren't too lazy to get wood for the fire. A freight pulled out there one night, and we rolled off half a ton of coal."

"Ever been to Mounds?"

"Yes. The yard bull there is dirty. He searched me one night to see if I had any money on me."

"That's the way it goes," said the raincoat as he continued drying his socks.

In the meantime, the bristle-headed Dutchman had removed his trousers, and sitting tailor fashion on a newspaper in his extremely clean under-drawers, carefully unwrapped some thread, needles and a square of dark cloth, and began to apply a patch. At intervals, one or another of the party arose and strolled through the thicket, gathering driftwood and dry branches for the fire.

"Well," said Chili, "I think I'll take a boil." He picked a fairly serviceable tin bucket from an assortment which lay near-by, filled it with river water and set it on the grill, adding a broken crate to the fire.

"Watch your socks, Johnnie, that's going to be hot." When the water was boiling, he went into the willows, took off his clothes, put on his trousers and coat again, and came out carrying his socks, shirt and underwear. These he tossed into the boiling water and poked with a stick.

A pair of loiterers from the city came along the bank above. No one paid any attention to them until they were gone.

"Were those bulls?"

"Naw; collars-and-ties."

"Bulls ever bother you here?"

"Naw. I've worked this town five times, and they ain't touched me yet."

"Me, too. I did the main drag all yesterday, but they never said a word."

While I sat smoking silently, the bronzed man had been looking me over. "You come in by the freight, buddy?"

"No, I have a houseboat on the river—on my way south."

"What do you do, drift?"

"No, I have a small motor."

"Say, that ought to be pretty beaner! You'll get to New Orleans in a week or so, I reckon."

Just then a yell went up from one of the other fires.

"That's those damn canned-heaters," added the bronze man in disgust. "They get a couple of shots into 'em and they're liable to do murder."

"Canned-heaters?" I inquired.

"Yes, *you* know—the red stuff! Solid alcohol for alcohol stoves. You buy it for ten cents a can."

"Hey, Slim," some one yelled from the other fire.

The thin youth rose. "Why don't they git some one else to fix their stuff for them?"

"They figure you won't drink any," said the bronze man, with a sudden grin.

"Well they're right, at that. Not while I'm on the road. I've seen too many of 'em goin' around on crutches with one arm off from tryin' to make a freight while they was crazy." He strolled off to the other fire. I strolled too. There were only three men there. Terrible looking wrecks, ragged and filthy. One sat leaning against a tree, another—ash-colored—lay back among the litter, while the third was trying with fluttering, half-palsied fingers, to pry the lid from a small red can.

He held it out to the youth. "Here, Slim. You strain it for us. That a good boy!"

"Why don't you lay off the stuff?"

"Jus' this can, Slim. Thas a good boy!"

"Where's the rag?" Finding a red-stained cloth near

by, he opened the can, put the cloth over its top, and turned it dexterously upside down over a larger can. Reddish liquid trickled through the rag, and the solid wax-like center came out into the cloth. He squeezed it gently, then harder, until the wax was free from liquid. He repeated the process with a second can.

"Here you are, Joe." He put the half-filled jar of red death into the shaking hand of the other.

"Thas a good boy, Slim."

I returned to the first fire. The man in tweeds had removed his clothing from the boiler and had hung them up on a near-by bush. Another member had appeared, a snub-nosed fellow with carrot hair on which were several patches of white.

"How did you make out, Irish?"

"O. K. I've been eating every minute since I went up-town, and that was three hours ago. I'm all in a sweat from it." He took a paper from his pocket and unwrapped a small cake of yellow soap. "Here's some fine stuff," he said, holding it up for inspection. "It don't stick to the paper, and it don't crumble. I've had it for months."

He went to the river's edge, salvaged a pan of water, and washed his hands and face, scrubbing his ears with the familiarity of frequent practice. I was beginning to revise my opinion of hoboes and dirt.

"I got a job," he said, as he stood drying in the sun with his arms stretched out from his body like a figure on an anatomy chart.

"Yeah?"

"Yeah; to-night, over at the freight house."

"I wouldn't work nights," said the bronzed man.

"Well, what are you goin' to do? The box factories and the saw mills pay you two dollars for twelve hours. I said to the boss at one of 'em, 'Where am I goin' to get me shoes when these wear through?' 'Go without,' he says."

The others nodded, and spat contemplatively. Silence fell over them only interrupted by an occasional husky whoop from the canned-heaters.

Slim rose, and stretched himself. "Well, I'm goin' to mootch along and see if I can find something."

"Where you going to flop to-night?" asked Chili.

"If I get a good break, I'll find me a nice, quiet cat house and rest comfortable."

"I'm at the Volunteers of America. Guest of honor," said the Irishman.

"I was there last night," remarked Slim. "The trouble with 'em is, they're only good for one session."

"That's right," agreed the other. "You have to get a permit from the chief of police. I went up to him and he said, 'That's for to-night, and that's all. If you don't get a job for to-morrow, you're through.' 'All right'

says I. 'I guess one day's enough to work this town.'
'See that it is,' says he."

"I'll come back with some chuck," Slim announced.
"Anybody want to contribute?" From nooks in their
vests and trousers, they brought forth a few tarnished
coins. I contributed too. Slim went up the levee toward
the town. By ones and twos, the others rose and drifted
off, with the exception of Chili, who remained beside
me turning his underwear by the fire. When they were
moderately dry, he went into the bushes and put them
on.

"I feel good," he said, coming back to the fire. "It
makes a fellow feel good to keep clean. You might
think, 'Bums and hoboes' and all that; but there's not
one of this bunch doesn't take a boil every week.
Not one of 'em is lousy; at least, not if he can help
it."

"How do you like the road?" I asked.

"Me? All right! On the road you're a free guy. You
don't have to punch a time-clock for nobody. Of
course, there's some drawbacks; you get cold and you
get wet. Some are bothered by one thing, some by another. I dread going to the first house for a hand-out.
Did you see that big brown fellow here? He don't
mind going to the first house, but when he gets a little
food in him, he turns shy and don't like to ask for
more."

"What do you think is the main reason for men hitting the road?" I asked.

"Well, it's mostly hard luck. Almost every bird you meet has something wrong with him. The Irishman used to be an acetylene welder, but he broke his right arm and can't use it. Slim, the kid, has the 'con.' The Dutchman was a watchmaker, but his eyes went bad. A few of 'em, like those canned-heaters, are just bums. But I should say that eight out of every ten you meet, are working men out of work. Men traveling."

The carrot-haired man sauntered back to say, "There's a water tap across the tracks, if you should want it."

"That suits me," said the other. They walked together up the levee. I went over to the canned-heaters' fire. Two of them sprawled motionless on their backs among the weeds. The third lay with his shoes almost in the fire. The frayed hem of his trousers had caught a spark and was smoking. He moved his feet uneasily, but could not seem to locate the source of his discomfort. I pulled his legs around and put out the spark. Then I climbed to the top of the levee.

It was getting late. Lights appeared on the freight dock where a steamer had just come to anchor. The smell of cooking was wafted upward from a row of small houses at the town side of the levee. I walked down along the railroad to the riverside street, and on past an importunate negro girl in the direction from which I had come. Where the ferry crossed the railroad, a heavy, florid man who looked like a detective, was talking to the traffic policeman. As I approached, he chopped off his sentence and stared at me with a look that was anything but hospitable, but which carried a flicker of surprise. "What t'hell!" I could almost hear him say; "a bum with lumberman's boots on!" I thought he was going to hail me up before him, but no challenging voice of the law followed me. I went on to the *Isador* where some one was waiting.

"Why, Boppo! You look as happy as though the millennium had come. Your face is dirty, and you're covered with burrs and smiles. Where have you been?"

This episode does not end as it should, for by every rule of conventional matrimony, she should not only have been scandalized but have made me change my clothes on the deck as well. Instead, she said, "I haven't seen you look so carefree in weeks. Go back and play with them to-morrow. It's good for you."

But I didn't go. Who wants to do what's good for you?

DRIFT

CHAPTER XXIV

I

BATON ROUGE is an active and wide-awake city. For one thing, it is the state capital. For another, the state university, newly installed in its beautiful, Spanish-esque buildings, brings to the city a large number of young people from Louisiana and its neighboring states. The sprightly effect of their presence is apparent. Street cars advertise, "The safest place on the street is *inside*." The Baton Rouge Welding Company declare, "We weld everything but broken hearts." Newspaper stalls with papers from a score of cities and in a dozen languages are to be seen. There one can find the *New York Staats-Zeitung*, the *Wall Street Journal*, and the *Greenwich Village Quill*.

The statehouse is a strange-looking Gothic pile, all turrets and ginger-bread, yet withal having considerable charm. From the river side, one who is near-sighted enough to miss some of the building's more minute indiscretions, might imagine that he was looking at a splendid mediæval castle, in the height of good repair.

In a little house in the negro outskirts of the town, I talked to two old colored men who had been slaves before the war. One was Thomas Herbert, Company I, 84th Regiment of Colored Infantry, U. S. A. He had been born and bred in Louisiana. "I was bo'n right up Bayou Sara road," he said. "My owners was in Baton Rouge and Bayou Sara. I was bo'n right here an' beat right here. I used to work plowin' an' hoein' cotton. Nothing else to do. Nothing, only what you tell me, what the boss tell me. If I didn't, then there *would* be something else." The old men looked at each other, nodding merrily.

"May I see your army papers?"

"Oh, yes, suh. We keeps them all the time." He showed me his old tattered Honorable Discharge from the army of the United States, a form similar to that used in the Great War. "I was mustered out in the 84th, Colonel Dickens in command. That papah stayed away from me for three years. Then Cap'n come and say, 'Tom, take care this papah. It's your livin'.' He gave it to me—bless him."

"And you get a pension from the government?"

"Yes, suh. Thirty dollahs ev'y month. She nevah miss!" Again they bubbled with silent laughter.

The other, even quieter than the first, was George Williams, private first class, of the 67th Missouri Infantry, U. S. A. He was born in Madison County,

Virginia, but had been in southern Mississippi when the war began. He had fought in several battles—at Mobile, and at Bull Run, and had been wounded, but not badly.

"Ah was twenty when Ah 'listed in eighteen an' sixty-one. That was in the 6th Missouri."

"How did you get north to enlist?"

"Oh, Ah jes' *crep'* north."

"And you were wounded?"

"Yes, suh, but it didn't mount to much, jes' in mah hand."

"How did it happen?" I asked.

"Ah was crawlin' from a trench to the Mississippi to get some watah."

"And they were firing at you?"

"Yes, suh. The balls was fallin' all round like hail."

"So you took a bucket and put down your rifle and——"

"No, *suh!* Ah didn't put down mah rifle. Doan you write that down." They shook again with bubbling merriment, and the other ancient softly slapped his knee in a gentle ecstasy of humor, saying, *"He put down his rifle!* Oh, Lord! *He put down his rifle!"*

"I see. You took a bucket and your rifle, and crawled along through the grass——"

"Grass? Weren't no grass!" He looked at me a mo-

"My owners was in Baton Rouge and Bayou Sara. I used to work ploughin' and hoein' cotton. Nothing else to do!"

ment, shaking with silent mirth, and then broke out, "Ah like you, cause you're funny."

"I like you too," I said. But I gave up the matter of the rifle and the bucket and the grass, saying, "You get money from the government, too, don't you?"

"Yes. Ah gets money too." He became serious. "Ah gets money, but Ah won't wish it much longer. Ah been here a day or two. Mah time's about out."

They became quite sober now, the two old men; sober with a quiet and simple dignity. Wrapped by a calm in which were both hope and wistfulness, they raised their eyes as though in contemplation of some distant, shining place.

"We're lookin' forward to pass over any time, now," said one. And the other added softly, "Yes, we're lookin' forward."

2

Rork and MacGovren, in their gamboge barque, made the levee at Baton Rouge three days after us. On the evening before we were to leave, they sat again with us in the *Isador* looking about with a restrained but perfectly natural interest in the boat that was to be theirs.

"I had a dream about you last night," Rork said.

"I dreamed I was going on a voyage in an aeroplane. First I had to start on a long runway and then fly out over a precipice. There was some trouble with my engine and I didn't think I could make it; so I came over to you and got your out-board motor for an auxiliary. We attached it to the aeroplane and started. I had some doubt about the marine propeller being much help, but you reassured me and showed me what a current of air it was making.

"I started down the runway toward the top of the precipice, but I felt sure the aeroplane wouldn't make it. In some lucky way or other, just as I got there, I was able to reverse the propellers, and stop just in time."

If dreams mean anything, certainly his dream meant this: that we might give him the *Isador,* that we might help him make a start with his writing, and give him such encouragement and assurance as we could; but when it came to the final flight of Bellerophon on his own modern Pegasus, no other man might help him greatly. He must assay that strange, uncertain passage into letters alone.

Meanwhile MacGovren had been looking over the blue paper books of our library. On his boat they were getting out of reading matter, he said. Might they take a few of these with them? Certainly.

They attacked the shelf with avidity. MacGovren,

frail, red-cheeked, intense, bowing over the books,
frowned with concentration as he chose half a dozen
titles. Rork, quieter and with humor back of his Irish
eyes, chose effortlessly. The contrast was interesting.
MacGovren's were:

Agamemnon, by Aeschylus.
Antigone, by Sophocles.
On Walking, by Thoreau.
The Man who Escaped from the Herd, by Thoreau
Twenty-Six Men and a Girl, by Gorki.
My Brother Paul, by Dreiser.

Rork laughed as he looked at them. "He won't read
much of anything younger than a hundred years. He
likes his wine old." But the books Rork chose were:

Oscar Wilde's Letters to Sarah Bernhardt.
Byron and the Women He Loved.
Travels of Marco Polo, by Finger.
Creatures That Once Were Men, by Gorki.
The Three Strangers, by Hardy.
Sarah Bernhardt's Love Letters to Sardau.

"He likes his wine *red*," laughed MacGovren.
"Gee, I certainly did get some rare ones," said Rork,
blushing furiously. "I'd better put a few of them
back."

"No use! We know you. It's too late to change now."

They looked over their selections a little while, then put them into their pockets, and rose to go. We said good-by more particularly than usual. Twenty miles below Baton Rouge, the *Isador* would leave the main stream of the river for a time, travel by certain of its bayous down to the Gulf, and, cutting across the land via other bayous, would return to the Mississippi at New Orleans.

3

Thus came our last day, for a time, on the river. Back of the levees the land was considerably lower than the Mississippi. If the levees went out, all this country would be ten feet under water. The rushing, mud-colored river was only half a mile wide now—but it was eighty feet deep. During each second, one million, five hundred thousand cubic feet of water passed a given point on the bank. Two and a half million square miles of territory had emptied their earth-laden waters into it. In the course of a year, the sediment that it was carrying to the Gulf was equal in quantity to a solid block of earth one mile wide, one mile long, and three hundred odd feet high.*

* These are "official" figures. From another official source comes the report that in a year the river "pours into the sea about a cubic mile of mud." (National Geographic Magazine, September, 1927).

And as for our own simple statistics, we had only twenty miles to travel before reaching the lock at Bayou Plaquemine. At six miles an hour, we should arrive in three and a third hours. We must make these last miles very good ones! We must make this a *very* good day. . . .

But for some reason or other—perhaps because of the very fact that we wanted to make it a good day—there arose a warm and rigorous conflict of ideas concerning the art of navigation. After a few miles of it, we agreed to call the battle off; and we went on, a little silent and crestfallen, because then, as so often in moments of best intention, we had not quite achieved as shining a goal as we had hoped. (However, we might have spared ourselves any severe regret; for the entire human race, from ambassadors to bootblacks seems to have run itself individually and collectively flatfooted on just such quests as that.)

Here at last was a shallow harbor in the bank, with the concrete lock rising beyond it. We shoved our way in among the massed logs and débris before the gates. The lock accepted the *Isador,* lowered it nineteen feet, opened its farther doors, and ejected us into the bayou beyond. The town of Plaquemine rose on each side of the narrow, irregular canal. We found a nook in the bank near other shantyboats. We tied to a tree, and slept with a sense of absolute security.

The skiff, which had been squeezed by some of the logs coming into the lock, leaked too badly to allow us to go on. We hauled it ashore, caulked it with oakum, and gave it a coat of boat pitch. The *Isador* too, needed a bit of overhauling and painting. These matters took several days. We talked to the houseboat people near us. They seemed not as alert nor as attractive as those we had met on the river.

"Come over," said my neighbor on the right, "and bring your missus."

He was a skinny, loose-mouthed, pale-eyed, brutal-jawed specimen, and he had pink hairs growing out all over his face like a shote. I did not go the first day, nor the second. Then I perceived a coolness coming over him. In fact, he glowered when I went by. I did not wish to be involved in a shantyboat brawl. When evening came, and he played his phonograph, I stood outside his door and was invited to enter.

The grimy walls were covered with thick, torn pads of newspapers to keep out the cold. A soiled double bed with no bedding on the dingy mattress occupied most of the cabin. On the middle of the mattress, stood a greasy, glass-based oil lamp. A stout, dark woman and a girl of sixteen sat sewing on the bed beside it. In the space between the bed and the door, the quavering phonograph was grinding out a strange assortment of reels, jigs, and ballads. As I listened I realized for the first time in my life that I was hearing American folk ballads played in the sort of setting from which they originated. Between records, we engaged in the small talk of the river—storms, boats, leaks, high water, destinations.

"Listen to this," said the shanty man, "here's a real one." And he played "The Freight Wreck at Altoona," a vocal solo accompanied by guitar, fiddle, jewsharp and mouth organ. Then he turned it over, and played another which told how

"There was a man in Tennessee
     Kinnie Wagner was his name,
He got into bad companee,
     A moidera he became.

" 'Twas down in Mississippi
     The trouble it began,
For Kinnie got a pistol there
     And shot him down a man."

"I knew that boy, Kinnie," observed the shanty man, when the ballad was finished.

"You did?"

"I soldiered with him and palled with him. We slept together at his mother's house; and for what you might call an ordinary friend, there wasn't a better man. He might have killed a few people, but he always had a good reason. They hung him at last, but they didn't get a squeal out of him, for he died game."

Of the two records, however, I think that "The Freight Wreck at Altoona" is to be preferred. If you are jaded by two much symphony orchestra, or Japanese poetry, or French pastry, try "The Freight Wreck at Altoona." * And if it doesn't cast a rare, momentary glow across your worn-out receptivity, then strike me all the colors of the rainbow, for I have prophesied in vain.

"Kinnie Wagner's trouble was," went on the shanty man, "that he didn't make nothing out of himself." Then, with his thin, weird face illuminated by the light of the oil lamp, he continued on what was probably his favorite theme.

"My people landed in Norfolk, Va., March 25, 1776, and one of them signed and argued the Declaration of Independence, the history of which may be found in Independence Hall, Philadelphia. I was 'mancipated by my parents, or rather, given away, when I was nine years old. When I was twenty, I was ignorant. You could have wrote my name with box-car characters, and I couldn't have read it. Now, I can write with pencil, or with pen and ink. I can write with both hands. There was something in me. . . .

"You can build, or tear down, that's what I say. There are good blood in people, but it can be droven

* Columbia Record, 15065 D.

out, or else built to. If I talk about things, it ain't because I seen 'em in newspapers, or postcards, or a ten cent novel. It's right here," he added, pointing to his narrow untidy forehead. "I didn't see the Liberty Bell on a postcard. I seen it in Philadelphia, in Independence Hall, and that's where it is right now."

"No it ain't, boss," said his wife.

"Yes it is."

"No it ain't."

"God damn it, yes it is!"

"No it ain't," she said impassively. "They've got it hanging on the city hall, all covered with electric lights —and I know how many is on it."

He glared at her, his degenerate face turning dull red.

"They moved it for the exposition," I put in, "but they'll put it back later on."

He grinned sheepishly, and rubbed his mouth with the back of his hand. "That's right. They'll put it back. And it ain't been rung—it ain't been rung—" he raised his voice, "since the death of General Frederick W. Funston, in 1917." He shot a victorious glance at me. I suppose there was pathos about him, but his presence was such that it was very difficult to feel it.

"You take these Mississippi River people down here," he went on; "you won't find many you can get in direct conflab with without learnin' what they really are. There was a family we knew—listen to this: there was a baby; how old was it?"

"About three days bein' a month," said his wife.

"All right. There was a baby about three days bein' a month old when the mother died. There was older children, but what did they care? While the woman was lyin' a corpse, they got out and played hide-and-seek. They clumb the bushes and milked the goats—I don't believe one of them shed a tear—while the baby was lyin' in there cryin' day and night.

"I went to the father, 'I'm sure you can see we're people with a heart in us,' I said. 'You haven't a daughter can take care of that baby. Let me and my wife take care of it. If you want it back any time, you can have it.'

"Well, he got together with the children, and they haggled over it some days. At last they brought the baby in to my wife and said, 'Missus—could you do anything for it?' She took it in her hands and looked at it, and laid it on the bed, and said, 'I think it's dyin'.' It did die, too, about one-thirty that evening.

"The next day, the man and his children came over. I guess you've seen people who were all thrilled up about goin' to some jubilee. That's the way it was with them. The funeral was a show for them."

"They didn't have no more kind feelin's for the baby than for the mother," put in the woman.

"Kind feelin's?" He rose up dramatically. "Do you know there's people on these bayous who have *swapped their wives,* with fishin' tackle thrown in to boot?"

"Do you know them?" I inquired.

"We do. And mothers who have traded their children for fishin' tackle. Look here—did you see that boy who was around last night?"

"Yes."

"Well, he's my son-in-law, and this girl's his wife. Back there on the Black River, when he was three years old, his mother traded him for some fishin' nets." The woman nodded in assent. The young girl went on sewing without raising her head.

"He seemed a nice lad," I remarked.

The shanty man and his wife exchanged doubtful glances. "Well—we're not entitled to say we dislike the boy. But it's like feedin' a hog all the corn he'll eat. He won't root any more; he'll go and lie down. Still, the boy's young and the girl's young. If I could only get them off this dog-goned river . . ."

"I suppose they're here because you are," I said.

"Yes; and I'm at a teetotal loss to this day to know why I started it. Well, I say, all you can do is to let your conscience guide you. That's all you can do. At one time, since I was on the river, I started to make whiskey. I was backed by the county officials. They gave me all the wood and water I needed, and I could have as many niggers as I liked. I started it up, but my conscience said, 'No, don't do it.' So I quit."

He lowered his head musingly, his light blue eyes were fixed on a pin-point of light that was reflected from the dial of the phonograph. Now he had forgotten us.

"I quit," he said half-aloud. "It was too damned dangerous."

THE TIDE

CHAPTER XXV

I

WE rose early, and continued down Bayou Plaquemine. We were in a new world and it was just at our
elbow. Roads lined with bungalows, each having a
wooden cistern under the eaves, carried on down the
bayou. Small lumber mills were having their morning
ration of cypress logs from rafts chained end-on-end
along the canal. Green fan palms grew in clusters along
the banks. Under the water oaks and cypresses hung
that beautiful bearded eeriness called Spanish moss. In
the water, green bulbs were floating in irregular
masses. These were water hyacinths. In two or three
months they would spread over the bayous, making
them difficult of navigation for marine propellers and
utterly impossible for square-nosed, cumbersome craft
like the *Isador*.

Now we were done with the town. Bayou Plaquemine had turned southward into the Black River. We
swept passed the gray huts and net-cluttered yards of
a few fishermen, noting that no matter how shabby a
man's house might be, his boat was painted, polished,

and apparently in most excellent repair. Then the forest closed in on each side, a semi-darkness of palms, vines and moss-girdled trees, with water from the high river chuckling wickedly in through the rank undergrowth.

We reached a perplexing junction where two streams ran together in the forest and departed down several different ways. Here on the only solid patch of ground we had seen for miles, stood a fisherman's house. We turned back, worked slowly up stream toward the house, and shut off the motor. Several women, and a gnarly old man, a regular *Pithecanthropus erectus*, gray-bearded like the trees, came out on the porch.

"Which way to Morgan City?"

"Thataway—yonder!"

We thanked him and went down the lane of water he designated.

"Did you see that cluster of houseboats hidden up the other bayou?"

"Yes. If I ever do a murder, you'll know where to find me afterward."

The forest shut in again. Huge woodpeckers, like African priests in black robes and flaring vermilion head-pieces, tapped a solemn mumbo-jumbo on the limbs of trees. The full, swift water below, the quickly moving foliage on each side, gave proof of our progress. About us, the ozone-laden air was fragrant and tonic. The *Isador* was no longer a mere insect lost on the immensity of the great river. Though grimly somber, the walls of the forest were in scale with the houseboat.

We moored for the night in a narrow aisle of water beside the black trunks of cypresses, being careful, however, not to rest on the shoots or "knees" of the young trees that rose up like clusters of sharp volcanic islands out of the water around the central trunk. At our side spread a thick field of hyacinths. There must be no misstep off the deck now, with a downward plunge into that firm-looking bed! The aërated bulbs appear as solid as a meadow, but their silken roots are suspended in deep water. One might slip down between the bulbs easily enough, but they would re-form immediately over one's head in a thick impenetrable mat.

The moon came up between the bearded trees. Bubbles rising about us on the water, made dark momentary circles, which grew and spread into concentric rings of light. Hoot-owls, each in his own territory, shrilled out their weird, low notes. Now one flew over into a domain not his own. Then the deep, mellow tones, like a *flute d'amour,* changed to a demoniacal wow-wow, aw-aw-AW—the laughter of a madman gloating over his victim.

2

When the motor started at daybreak, small green sections broke loose from the hyacinthine main-land and floated off down stream to find new waters to conquer. We followed and passed them, coming at last to another group of gray, pathetic houses, almost completely shut off from the world. But never in our journey had we seen larger or better kept john-boats. Two little boys, perhaps six and nine years, came along beside us in a dory driven by a heavy engine. Just ahead the water was divided left and right, with a substantial gray cabin on the land between. "Which way," I called again, "to Morgan City?"

The older lad stopped the motor instantly.

"Which way to Morgan City, son?"

"Dis-yere way!" He pointed to the left.

"Thanks. Are you going to school?"

"Yes—thar—." He pointed toward the weathered shack on the bank. We grinned in unison, for all men understand and sympathize with each other about school.

On the bayou below was the Pelican Fish Company —a houseboat and fish-market moored to the bank. "Alligator Hides, Furs, Frogs, Fish, Turtles," it announced on its gunwale. A bright, orange-colored barrel stood on the front deck with a three hundred pound man in a pea-green sweater leaning on it. "Hey! Hey!" he called to his companion inside the cabin. They looked at the *Isador* and burst into delighted laughter. No doubt they had never seen a houseboat with a motor on it before. The *Isador* waddled calmly on its way without so much as crinkling a deck board. It had not gone two thousand miles down the great river to be bothered by laughter in a bayou!

A mile farther on, we came to a two-room houseboat tied under a cluster of moss-hung trees. The doors and windows were open. The front room was nearly filled by a broad, white bed with two immaculate pillows laid just so, and a snowy counterpane. There were three women on the boat. They came to the door and looked at us timidly. They wore little sunbonnets and tight-fitting waists. Their skirts, which touched the floor, were rounded out with many unseen petticoats.

Ten miles farther on came the first village we had seen since Plaquemine. Here the bayou was obviously the village street, lined with one-story houses of silvery, unpainted cypress, and shaded by great shrouded oaks. These cast their broken shadows over the bayou, at the sides of which the brightly painted john-boats flashed out with carnival colors in the intervening patches of sunlight. Two row-boats were approaching with loads of dried moss. The oarlocks were somewhat raised above the gunwales and the rowers stood up facing forward, as they do on the canals in France. When I stopped at the general store of the village for the usual gasoline, some youths came in inquiring of the storekeeper, "Est-ce que vous avez des 'Camail' cigarettes?"

Beyond the village a lone fisherman was pulling black hoop-nets up into his skiff. Fish of various kinds jumped and capered in the bottom of his boat. Our course lay near him; the waterway was only a hundred feet wide.

"How are they biting?" I called. He gave me a pleasant, inquiring look, but did not answer. "He must have been French," I said to the mate when we had passed. "I shall certainly write it down that we met a man who did not understand English."

"When you are fishing with a net, fish don't *bite,*" she said.

Oh well, of course . . .

Silence on the bayou.

As we progressed, the channel opened into a wide lake, across the center of which a curving line of piles pointed the way toward Morgan City. Without these a newcomer must inevitably have been lost among the islands that surround the town. The shores approached within a half mile of each other, Morgan City being on one side, and Berwick on the other—two flat towns emerging from the water and joined by a long, low bridge.

We turned to the left and sought a landing place above Morgan City in a little bay between some anchored fishing boats. I had just signaled the mate to cut the motor to half speed, when the *Isador* with a profound shudder, climbed out of the water on a submerged pile, and hung there, quaking, with the bows and part of the bottom in the air. We quaked too! Had our second-hand planks cracked? Planting the pike pole on the lake bottom, I mounted the sloping deck. Fortunately, after a foot or two of silt, the bottom was solid. The pole held. By bracing myself against the cabin's front end, while my colleague hung out over the back deck for leverage, I was able at last to push the boat off the piling.

We went on toward the bridge. Its broad band of T-iron was very close to the water. The *Isador* could by no means pass under it without having the chimney forcibly removed. We skirted across to the Berwick side where one of the spans was a turntable. The mate blew a whistle which we had acquired for just such a pass. Workmen who seemed to be making repairs, stood still on the turntable and looked at us. Plainly, for the time being, it did not open.

Where the bridge left the shore, there was a short

section with a slightly higher clearance than that of the rest of the structure. But the current was strong along the bank, and a few feet south of the bridge a wooden shed jutted out into the river. Could we make the narrow passage under the bridge and then turn out in time to avoid the building? We could try. But as we started for the narrow place, a fishing boat darted in from the other side; so, since our motor would not reverse, we had to turn again up stream, finally passing under the bridge at an angle we had not wished. The shed was immediately before us. The houseboat refused to turn out for it. I rushed to the back deck and shut off the motor. In spite of great effort with the pole, we made straight for the solid side of the shed.

There was a splintering crash. One end of the shed's siding bent inward, cracking under the strain; but instead of breaking off, the heavy cypress boards sprang back into place. The houseboat bounced away, slid around a pile, and made off with the utmost intelligence into open water! We looked ourselves over for damages. The mate, the *Isador* and I were intact. Somewhere in the stress of the moment, the mate had lost another slipper.

South of the town on a wide point lined with fishing smacks, john-boats, trappers' tugs and shantyboats, we found a spot which seemed unoccupied.

"Give me a rope," said an old man on the shore, "I'll

help you in." I passed him a line, but as we came in toward the shore, we struck gently against an impediment.

"What's that?"

"Oh, it's just an old barge that's sunk. You'll come in over it as soon as the tide is up."

The tide. We knew it would be here, of course, for the Gulf was only eighteen miles to the south. Certainly we had come south past Vicksburg and Memphis and Baton Rouge. The pine and spruce of the north had given place to sycamore and ash, then to live-oak and cypress, bearded by the gray moss. But here, beyond all variation in climate or foliage or accent, beyond all other proof of our journeying, was a thing, vast and irrefutable. Here was *the tide*.

THE BAYOUS

CHAPTER XXVI

I

On three sides of the flat south-pointing nose of land which bore the town of Morgan City, several broad, subdividing channels swept southward to the Gulf. We gathered together some lunch, fastened the motor to the skiff and, leaving the houseboat at its moorings, started down one of the bayous toward the south. The mate was on the middle seat, I at the back beside the motor. There was good color in her cheeks after these months, and gayety in her eyes; and, as her hair blew back in the freshening wind, she looked at me and laughed with exhilaration at the present small adventure. But she did not feel how the rudder was tugging at its ropes, nor seem to realize the strength of the wind, nor know at what a nice angle I had to meet the crisp, salt waves. She paid no attention to the steering at all. Was she actually relying on my judgment— after all these miles and months? That settled it! We would take no chances now. I stopped at an inlet where fishermen were mending their nets and went ashore.

"We want to go down to the Gulf. Would you risk it in this wind?" I inquired.

They looked at the skiff and shook their heads. "No, we wouldn't go outside to-day, even with our own boats."

I started the motor and turned the skiff back up the bayou. She looked at me inquiringly.

"It's too rough; we can't make it."

"All right. Let's go for a ride." So, like the two motormen who spent their holiday riding on the street-cars, we tracked down into a narrower bayou and had lunch under a group of cypresses, beyond which appeared the quite novel spectacle of automobiles passing along a road.

The wind died down early in the afternoon. We regained the great bayou, turned south, and made a dash down a broad expanse of lake bounded by low horizons; then across the lake past a ragged line which marked the end of the thickets and the beginning of swamp grass. Now the distant grass melted imperceptibly into the blueness of Atchafalaya Bay,* while the skiff rose and fell slowly on swells from the Gulf. And all this time there had been growing in me a great and increasing respect for the fiery old Spaniards, who, with no maps, and with only their crude instruments of navigation, entered these broad waterways from the

* Called Shaffel-eye Bay.

Gulf when there were a thousand similar flat channels to choose from. Imagine trying to find your way back between the same two islands that you had left months or years before. Sometimes they made mistakes. The strange part was that once leaving, they were ever able to return at all.

A larger wave than the others splashed over the front of the skiff. We had seen and felt the Gulf. That

A bayou oyster boat

was enough; besides, the wind was bestirring itself a little after its midday repose. We would do well to come in out of the open before it got the sleep out of its eyes and recognized us. Half an hour later we had recrossed the lake and had come again into the curving tree-edged protection of the narrower bayou. We skirted the shore watching the isolated groups of fishermen's huts and the chunky, tight-cabined fishing tugs, pulled up on the sand. Strange people—these fisher-folk—of strange, mixed races. Here French, Italian, Spanish, Kanakas, West Indians, Japanese

The tombs in the ancient cemeteries of New Orleans were raised above the ground since water lay only a short distance below the surface.

and Mexicans intermingle and marry, fusing into a race of water gypsies indigenous to the bayous alone, who fish, trap and loaf, living somehow through the floods and the terrific storms that sweep upward from the Gulf.

Something round and flat and russet was floating near the shore. It looked like nothing so much as a large turtle shell. I circled back to it thinking that if it were clean, I should send it to a brother of mine, who is studying medicine at Harvard; he, who as a little fellow only a few years ago, had written to me, "My birthday will be in nine days more. I expect to hear from you soon." Lord how the time had flown! Now he was twenty-two, and nearly a doctor; some one to feel your pulse and tell you that you weren't really sick at all, even if the death rattle were in your throat. My reverie was interrupted by a squeak from the mate. "Oh! it's not a turtle shell!"

I looked. "That's so. It's a——"

"Don't go near it; don't go where I can see it."

"Why, it's only a——"

"No! Don't tell me what it is. I don't want to know!"

We circled away and went on. What a state she was in! How can a man know anything about a woman anyway! Sometimes a woman who isn't squeamish at all, will suddenly become as squeamish as possible— even though she may be the only woman who has dared the Mississippi from end to end in a small boat. Any man who expects the same behavior from his feminine companion on all similar occasions must suffer many a shock. Very perplexing, but undeniably pleasant. Why pleasant? Because it gives a man such a gratifying sense of his own solid dependability.

I suppose that enough time has elapsed so that she would not mind reading what it was that was lying there on the water. It was a——

On second thought, I don't think I'll take a chance.

2

We talked to the old man, who had helped moor the *Isador*, about the bayous we had seen north of Morgan City. His daughter was a schoolteacher in a bayou settlement near Teche, and he himself knew the bayou people well. The girls, he said, seldom went beyond third or fourth grade in school. For by that time, they were usually married. Sometimes, when a little girl of fourteen or so was married, and was well off so that she could keep coming to school, she brought her baby with her. The boys left school even a little younger than the girls. Once in a while there would be a boy of fifteen or sixteen who was ambitious, and who would come back to the school. But the little girls gave him no peace and were at him from morning till night. By the end of the year, he was always married too.

Worse than the girls, said the old man, were the mosquitoes. In summer, they were "something enorme." When the children went to school, their legs would be covered by mosquitoes, like *brown fur*. They would smooth their hands over their legs, and their legs would turn red with blood as though they had been painted.

There were a few places where oil was found in the swamps. The bayou people knew where it was, and they sometimes smeared themselves with it. But it did not give perfect protection against the mosquitoes, which always came up at a certain time before sunset. It was better to make a heavy, stinking smudge of wet moss and fill the whole house with its fumes, shutting the doors and windows and sleeping in it.

"The bayou people don't need schools," added the old man, "what they need is moving pictures. That's something you ought to have—a boat with moving pictures on it. A fellow came along here a year ago with a boat about fifty feet long, and a picture outfit. He stopped at all the landings along Bayou Shane and Bayou Black, and when he came to give a show, every seat was full. Advance agent? No, indeed. He'd give a couple of niggers tickets to his show, and they'd run down the bayous with the news. People came from miles around, even from Morgan City. There's a picture show here in town—but people wanted to see pictures on a boat. That's the sort of business you ought to have."

"It sounds very interesting. What became of him?"

"He was drowned. He lost his outfit and his life in a storm in one of the bayous."

"And that's the kind of business you advise me to go into?"

He shook his head whimsically. "Well, I don't know how it is with you, but I believe when a man's time is up, it's up. I believe in destination."

And since he had brought up the subject of destination, we were forced to remember that we had one too.

Carefully avoiding three right-hand turns which led directly to the Gulf of Mexico, the *Isador* turtled slowly down Bayou Shane into Bayou Black. There was practically no current now, to help us on our way. We traveled about three and a half miles an hour. Bayou Black was well named—a dismal, sinister water-canyon through a lowering cypress jungle, shut in by giant vines and draped with the bearded parasite moss. There was a feeling of wickedness about the place, a gloating, exultant fecundity of vegetation and insect life. There were no settlements here, only an occasional house clinging to a strip of earth between the bayou and the jungle. Lines stretched among the trees, and on these hung rows of black, drying moss. Later the moss would be brought to the trading post which was located where two bayous met. We talked to the trader there. Ten thousand pounds of moss had been weighed the day before, and shipped north to automobile factories where it would be used for filling cushions.

The aspect of Bayou Black changed. Narrowing to a fifty foot canal, it wound through the midst of plantations. There were roads on each side now, and small houses facing the road, with their backs to the canal. The poorer dwellings had no glass in the windows, but solid wooden shutters to keep out the rain. Little truck gardens ran right to the edge of the six foot bank beside the canal. Negroes, their mouths hanging open with surprise, came out of the houses to look at the *Isador*. There were hundreds of them. We went down a landscape punctuated with glistening white teeth.

Dozens of bridges spanned the canal. Some of these were rickety foot bridges, others would bear the weight of a wagon or motor car; always they turned by pivoting on a mid-channel pier. Sometimes darkies pushed them around, sometimes white men. Most of the bridge men responded to my whistle and had the draw open by the time the *Isador,* going at half speed, came to the bridge. Once an old French woman and three little boys strained their bridge around.

Only one, a white man, sought any honorarium for his work. I had stopped the boat at the near side for his bridge had not been opened. He sauntered up with his helper.

"I am absolutely under orders not to open the bridge for any boat that will not go under. Won't your boat go through there?"

"No, it won't quite make it."

"Isn't the chimney removable?"

"The chimney may be, but the roof isn't."

He looked at me sharply. What kind of a shanty man was this anyway, who was laughing good-naturedly? A regular shanty man should have been turning red and apologetic, should have been offering him some of the little money he had managed to get together. But this one was only merry. So the bridge man took one more look at us, opened the bridge with unexpected celerity, and we passed on.

Clouds like white cotton-tufts scudded across the sky under the flick of the wind. A pickaninny sat eyeing us in the fork of a tiny tree, still and shining as a large black plum. On the bank beside him, we saw for the first time in our lives, a cow with a double chin. Here was a temporary bridge of the pontoon type—an incredibly clumsy wooden barge with a heavy superstructure of beams across it. As we approached, two dark men who looked like Mexicans, ran out on the bridge, unbolted the ends, and, with the help of a winch and drum and steel bars, attempted to swing the ponderous barrier to one side. It stuck. They worked at it feverishly, with all the good will in the world. Time after time they pried it nearly free from the end supports with their steel bars, but the hellish thing kept sticking like a new stint designed for Sisyphus.

"I sorry I kip you waiting," cried the older of the two. "I lak to have the breedge open when the boat kam. I hope pretty soon they begin new breedge."

"Will you have charge of the new bridge?"

"I tink. Least, I hope. I been here two years."

We left them levering their heavy sorrow back into place, passed under another bridge with an inch or two to spare, and turned for the night into the busy canal of the town of Houma where the oystermen come in with their cabined dories from the oyster beds. Their boats, the *Reine,* the *Young Joseph,* the *Good Mamma,* the *Esperoire,* the *Bon Jour,* lined the canal. Dusky men within talked French and whatnot to their dusky women. Laughter rose from the cabins at the *Isador's* "egg-beater." The oystermen thought of us as competitors. And what kind of an outfit was that, *mon Dieu,* to go after oysters in!

On then, across miles of flat marshland, with the clouds dipping down to their images in a thousand broken pools below; until, by virtue of a few low dikes, the marsh turned into magnificent fields of black, even furrows, awaiting the early sowing of spring; while the canal, not to be outdone by the fields, led on to Lockport and the Bayou LaFourche.

We tied beside a bridge while I bought gasoline and filled the always thirsty water pail from a cistern back of the town garage. As usual, half a dozen unoccupied young men appeared from nowhere, struck silent by my Minnesota boots. Had I come far? Yes, from beyond St. Louis, even from beyond St. Paul. In a boat? Yes, a houseboat. They walked with me to the canal side to see such a boat, it being hidden by the twelve foot bank. As we looked down, there, great Heaven, was the mate standing nearly on her head on the front deck and holding on with one foot, both arms in the water and an expression of rapt bliss on her face as she gazed down into a small metal sieve in her hand.

I approached alone. "What *under* the sun are you doing? All those men up there——"

"See, I've caught a tiny crawfish!" She had indeed —with great emphasis on the tiny. He was nearly half an inch long. She ran and got a pail of water for him; and no sooner had we left the town than she was down again on the front deck, and when she dipped up another out of the moderately clear water as we plowed along, she got into such a wild state of enthusiasm that I made her fast with a line and held the end of it while I steered the boat, so she wouldn't go overboard with her foolishness.

When she had caught half a dozen, she cried, "Come on—you catch a few!"

"No."

"Yes—come catch some." And she was so insistent that damned if I didn't have to give her the rudder line and get down on my belly on the deck and catch crawfish so as not to mar the fine edge of her gayety.

"Put your arm down in the water, and hold the sieve with the top just below the surface. That's right." Presently I caught one, and then another as it shot away through the green water; whereupon, I relinquished my place to her, and she stayed there all afternoon, now catching a very little fellow, now a somewhat larger one, but never any more than an inch long.

Later, we dropped one in boiling water, and it turned slightly pink, a martyr to domestic science. Then, of course, some one had to taste it, and when he did, another martyr to domestic science was instantly had, because the small insect tasted vile. So, after all the fuss and feathers of the afternoon, we turned the others back into the bayou. (But really I, too, was quite content, for I had seen her happy as a small girl at play.)

THE JOYOUS CITY

CHAPTER XXVII

I

In its time, Bayou LaFourche has been a picturesque and writer-haunted stream. Many of the early
French expatriates from Canada settled along its
marshy sides. In Donaldsonville, at its head, where
water from the Mississippi formerly flowed into the
bayou, there is a tree called the Evangeline Oak, in
memory of her who sought for so many long years for
her beloved Acadian.

Now LaFourche has been blocked off from the great
river. Like Bayou Plaquemine, except in exorbitant
flood, it is no longer subject to the rise and fall of the
Mississippi. The high green levees running for miles
close along its sides have been cut through in many
places showing glimpses of fertile farmland beyond.
Down the twenty miles that separate Lockport from
the village of LaRose, houses follow one after another along both sides as closely as along a country
road at the edge of a village. Except for the presence
of the negro, the physically picturesque elements have
gone from LaFourche. True, the natives still call to

each other in peculiar French across the canal, but most of them have Ford cars. What remains is only that which is to be found anywhere else in the south country.

We stopped at LaRose, where, at right angles to the bayou, a government canal cut straight as a slightly-bent arrow to Lake Salvador, eight miles distant. At

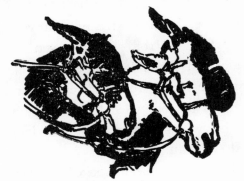

Pharaoh's hosses

our whistle the bridgeman looked out to make sure that we were not a boat that looked official, then kept us waiting half an hour while he finished his breakfast. Coming out at last he asked quite gruffly—to cover his offense—the name of our boat and how we had arrived there, information which was almost none of his business. Finally he unwound the bridge, and we went on past his little show of authority, toward the greater worry that was Lake Salvador.

On a large-scale map of the United States, Salvador

is barely a dot. But when you get to it, particularly in
a houseboat driven by an out-board motor, you'll find
that it is twenty miles long and eight miles wide. As we
came out of the canal into the lake, a light breeze
splashed certain small waves against the boat's flat
nose until the spray flew up into view, bringing with it
the old, old question, "To go, or not to go?" But as so
frequently before, the forward motion of the *Isador*
settled the matter for us and we went on. Soon the
morning settled down into such a day as would have
been the envy of Como or Maggiore, with voluptuous
clouds painted in a gay moment by some celestial Ru-
bens (in ethereal memory, perhaps, of the gifted
Marie F.).

A bulky lighthouse rose to the right at the apex
of a tree-girded bay. We passed it, came into a narrow channel, turned to the left, and found ourselves
in the loveliest bayou of all. Here were wide grassy
banks with fishermen's houses under superb live-oaks
and cypresses, from which dripped the clustering moss;
here were arborescent vines twining among the rank
undergrowth of palms. Here were dense timbered
thickets, ending in the somber frustration of cypress
swamps. Here were flowers, fragrant and exotic, and
the sound and sight of innumerable birds which were
led in color by the cardinal, and by the wood-thrush in
song.

For two days we traveled without haste along the luxuriant bayou, having nothing more to bother about than the nightly sword-dance of the mosquitoes before our door. At last, reaching the end of the bayou, we went down four miles of straight canal, which ended abruptly in three bridges before the steel gates of a lock. We moored to the bank amid a dozen or two oystermen and cabin boats and government launches in the two-hundred-citizen village of Harvey, then walked a few yards up the by-road, and climbed the grassy bank beside the lock. There, swirling along a few feet before us, was the frothing, Brobdingnagian, magnificent old Mississippi; and just beyond, the municipal docks of the joyous city of New Orleans.

2

We took the ferry—then, on the other side, a street-car whose name was Tchoupitoulas, and came down through miles of palms and smells and negro houses and iron balconies and fruit markets, to the center of the city. Reserving its sights and sounds as something to be enjoyed later, we searched up and down the long water-front for a mooring-place for the *Isador*. The huge docks, the many-thousand-ton fruit and cotton and coffee steamers, the enormous warehouses with ten-foot waves from sea-going tugs dashing against

The "Quarter" of New Orleans abounds in mellow courtyards with rich foliage and hundred-year-old walls.

their piling would certainly be strange and rough neighbors for the gentle-mannered little houseboat.

However, just at the foot of Canal Street, behind a large gay river steamer called the *Island Queen,* we found a little pocket that would hold the *Isador.* Canal Street is the greatest artery of New Orleans. Its esplanade runs directly to the river. Here, above all places, would be the spot from which to see the city.

Two evenings later, as we returned to Harvey on the ferry, from the Dock Commissioner's office, we heard the irregular put-put of a badly-tuned motor on the river behind us. Certainly we had known that uneven snort and sputter before. Looking out across the water, we saw a small skiff coming toward us. Rork and MacGovren, of course—their boat tossing about like a splinter in the wake of a ferry. They tied near the lock, and dined with us on the *Isador.*

They had arrived a day or two earlier and had moored their houseboat two miles above us near Audubon Park. What with Gulf winds and an opposing current, the river had given them a bad time from Baton Rouge. Once their dory with the engine in it, taking fright at something, had leapt up on the back deck of their houseboat and refused to get off. There had been some compensation for their difficulties, though, for they had met a traveling preacher who not only had his houseboat and his wife with him, but a farmboat too, with many chickens and nine goats on it. He was full of good works, but so short of gasoline for his launch, that he had taken six months getting seventy miles up the river from New Orleans. That would make writing!

Rork, who had been so silent when we first met, had gradually become more and more fluent. Now it was MacGovren who listened quietly. Shyness had come over him. Perhaps he thought that we now found Rork more attractive. Since Rork had begun to talk and to find himself, MacGovren seemed to have begun to suffer and to have misgivings about his own value. The fact that he was embarrassed over nothing may have made his discomfort greater still. He may have even brought himself to the place of believing that it was Rork who was to have the *Isador*. My sympathy went out to him and I wanted to say, "Don't worry, dear man, about your sensitiveness. Even if you doubt yourself and mistrust yourself for a time, that won't hurt the quality of your work; for by looking into yourself and seeking within for the reason of the man you are, you shall come to understand other men and women and their intrinsic values always better and better." But there was no opportunity to say it.

The next morning, the mate and I took the *Isador* through the lock, and down two miles of tumultuous

river to its new berth back of the *Island Queen*. And
now the city lay before us.

3

New Orleans is twenty-three miles long and nine
miles wide. Normally, it is from four to seven feet below the level of the river. In high water, eighteen to
twenty feet below. But that does not matter. The spirit
of the place is miles high. For color, for sparkle, for
gayety, there is no other city in the country to compare with it.

Canal Street, once a bayou where the alligators
roared, divides the city into the old and the new. The
new section is a district of municipal conformities. It
has its standardized business blocks, its banks, broker-
age house, barbershops and hotels; it has its Liggetts,
Child's, Woolworths, Thompson's Lunch, Loew's, and
other sub-classic institutions. But it is in the old quarter, east of Canal Street,—the Vieux Carré—that the
city has a municipal jewel beyond price.

As long ago as 1718, on the low, undrained *marais*
between Lake Ponchartrain and the Mississippi, Bienville began building a city. He laid it out in a parallelo-
gram, with a parade ground near the river front where
the troops might form, and mount guard, and drop

their muskets in the mud, for the pleasure of small boys and the Kings of France.

Back of the Place d'Armes, the city was laid out as regularly as possible, a few blocks wide and a few blocks long, with street-names such as Chartres, Dauphine, Bourbon, Burgundy, Orléans, and others that were called up by heartache or loneliness or pride. In time, within this square city—later protected by a fifteen-foot rampart and a forty-foot moat, complete with drawbridges and five forts—grew up the quaint, old-world houses, courtyards and atmosphere that remain to us in the Vieux Carré.

The early history of New Orleans, with its floods, pestilences, pirates, and changes of government from France to Spain and later back to France, contains a hundred incidents of compelling interest. For example, there is the story of the "Cassette girls." Prior to 1727, large numbers of girls and women had been sent to New Orleans from houses of correction and hospitals of France to suit the salty dispositions of the first swash-buckling pioneers. But as the better class of citizenry increased, there came a call for helpmates of a little higher quality. Whereupon came the "Cassette girls," poor but all-right young women, each of whom had been supplied by the king with a cassette or little chest, full of clothes. Ursuline nuns, who had long been in the city, took charge of the girls upon their arrival.

Thanks to the young blades of the colony, however, this arrangement was only temporary; and "many well-known New Orleans families trace their origin back to the marriage of some gallant French gentleman with a lovely *fille de la Cassette.*"

This and other delightful incidents may be found in the excellent guide to the city published by the New Orleans *Times-Picayune,* a newspaper old in years, but exceedingly young in heart.

Walking along the narrow streets of the Quarter, under the remarkable wrought-iron tracery and trellis work of the balconies, one catches a glimpse of small, fountained courtyards where shafts of sunlight play on century-old walls, or filter into rare patterns under the rich foliage of palm and banana tree and magnolia. At the back are the old slave quarters, now changed into apartments, in which almost any man might live with enormous content. What a cycle of habitation the old Quarter has had! After the pioneer days, it was occupied by the élite of the town, Creole * families, the best society of New Orleans. Then came the War and its following desolation. The slave quarters which had sometimes held seventy or eighty slaves were empty. The better families moved away to a new part of the city. Only the poor and a few of the

---

* Creole: A descendant of French or Spanish (or French and Spanish) settlers in the gulf States, preserving their speech and culture.

very proud, remained behind their closed blinds. Foreign immigrants came in, Sicilians of the lowest type, making a slum which became a rendezvous for prostitutes and their accompaniment of rakes and thugs. Then a few artists came in and others who appreciated the charm of the old streets and houses. Gradually the tone of the Quarter improved.

Now it is filling up again, attracting, after the manner of Greenwich Village, its quota of pseudo-Freudians and gifte shoppes, and human dismalia who pester hell out of artists by talking to them about something of which most artists care nothing, called "Art." But I do not think they'll spoil it, because the Quarter has already been through a more searing baptism of fire than they can give it. And as for the physical aspect of the place, there is a municipal building committee which sees to it that "repairs" on the old buildings do not, peradventure, blossom into ten-story apartment houses.

4

At the corner of Chartres and St. Louis Streets rises a beautifully proportioned French house of old gray-painted plaster. The mansard roof, cut by five round-topped dormer windows, slopes up at that slight angle which you will find in Avranches or Meudon or Nantes. There are four chimneys irregularly placed on the roof, and in the center a black cupola. Across the front of the second and third floors are seven windows. These are hidden by faded green shutters except for two on the third floor near the center, which are open, disclosing the rich yellow-ocher window frames. The ground floor is occupied by the Napoleon Grocery and Café.

Walk down St. Louis Street, then turn around again and look at its weathered gray walls, its mansard roof, and its blue-green blinds against the bright billboards where the old St. Louis Hotel stood, with Royal Street beyond. It is a part of France—and it should be, for this house was built for Napoleon Bonaparte himself by those who expected to help him escape from St. Helena. He died, however, before the plan could be carried out.

Three doors down Chartres Street is another dwelling bearing the legend, "This house was built for Napoleon Bonaparte." That, it would seem, is not correct. I was assured most emphatically by a fine lady who had spent her girlhood in the corner house and whose father, I found later, was a friend of Louis Philippe, that the *maison* with the cupola *is* the Napoleon house.

5

Alone or with pleasant companions we browsed about day after day, coming back at night to our berth in the lee of the *Island Queen*. At eight o'clock on the first evening, we had been surprised to hear the great ship bellow forth with the thunderous toots and wheezes of a steam calliope on its upper deck; still further surprised, when at eight thirty P. M., to the accompaniment of the music of a large orchestra, it started down the river with hundreds of pleasure-seekers aboard, leaving a mile-wide stretch of choppy water in which the *Isador* lurched and rolled disastrously.

However, the *Island Queen* returned at eleven, and at twelve the dancing was over. Shortly, we regulated our absence to its own, spending our evenings as well as our days in the city. We went to its theaters and its restaurants; some of the latter were good, some were not. Some have been praised so highly that they have become quiveringly self-conscious of the excellence of their food, and hence, uncomfortable. At Antoine's, for example, several of the waiters were patronizing to a degree that would not be tolerated for a minute in any foreign city, except by Americans. I prefer La Louisiane around the corner. There the atmosphere is thoroughbred, the food is good, and they let you alone.

Above the other restaurants, I like Madame Begue's on the old Place d'Armes, which is now called Jackson Square. It is located on the second floor of one of the two Pontalba buildings which flank Andrew Jackson's statue. The hallway is old and shabby, and the restaurant itself is not much better. But the business has been in the family for two hundred years, and the food you get there is not of Paris,—you can find something approximating Parisian food in several cities in the United States—it is that of a good restaurant in a provincial city in the south of France. A young girl will wait on you. Her name will be Pauline or Nicoline Begue; and you will retain the same knife and fork for all your courses. You will eat good, simple food; and afterward, in great peace, you will go out along the old side-streets with their square cobblestones set diamond-wise, cobblestones which, at the suggestion of some very shrewd governor, were brought over as ballast in the ships of long ago. Even on the newly-paved streets where the old cobbles are forgotten, they are not gone. The new paving is laid above the old.

You may go to the Little Theater—the *Petit Théatre du Vieux Carré*. As you reach the Cabildo, that ancient palace of the Spanish governors, now used as a museum, perhaps you may come upon such a symbol of the gayhearted city as we did. Going along St.

Peter Street, we saw a light inside the Cabildo, shining through one of its ground-glass windows; and there against the window in that old building of the Spanish grandees where Lafayette was later entertained, was the silhouette of two young people who thought they were quite hidden, kissing each other rapturously, for all the world to see.

Later, you may saunter up to the equestrien statue of Andrew Jackson in the Square, and if it is not too dark, you will note that his sword, which has fallen off at some time in the past, has been fastened on again upside-down; and you may hope that no one will change it back again, for it makes the bronze statue of the fiery old warrior much more human than it could possibly have been before.

6

The collegians came down to see us once again, climbing out over the piling of the old coffee dock to say good-by. Their houseboat was already in the mouth of the Industrial Canal below the city, awaiting ours. They would get a fisherman with a launch to pull the caravan through the canal, up Lake Ponchartrain, and back into Bayou St. John to a mooring place they had found in the city. If it suited our plans, they would call for the *Isador* at three the following afternoon.

7

We were ready at two. We sent our bags and the boxed motor to the near-by station, our trunk and hand luggage to the St. Charles Hotel. We gave the boat a last inspection to make sure that it was shipshape and clean. We were leaving it just as we had lived in it —the stove filled with fuel, dishes in the cupboard, water in the water-keg, the library and lamp on the book-case, the green curtains at the windows, and the gay cushions—not quite as gay as they had been two thousand miles earlier—on the couch. We put the key on the shelf outside the door, and went away.

After dinner, we wandered back to the river front. The *Island Queen* was brilliantly illuminated for her nightly voyage. (*Had they taken it away?*) We went slowly around the corner of the Esplanade, and looked at the narrow space of water between the great boat and the coffee dock; and then the former mate of the *Isador* was saying, "It's gone. Our poor little, funny little boat! It leaves a great emptiness against the river." We turned silently away.

The myriad lights of the *Island Queen* attracted us. Soon she would be heading out there into the darkness. Moonlight to-night on the Mississippi. We looked at each other. A bell on the bridge, vibrating under the slow strength of a man's arm, sounded the warning signal. One . . . two . . . three. . . . One . . . two . . . three. . . .

"Come on!" We hurried aboard. With a rush of steam, the light-studded gangplank rose high above the narrow moat of water. The hawsers unwrapped from the pierheads. The whistle roared hoarsely, spluttering careless drops of water on the deck.

"Turn 'er out slow, sir." The ship eased slowly away from the row of piling where the *Isador* had lain.

"All right, sir. She's clear."

People were dancing on the broad, shining floor; a burst of laughter and the bleat of a saxophone came out to us through the open door.

We climbed to the upper deck. No other passengers were there; only the steersman, well forward on the enclosed bridge. Beyond the rail, its darkened waters moving with tremendous power, surged the great river. What force! What inexorable tenacity of purpose!— flowing like that down through the days and nights, down through the cycle of the years. If a man, learning the lesson of that irrepressible tide, could set himself to a certain goal, freeing himself from all lesser things, casting aside all trivialities——

Some one put her arm on mine. "They're dancing downstairs," she said.

"Yes?"

"Yes. They're dancing downstairs——"

HAROLD SPEAKMAN (1888–1928) was a writer and artist who was educated at the Art Institute of Chicago. He was the author of eight books, including three other travel memoirs: *Beyond Shanghai, Hilltops in Galilee,* and *Here's Ireland.*